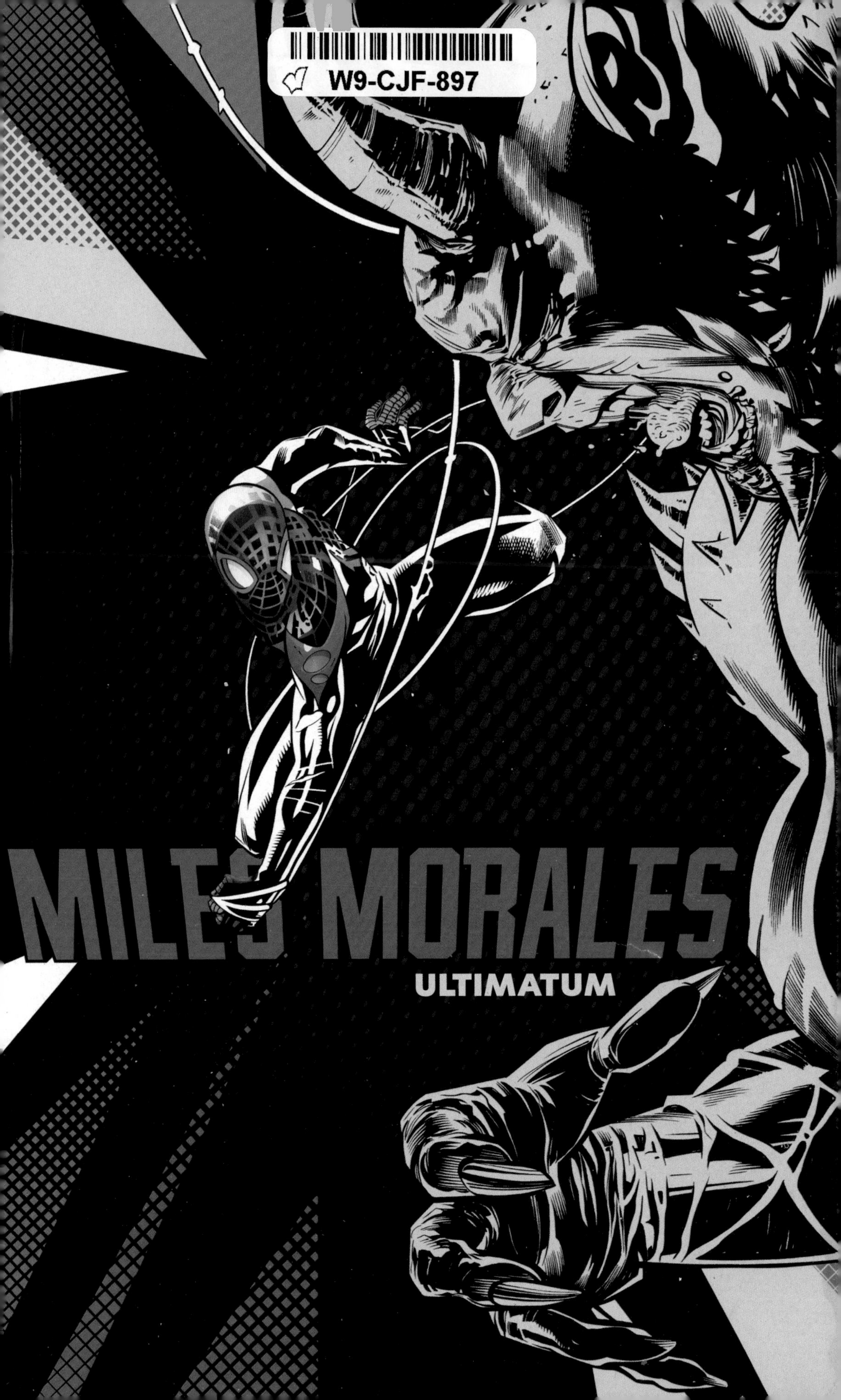

MILES MORALES
ULTIMATUM

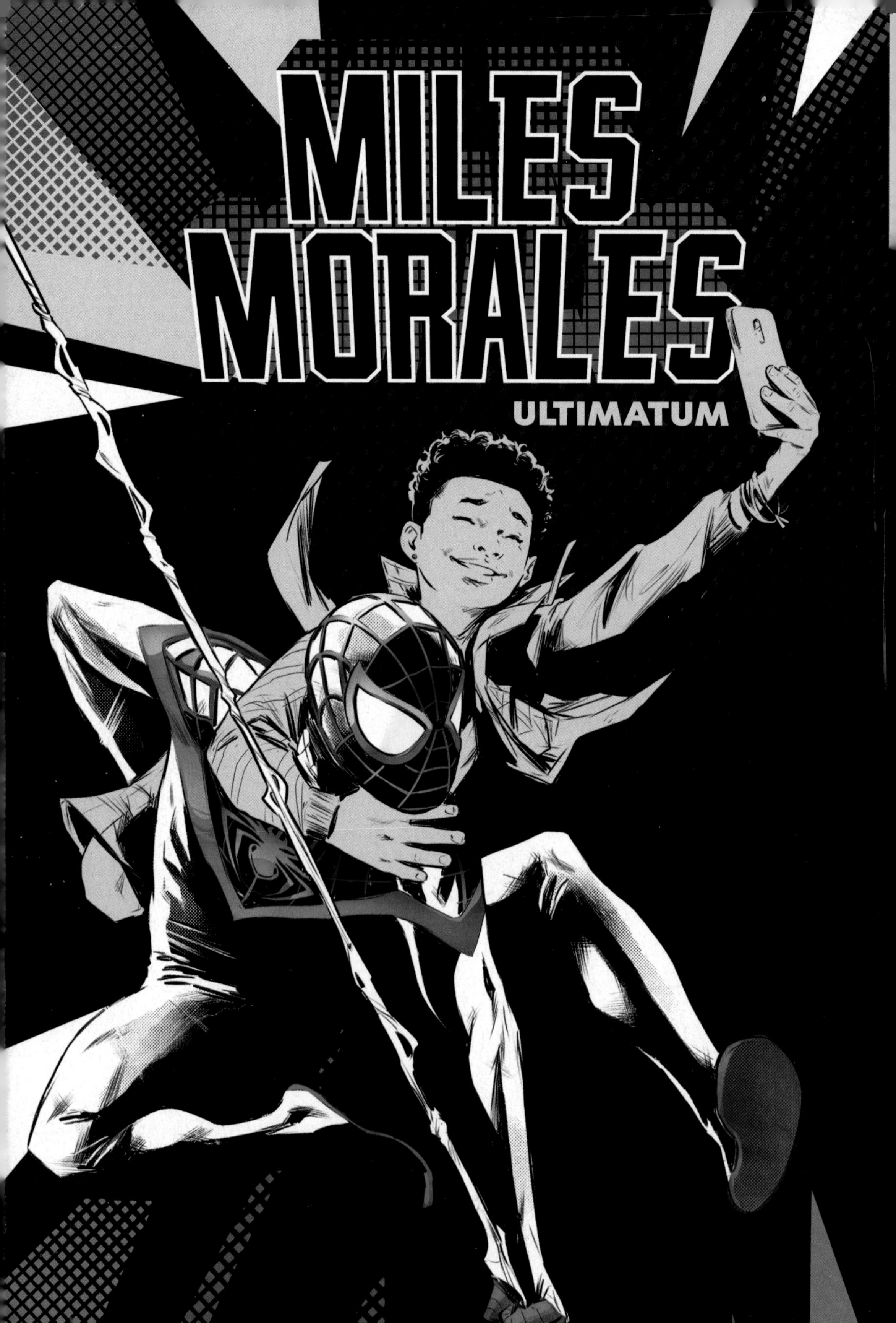
MILES MORALES
ULTIMATUM

MILES MORALES VOL. 4: ULTIMATUM. Contains material originally published in magazine form as MILES MORALES: SPIDER-MAN (2018) #16-21. First printing 2021. ISBN 978-1-302-92017-3. Published by MARVEL WORLDWIDE, INC., a subsidiary of MARVEL ENTERTAINMENT, LLC. OFFICE OF PUBLICATION: 1290 Avenue of the Americas, New York, NY 10104. © 2021 MARVEL No similarity between any of the names, characters, persons, and/or institutions in this magazine with those of any living or dead person or institution is intended, and any such similarity which may exist is purely coincidental. **Printed in Canada.** KEVIN FEIGE, Chief Creative Officer; DAN BUCKLEY, President, Marvel Entertainment; JOE QUESADA, EVP & Creative Director; DAVID BOGART, Associate Publisher & SVP of Talent Affairs; TOM BREVOORT, VP, Executive Editor; NICK LOWE, Executive Editor, VP of Content, Digital Publishing; DAVID GABRIEL, VP of Print & Digital Publishing; JEFF YOUNGQUIST, VP of Production & Special Projects; ALEX MORALES, Director of Publishing Operations; DAN EDINGTON, Managing Editor; RICKEY PURDIN, Director of Talent Relations; JENNIFER GRÜNWALD, Senior Editor, Special Projects; SUSAN CRESPI, Production Manager; STAN LEE, Chairman Emeritus. For information regarding advertising in Marvel Comics or on Marvel.com, please contact Vit DeBellis, Custom Solutions & Integrated Advertising Manager, at vdebellis@marvel.com. For Marvel subscription inquiries, please call 888-511-5480. **Manufactured between 1/1/2021 and 2/2/2021 by SOLISCO PRINTERS, SCOTT, QC, CANADA.**

Saladin Ahmed
WRITER

Cory Smith (#16), Carmen Carnero (#17-19) & Marcelo Ferreira (#19-21)
PENCILERS

Victor Olazaba (#16), Carmen Carnero (#17-19), JP Mayer (#19), Wayne Faucher (#20-21) & Marcelo Ferreira (#20)
INKERS

David Curiel
COLOR ARTIST

VC's Cory Petit
LETTERER

Javier Garrón WITH David Curiel (#16-19, 21) & Chris Sotomayor (#20)
COVER ART

Lindsey Cohick
ASSISTANT EDITOR

Kathleen Wisneski
EDITOR

Nick Lowe
EXECUTIVE EDITOR

SPIDER-MAN CREATED BY Stan Lee & Steve Ditko

COLLECTION EDITOR **JENNIFER GRÜNWALD**
ASSISTANT EDITOR **DANIEL KIRCHHOFFER**
ASSISTANT MANAGING EDITOR **MAIA LOY**
ASSISTANT MANAGING EDITOR **LISA MONTALBANO**
VP, PRODUCTION & SPECIAL PROJECTS **JEFF YOUNGQUIST**
BOOK DESIGNERS **SALENA MAHINA** WITH
JAY BOWEN & **MANNY MEDEROS**
SVP PRINT, SALES & MARKETING **DAVID GABRIEL**
EDITOR IN CHIEF **C.B. CEBULSKI**

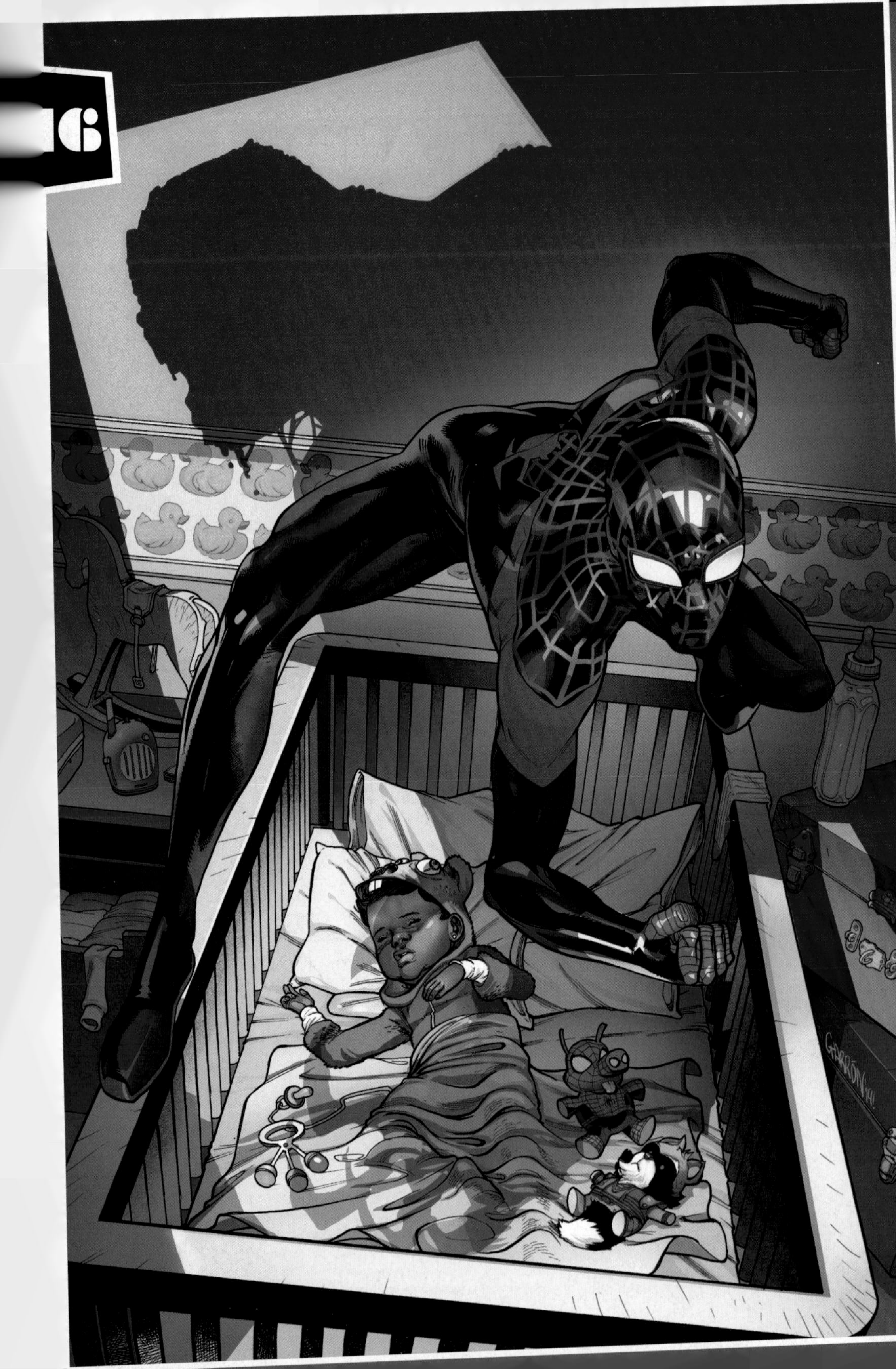
16

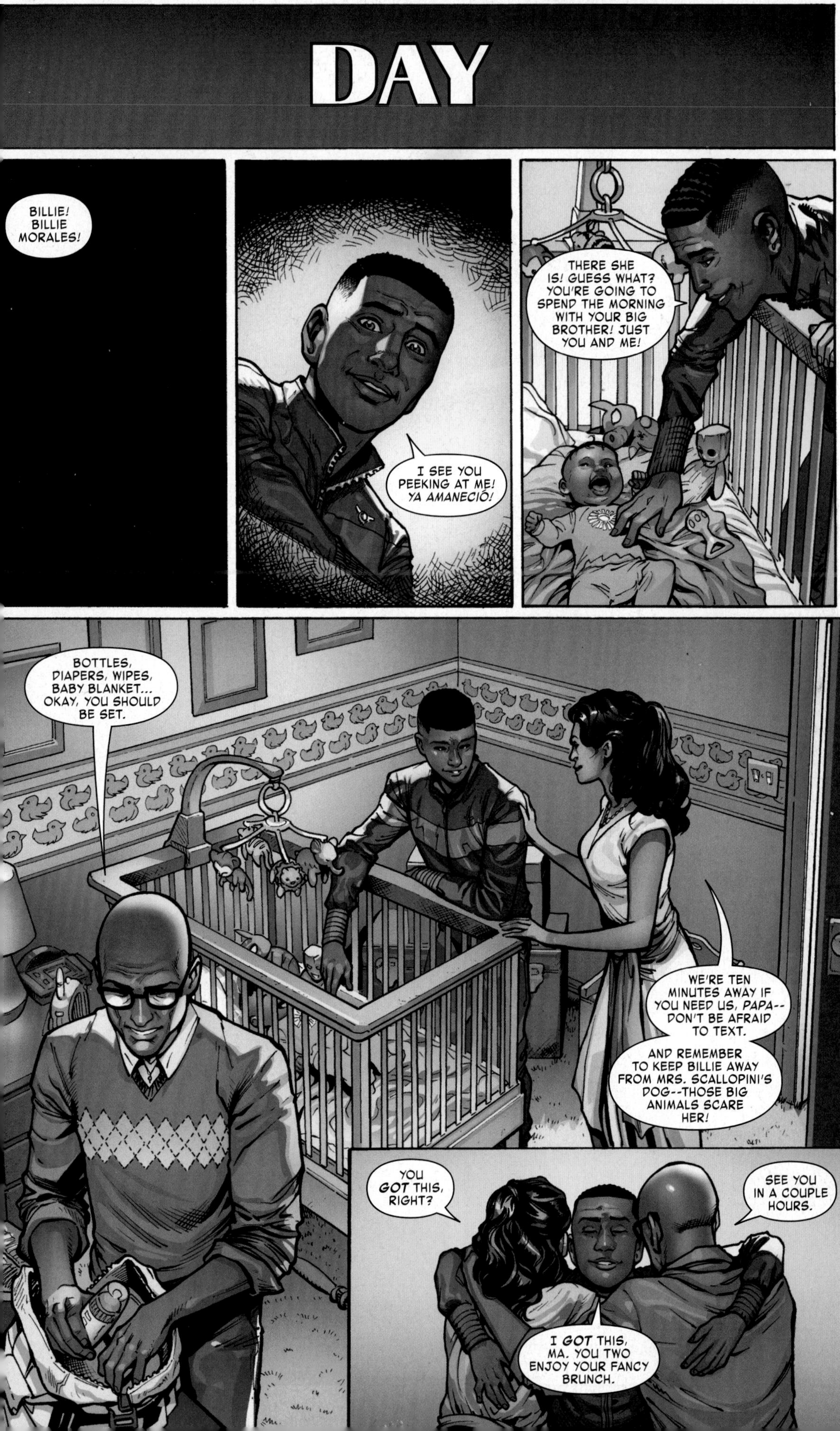

DAY
BILLIE! BILLIE MORALES!
I SEE YOU PEEKING AT ME! YA AMANECIÓ!
THERE SHE IS! GUESS WHAT? YOU'RE GOING TO SPEND THE MORNING WITH YOUR BIG BROTHER! JUST YOU AND ME!
BOTTLES, DIAPERS, WIPES, BABY BLANKET... OKAY, YOU SHOULD BE SET.
WE'RE TEN MINUTES AWAY IF YOU NEED US, PAPA--DON'T BE AFRAID TO TEXT.
AND REMEMBER TO KEEP BILLIE AWAY FROM MRS. SCALLOPINI'S DOG--THOSE BIG ANIMALS SCARE HER!
YOU GOT THIS, RIGHT?
SEE YOU IN A COUPLE HOURS.
I GOT THIS, MA. YOU TWO ENJOY YOUR FANCY BRUNCH.

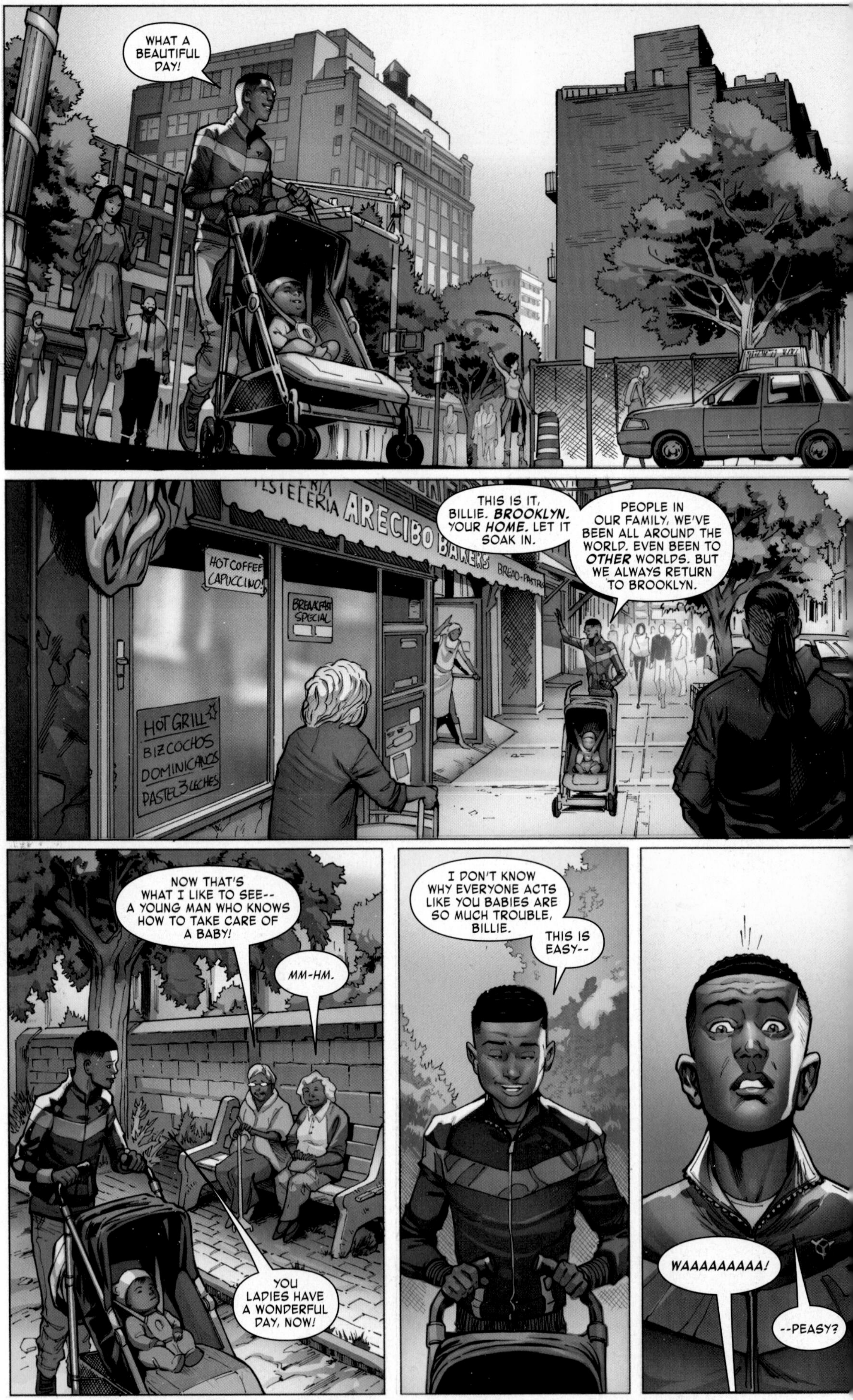
WHAT A BEAUTIFUL DAY!
ARECIBO BAKERS
HOT COFFEE CAPUCCINO!
BREAKFAST SPECIAL
HOT GRILL BIZCOCHOS DOMINICANOS PASTEL 3 LECHES
BREAD-PASTR
THIS IS IT, BILLIE. BROOKLYN. YOUR HOME. LET IT SOAK IN.
PEOPLE IN OUR FAMILY, WE'VE BEEN ALL AROUND THE WORLD. EVEN BEEN TO OTHER WORLDS. BUT WE ALWAYS RETURN TO BROOKLYN.
NOW THAT'S WHAT I LIKE TO SEE-- A YOUNG MAN WHO KNOWS HOW TO TAKE CARE OF A BABY!
MM-HM.
YOU LADIES HAVE A WONDERFUL DAY, NOW!
I DON'T KNOW WHY EVERYONE ACTS LIKE YOU BABIES ARE SO MUCH TROUBLE, BILLIE.
THIS IS EASY--
WAAAAAAAAA!
--PEASY?

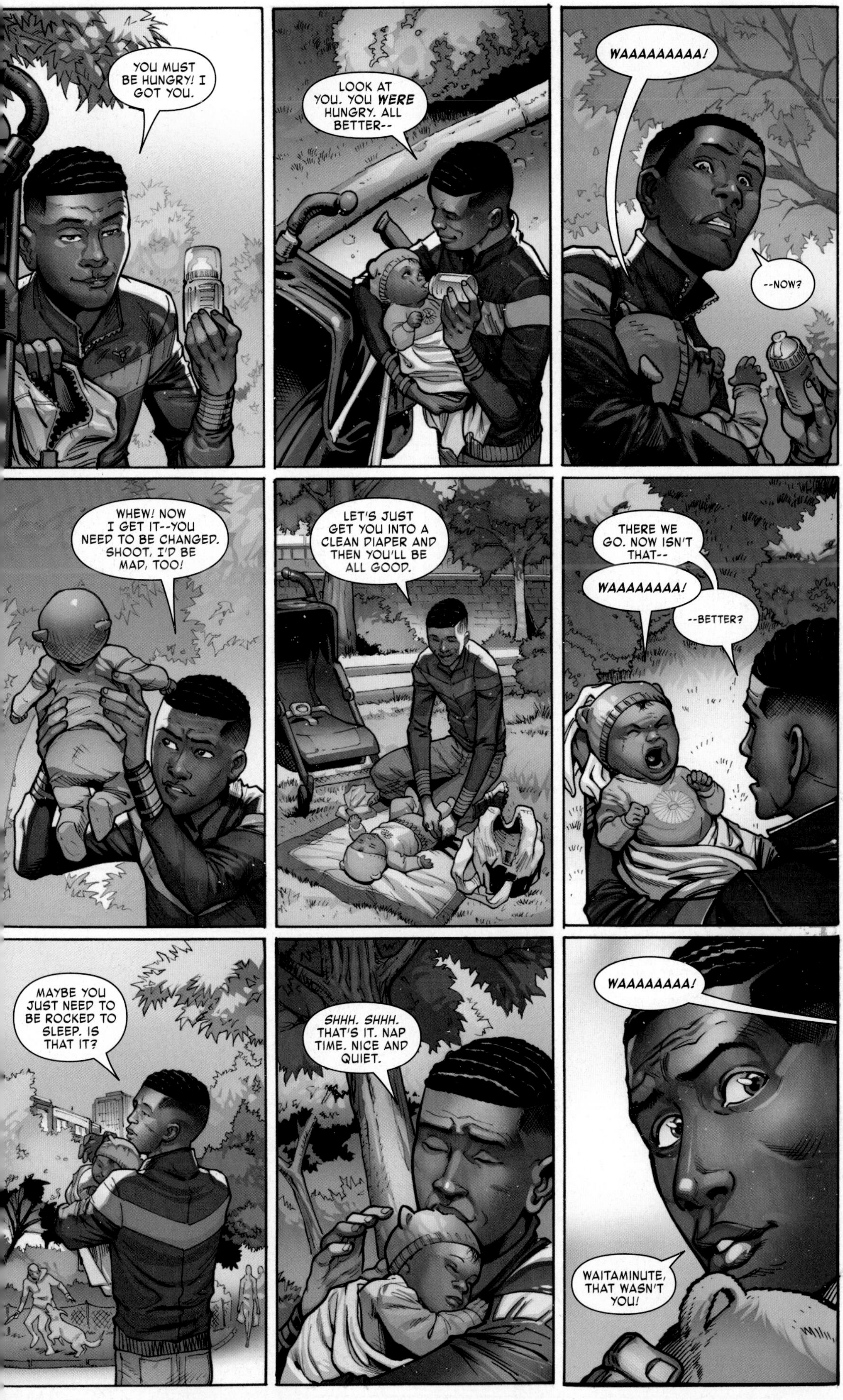
YOU MUST BE HUNGRY! I GOT YOU.
LOOK AT YOU. YOU WERE HUNGRY. ALL BETTER--
WAAAAAAAAA!
--NOW?
WHEW! NOW I GET IT--YOU NEED TO BE CHANGED. SHOOT, I'D BE MAD, TOO!
LET'S JUST GET YOU INTO A CLEAN DIAPER AND THEN YOU'LL BE ALL GOOD.
THERE WE GO. NOW ISN'T THAT--
WAAAAAAAA!
--BETTER?
MAYBE YOU JUST NEED TO BE ROCKED TO SLEEP. IS THAT IT?
SHHH. SHHH. THAT'S IT. NAP TIME. NICE AND QUIET.
WAAAAAAAA!
WAITAMINUTE, THAT WASN'T YOU!

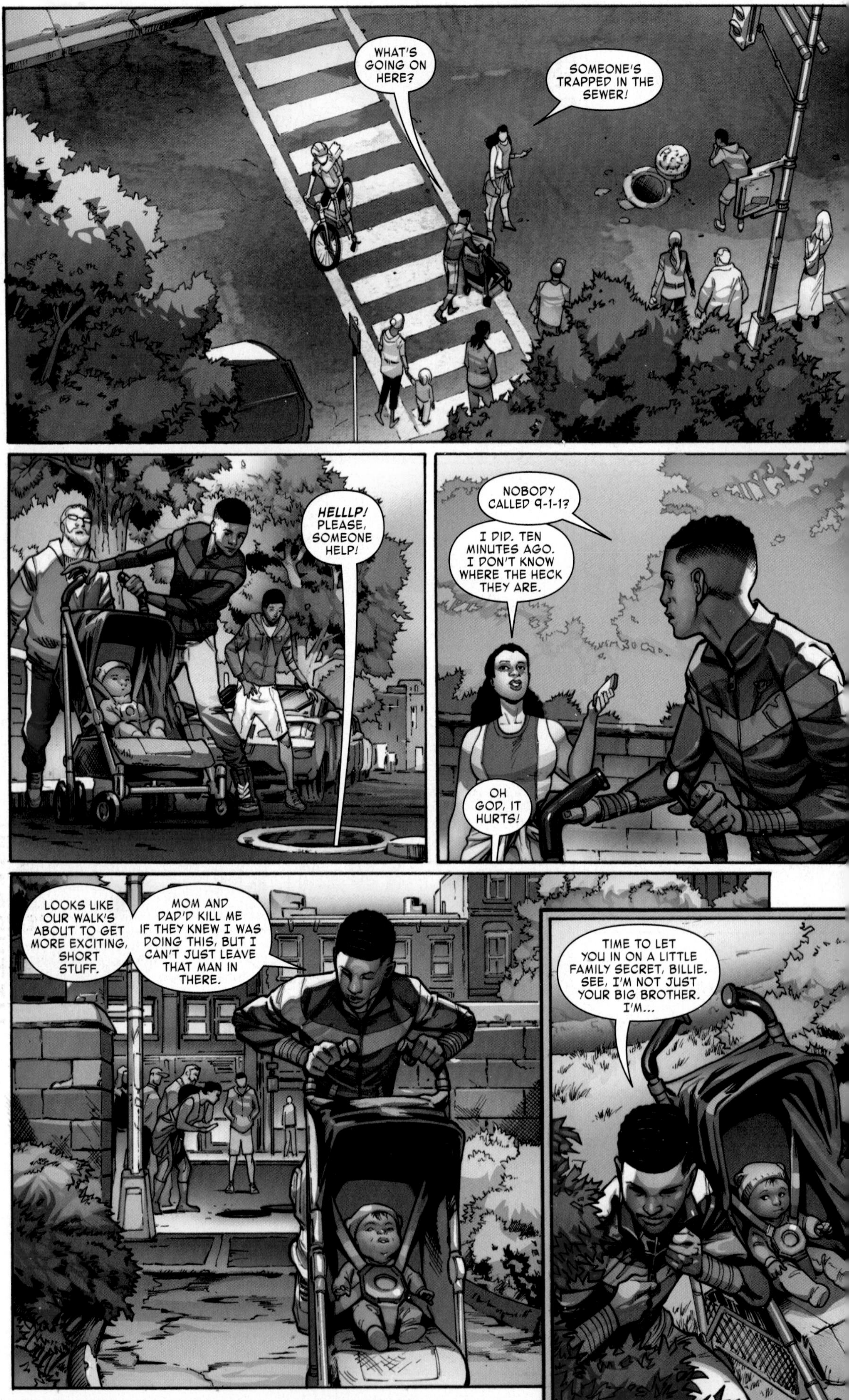
WHAT'S GOING ON HERE?
SOMEONE'S TRAPPED IN THE SEWER!
HELLLP! PLEASE, SOMEONE HELP!
NOBODY CALLED 9-1-1?
I DID. TEN MINUTES AGO. I DON'T KNOW WHERE THE HECK THEY ARE.
OH GOD, IT HURTS!
LOOKS LIKE OUR WALK'S ABOUT TO GET MORE EXCITING, SHORT STUFF.
MOM AND DAD'D KILL ME IF THEY KNEW I WAS DOING THIS, BUT I CAN'T JUST LEAVE THAT MAN IN THERE.
TIME TO LET YOU IN ON A LITTLE FAMILY SECRET, BILLIE. SEE, I'M NOT JUST YOUR BIG BROTHER. I'M...

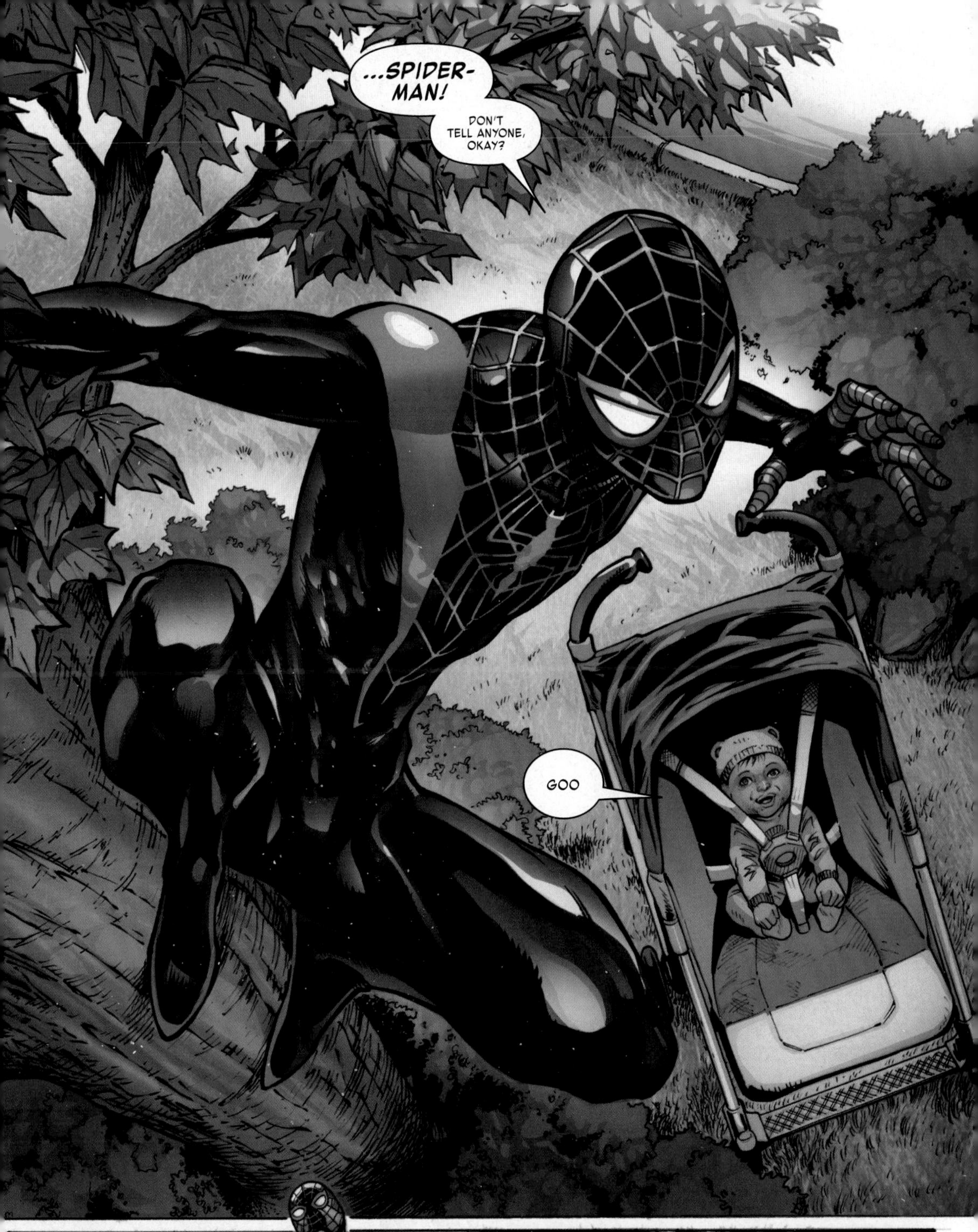
...SPIDER-MAN!
DON'T TELL ANYONE, OKAY?
GOO

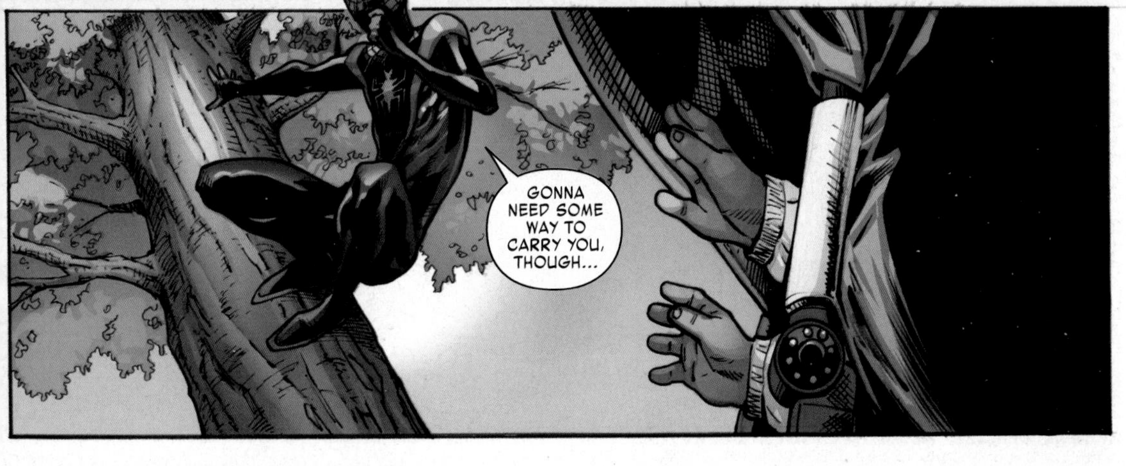
GONNA NEED SOME WAY TO CARRY YOU, THOUGH...

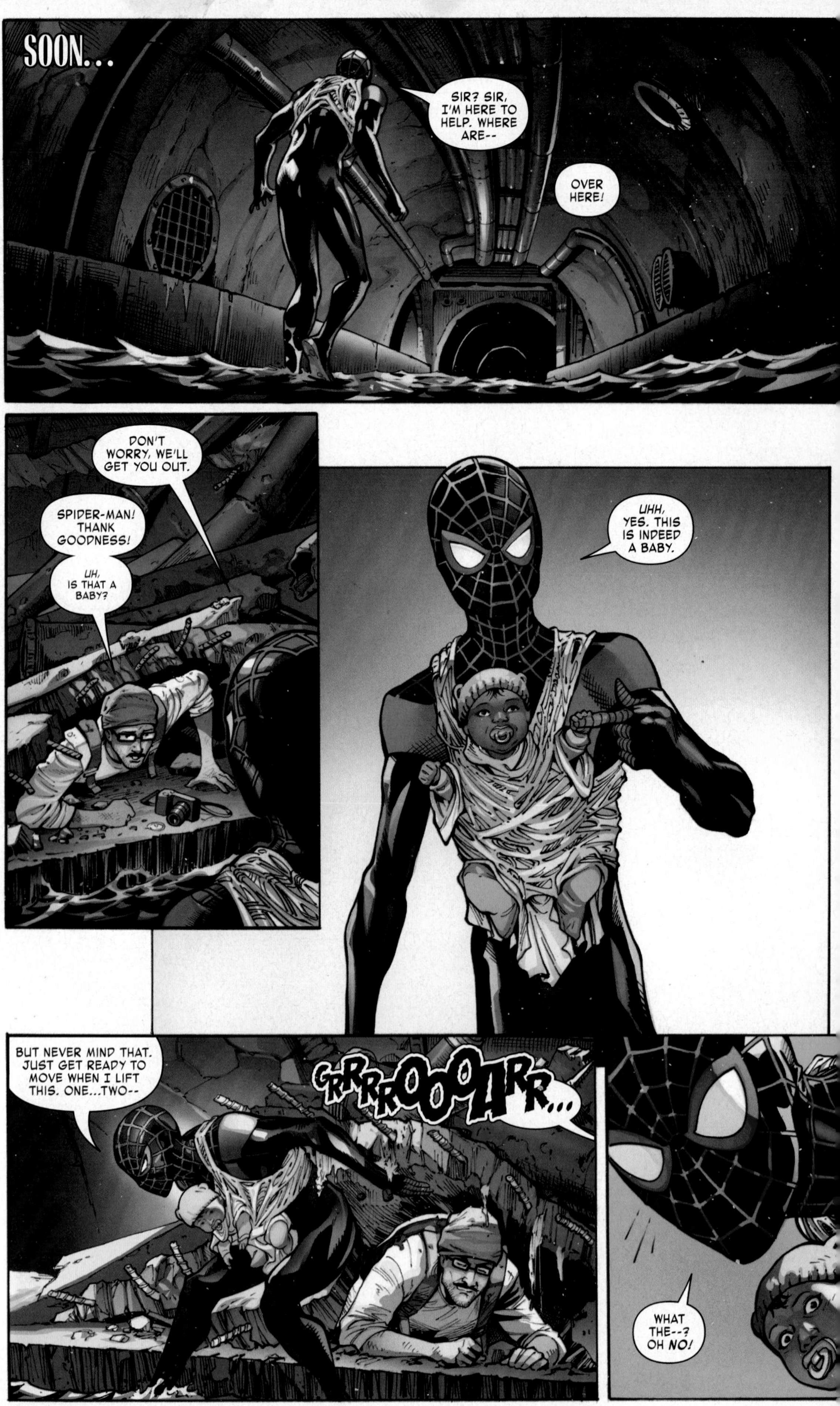
SOON...
SIR? SIR, I'M HERE TO HELP. WHERE ARE--
OVER HERE!
DON'T WORRY, WE'LL GET YOU OUT.
SPIDER-MAN! THANK GOODNESS!
UH, IS THAT A BABY?
UHH, YES. THIS IS INDEED A BABY.
BUT NEVER MIND THAT. JUST GET READY TO MOVE WHEN I LIFT THIS. ONE...TWO--
GRRRROOOOARR...
WHAT THE--? OH NO!

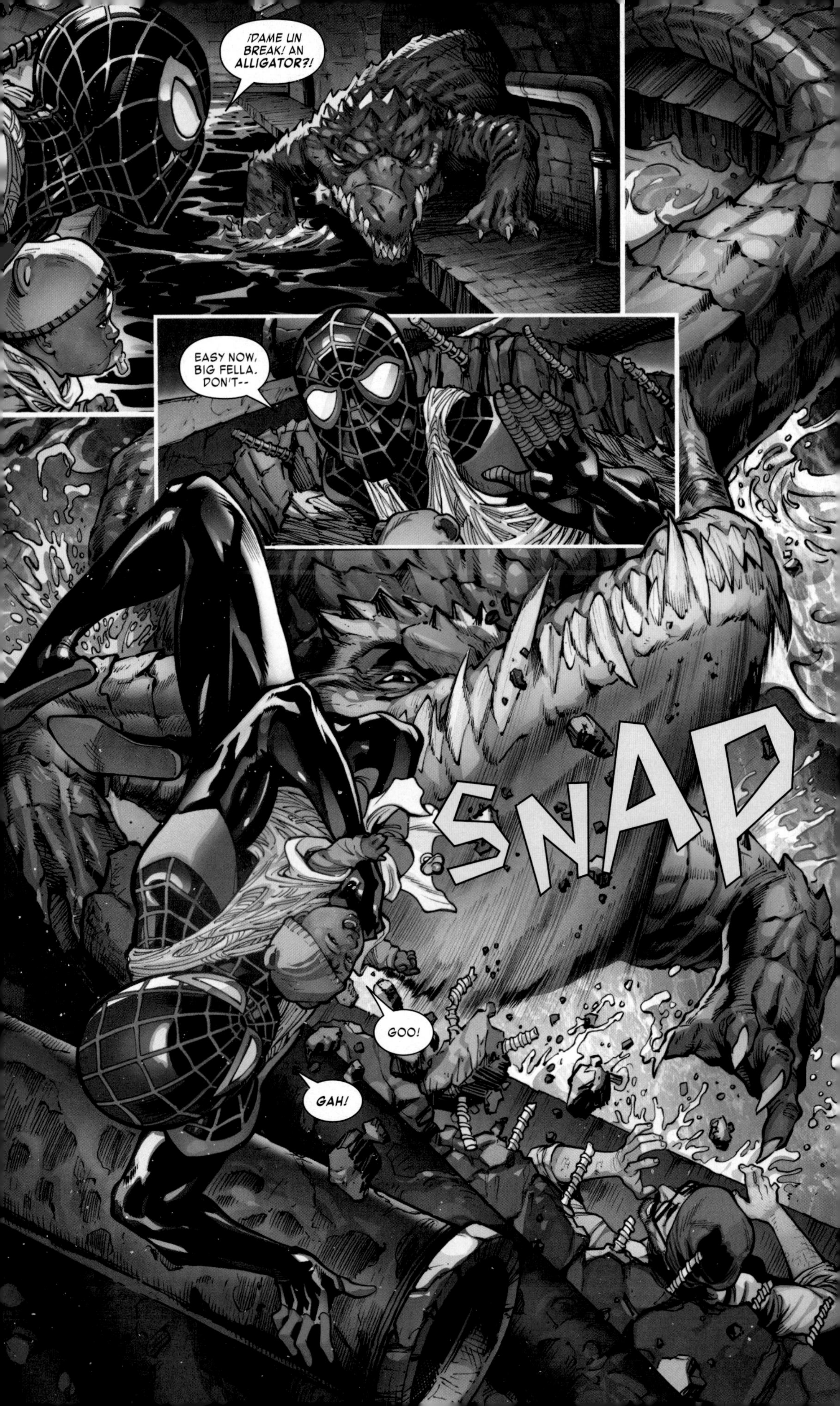
¡DAME UN BREAK! AN ALLIGATOR?!
EASY NOW, BIG FELLA. DON'T--
SNAP
GOO!
GAH!

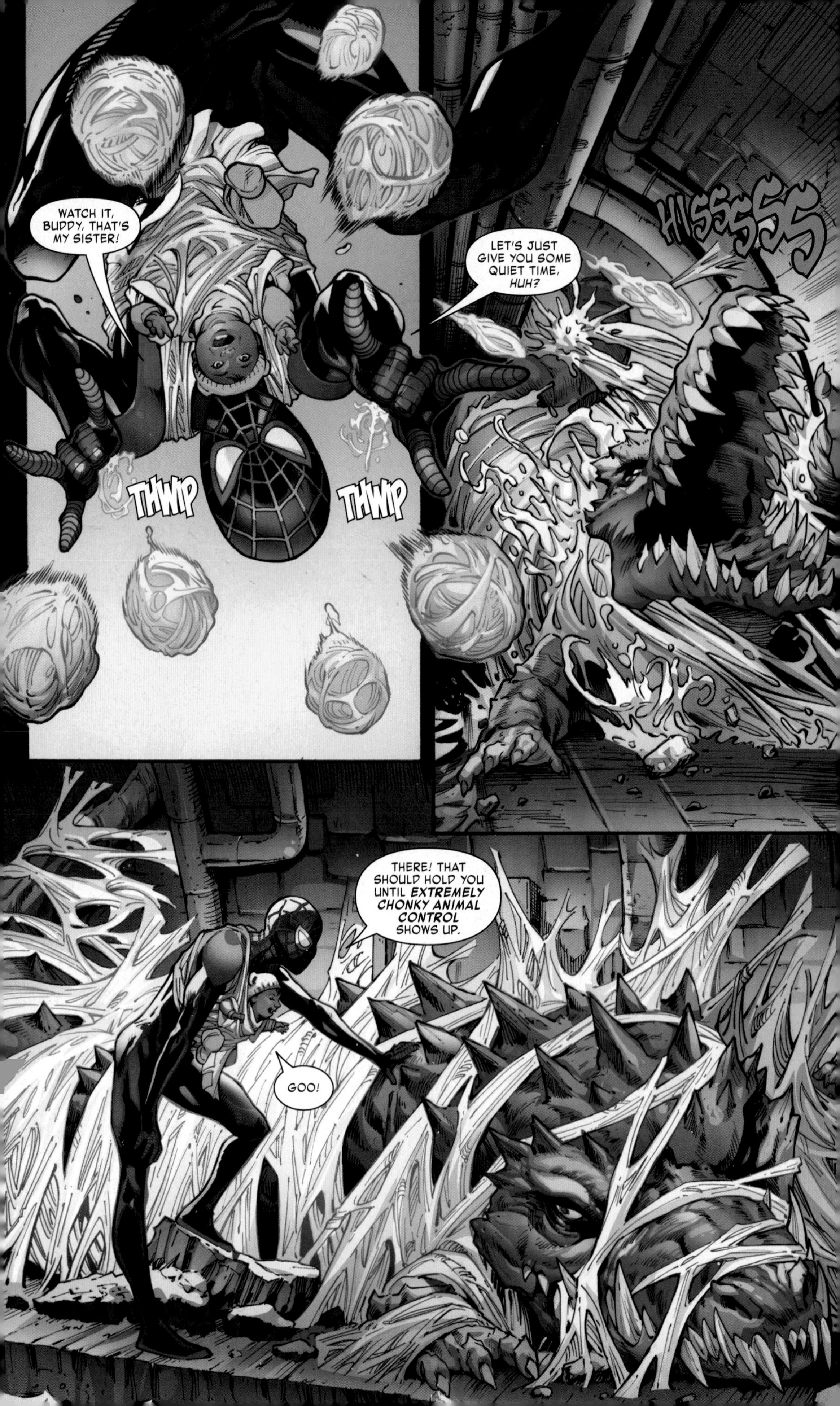
WATCH IT, BUDDY, THAT'S MY SISTER!
THWIP
THWIP
LET'S JUST GIVE YOU SOME QUIET TIME, HUH?
HISSSSSS
THERE! THAT SHOULD HOLD YOU UNTIL EXTREMELY CHONKY ANIMAL CONTROL SHOWS UP.
GOO!

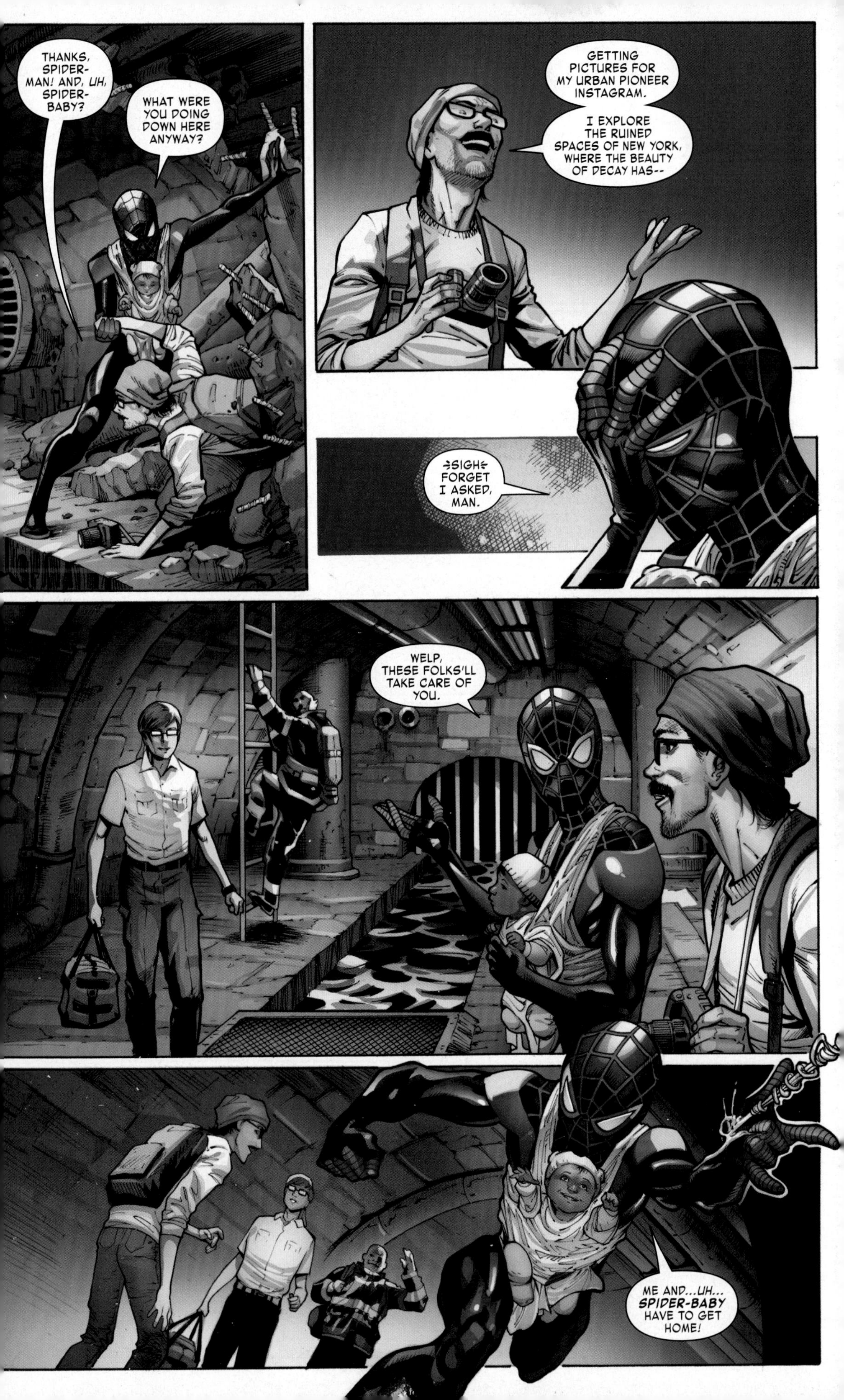
THANKS, SPIDER-MAN! AND, UH, SPIDER-BABY?
WHAT WERE YOU DOING DOWN HERE ANYWAY?
GETTING PICTURES FOR MY URBAN PIONEER INSTAGRAM.
I EXPLORE THE RUINED SPACES OF NEW YORK, WHERE THE BEAUTY OF DECAY HAS--
SIGH FORGET I ASKED, MAN.
WELP, THESE FOLKS'LL TAKE CARE OF YOU.
ME AND...UH... SPIDER-BABY HAVE TO GET HOME!

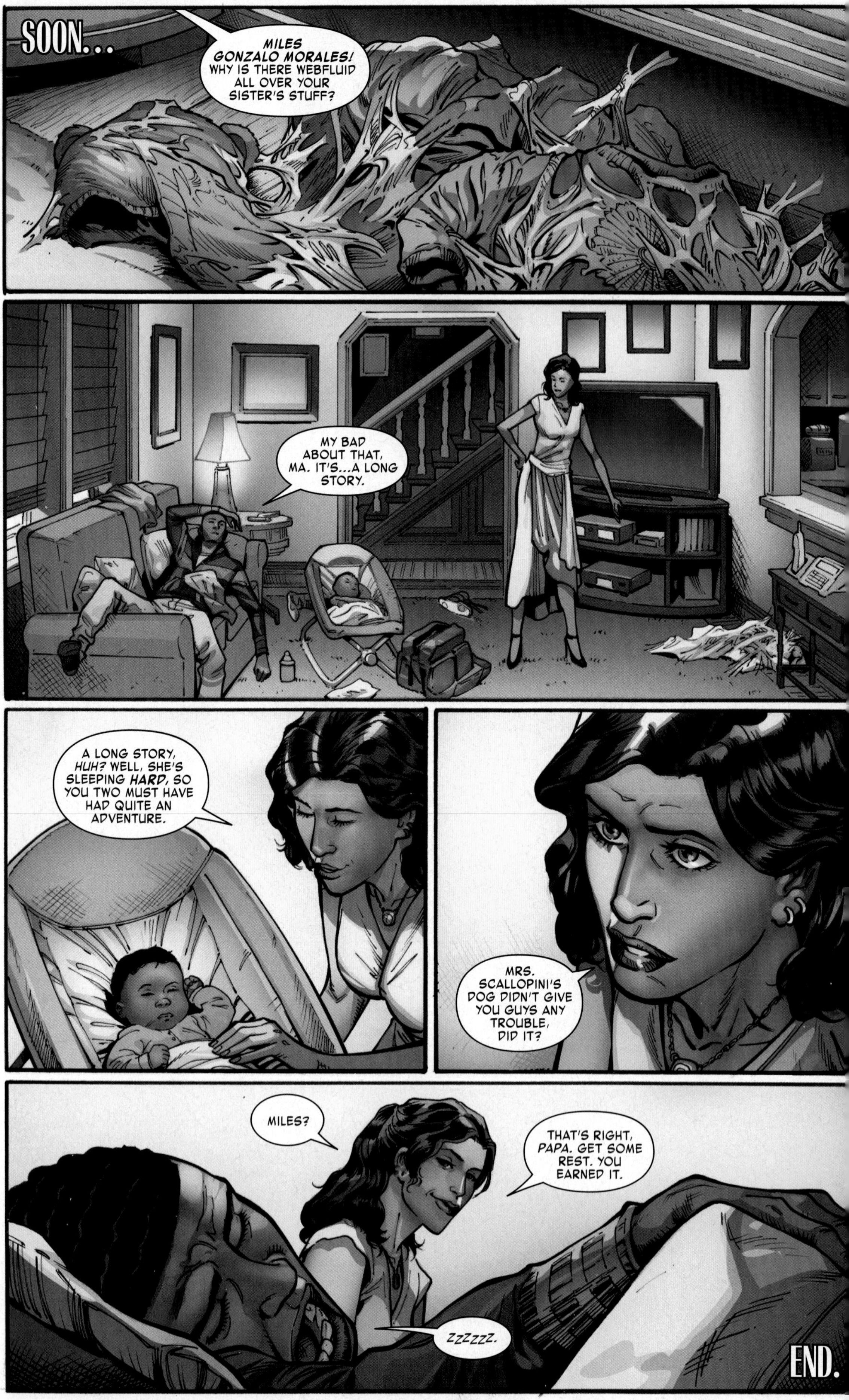
SOON...
MILES GONZALO MORALES! WHY IS THERE WEBFLUID ALL OVER YOUR SISTER'S STUFF?
MY BAD ABOUT THAT, MA. IT'S...A LONG STORY.
A LONG STORY, HUH? WELL, SHE'S SLEEPING HARD, SO YOU TWO MUST HAVE HAD QUITE AN ADVENTURE.
MRS. SCALLOPINI'S DOG DIDN'T GIVE YOU GUYS ANY TROUBLE, DID IT?
MILES?
THAT'S RIGHT, PAPA. GET SOME REST. YOU EARNED IT.
ZZZZZZ.
END.

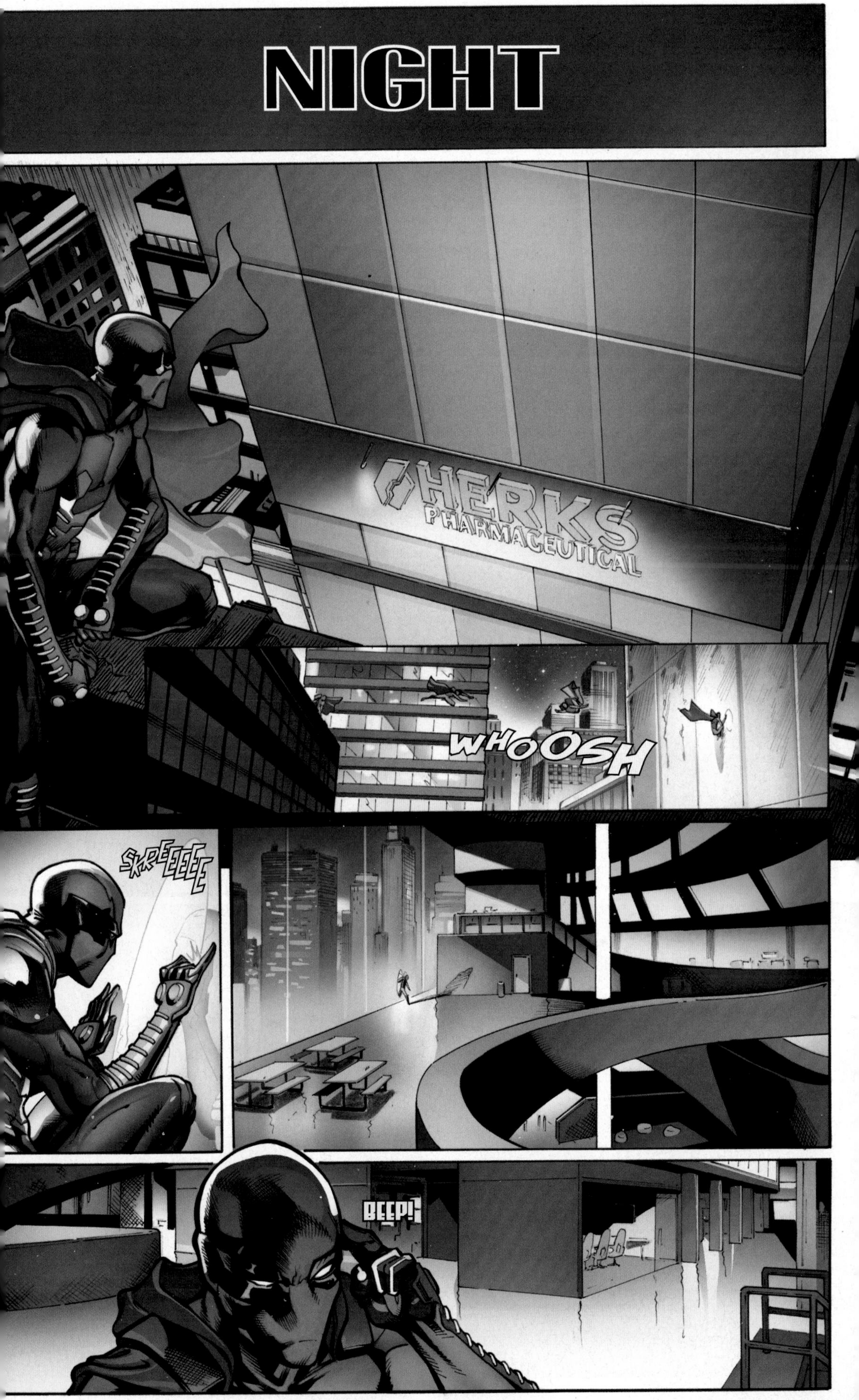

NIGHT
HERKS
PHARMACEUTICAL
WHOOSH
SKREEEEEE
BEEP!

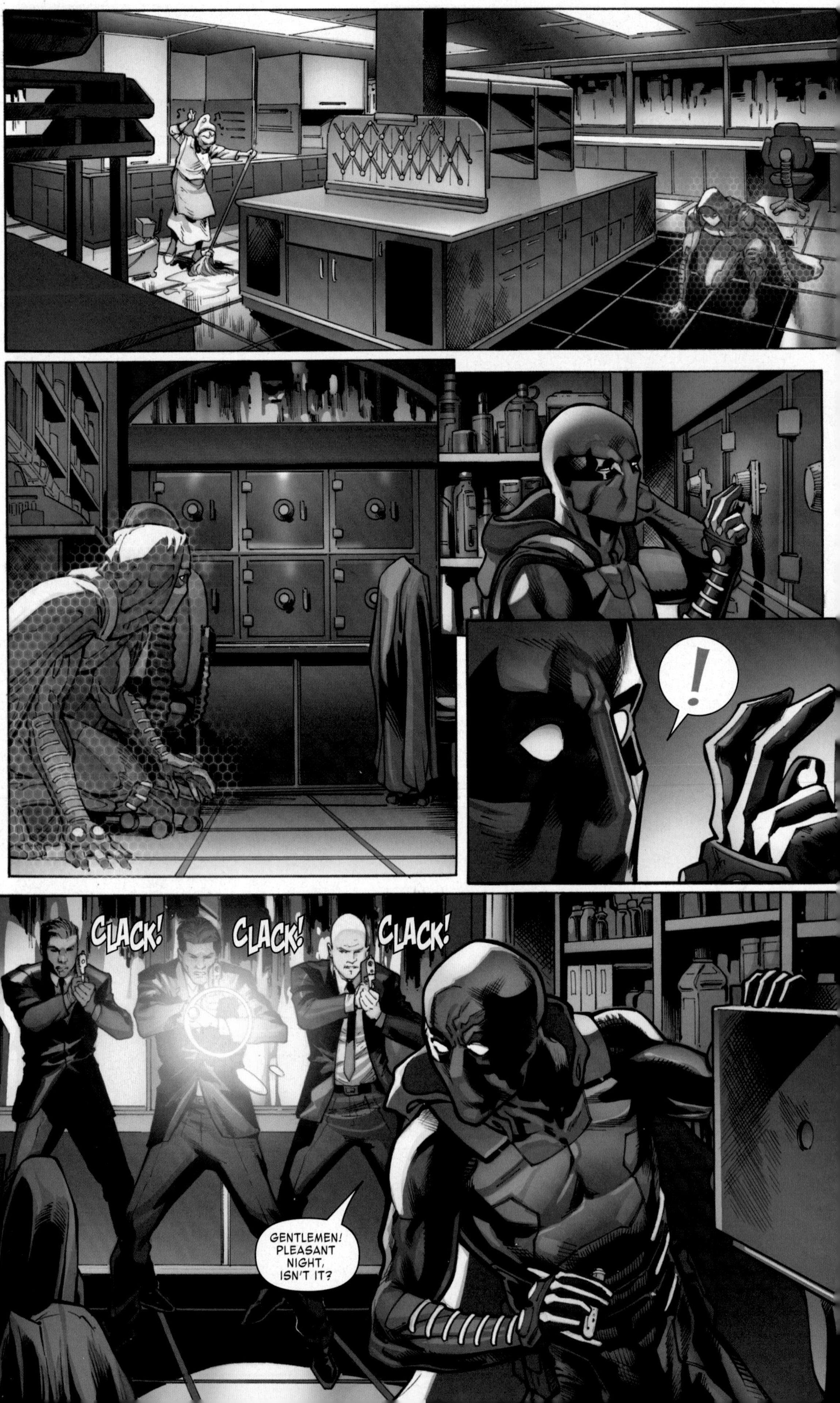
!
CLACK!
CLACK!
CLACK!
GENTLEMEN! PLEASANT NIGHT, ISN'T IT?

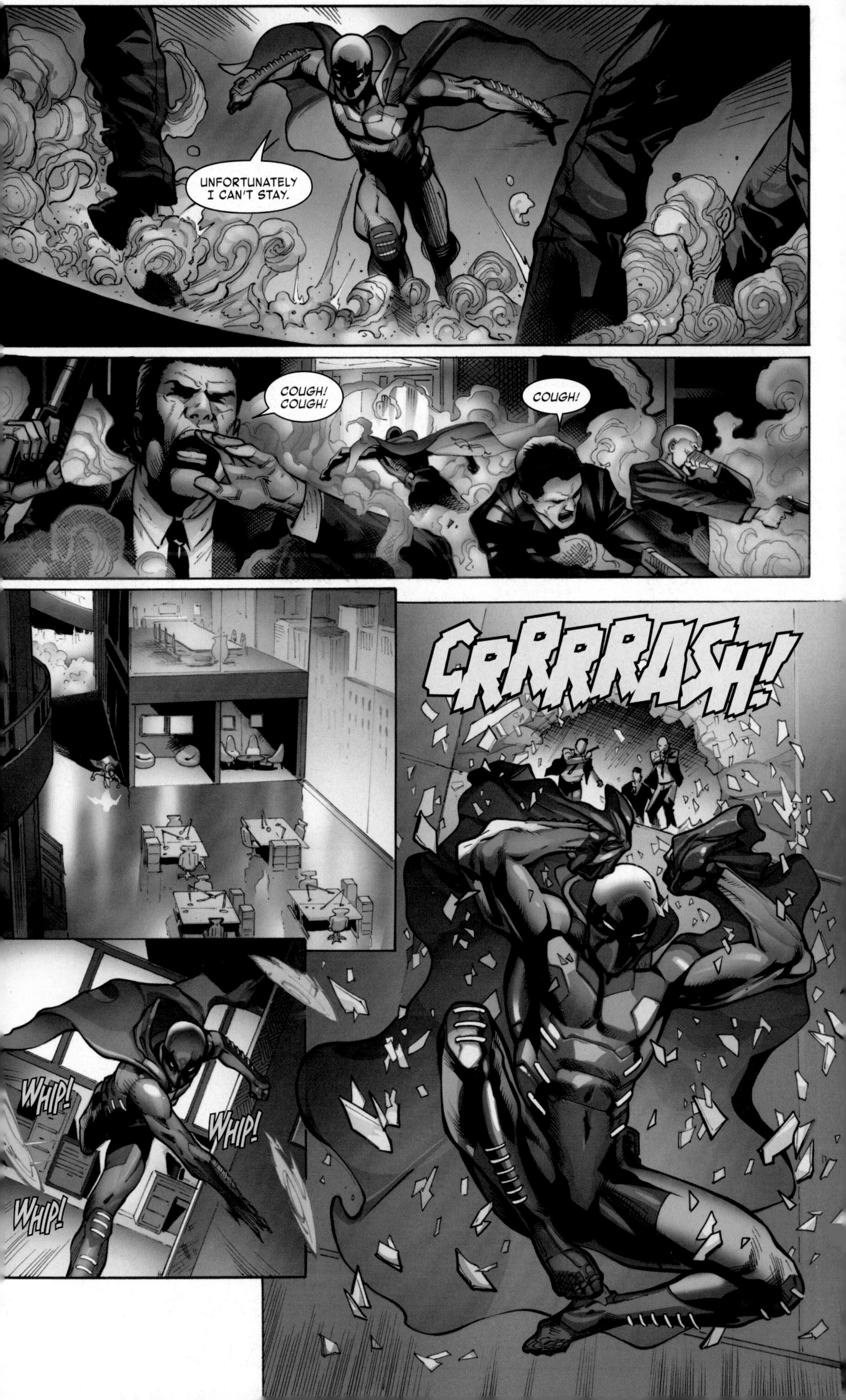
UNFORTUNATELY I CAN'T STAY.
COUGH! COUGH!
COUGH!
CRRRRASH!
WHIP!
WHIP!
WHIP!

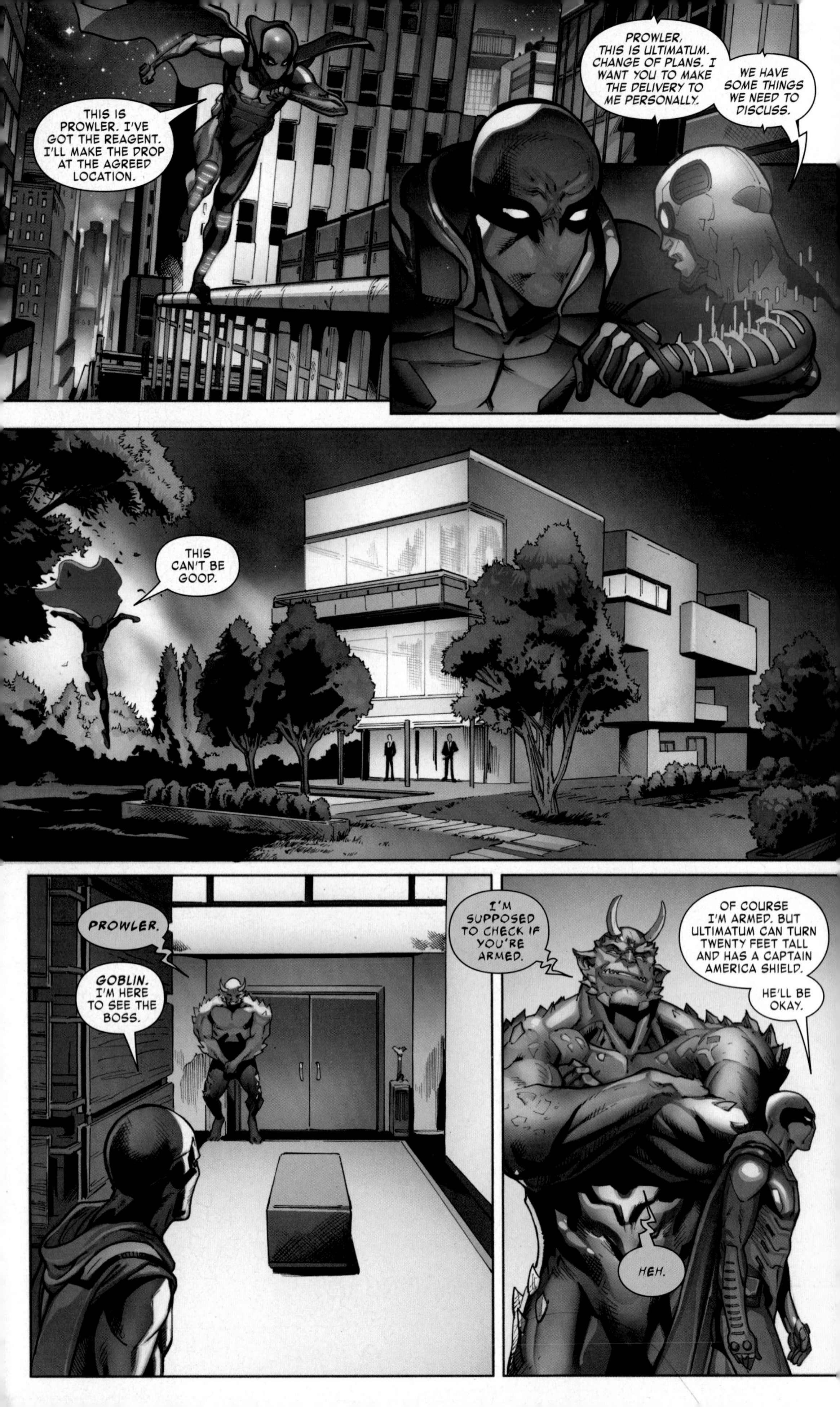
THIS IS PROWLER. I'VE GOT THE REAGENT. I'LL MAKE THE DROP AT THE AGREED LOCATION.
PROWLER, THIS IS ULTIMATUM. CHANGE OF PLANS. I WANT YOU TO MAKE THE DELIVERY TO ME PERSONALLY.
WE HAVE SOME THINGS WE NEED TO DISCUSS.
THIS CAN'T BE GOOD.
PROWLER.
GOBLIN. I'M HERE TO SEE THE BOSS.
I'M SUPPOSED TO CHECK IF YOU'RE ARMED.
OF COURSE I'M ARMED. BUT ULTIMATUM CAN TURN TWENTY FEET TALL AND HAS A CAPTAIN AMERICA SHIELD.
HE'LL BE OKAY.
HEH.

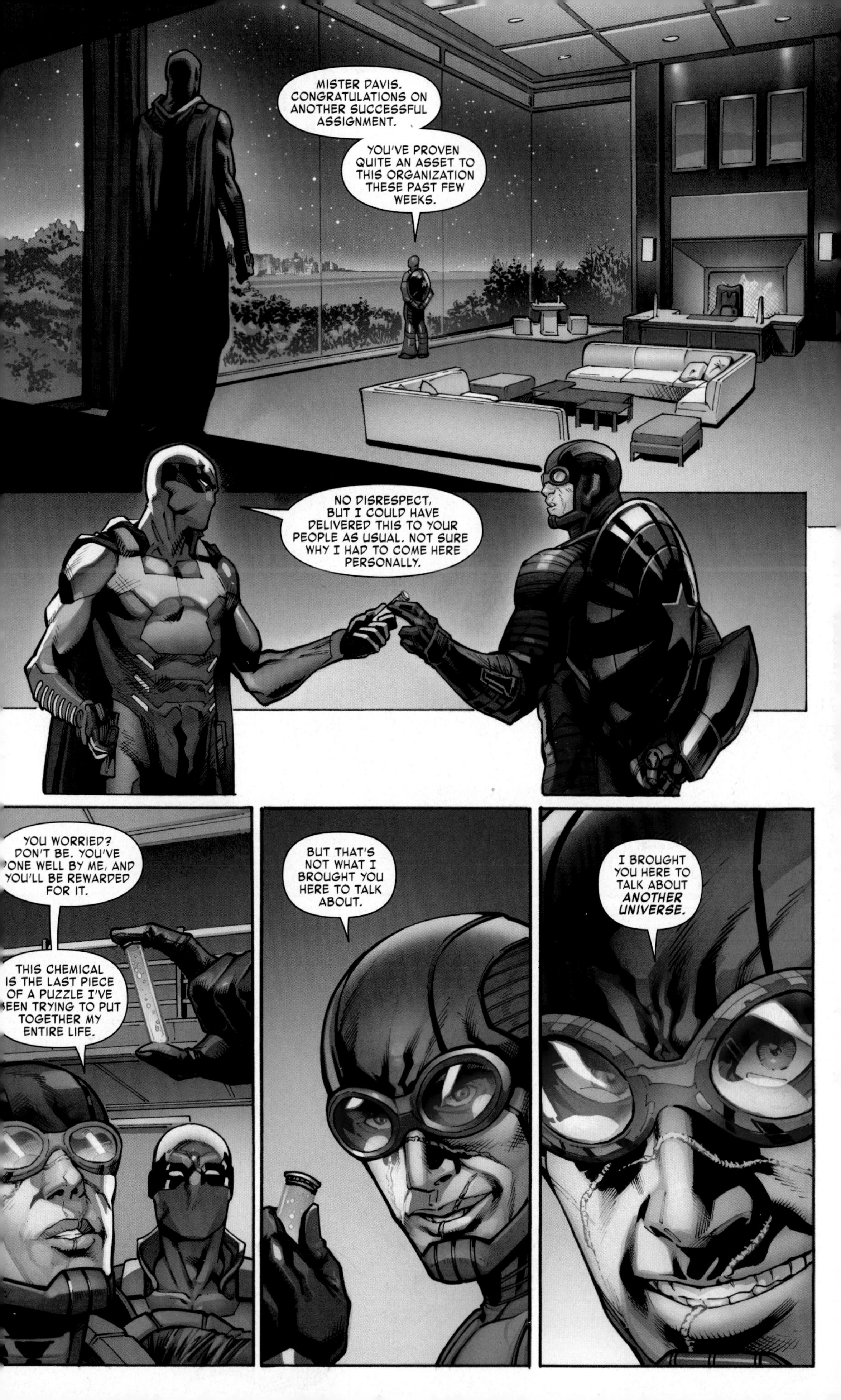

MISTER DAVIS. CONGRATULATIONS ON ANOTHER SUCCESSFUL ASSIGNMENT.
YOU'VE PROVEN QUITE AN ASSET TO THIS ORGANIZATION THESE PAST FEW WEEKS.
NO DISRESPECT, BUT I COULD HAVE DELIVERED THIS TO YOUR PEOPLE AS USUAL. NOT SURE WHY I HAD TO COME HERE PERSONALLY.
YOU WORRIED? DON'T BE. YOU'VE DONE WELL BY ME, AND YOU'LL BE REWARDED FOR IT.
THIS CHEMICAL IS THE LAST PIECE OF A PUZZLE I'VE BEEN TRYING TO PUT TOGETHER MY ENTIRE LIFE.
BUT THAT'S NOT WHAT I BROUGHT YOU HERE TO TALK ABOUT.
I BROUGHT YOU HERE TO TALK ABOUT ***ANOTHER UNIVERSE.***

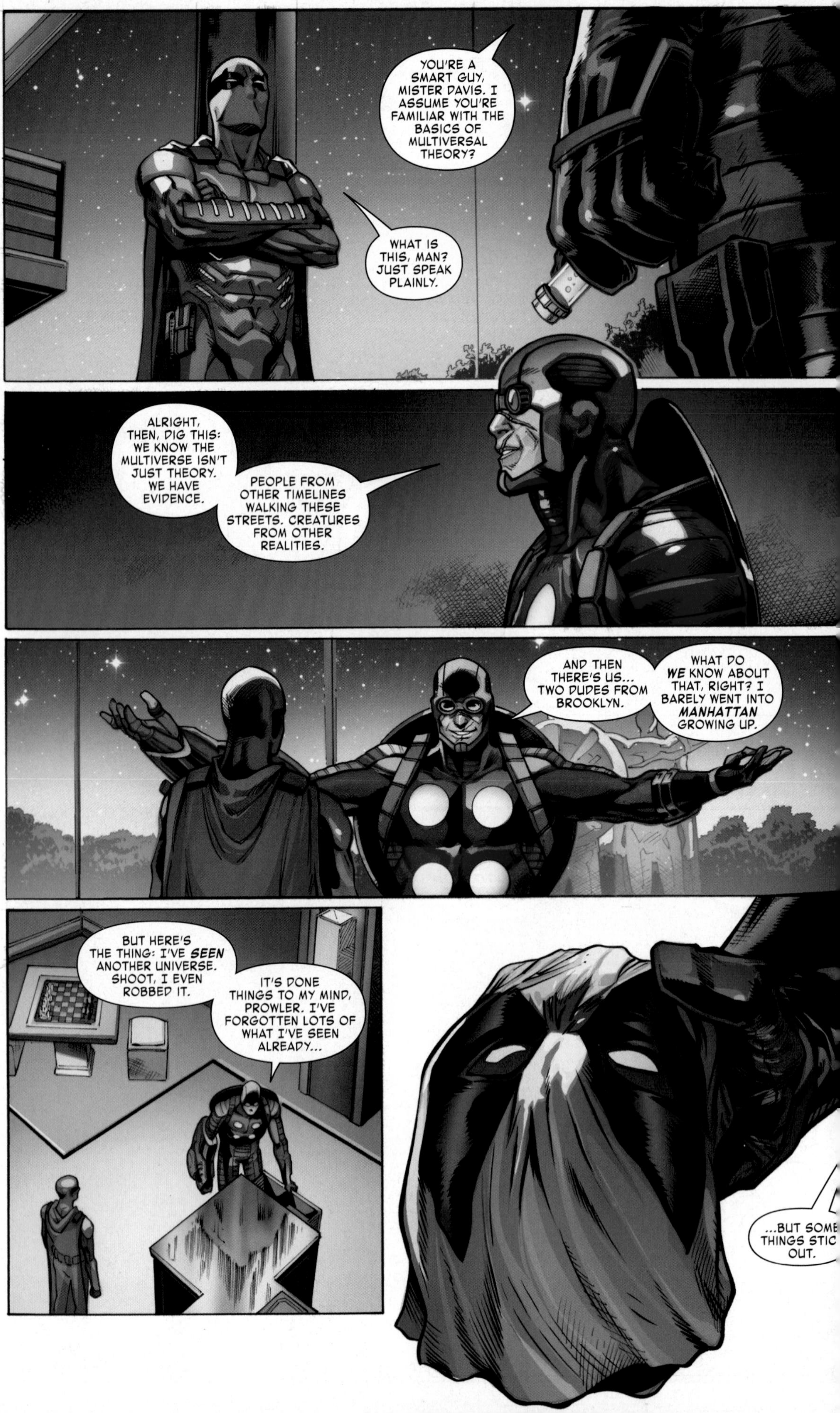
YOU'RE A SMART GUY, MISTER DAVIS. I ASSUME YOU'RE FAMILIAR WITH THE BASICS OF MULTIVERSAL THEORY?
WHAT IS THIS, MAN? JUST SPEAK PLAINLY.
ALRIGHT, THEN, DIG THIS: WE KNOW THE MULTIVERSE ISN'T JUST THEORY. WE HAVE EVIDENCE.
PEOPLE FROM OTHER TIMELINES WALKING THESE STREETS. CREATURES FROM OTHER REALITIES.
AND THEN THERE'S US... TWO DUDES FROM BROOKLYN.
WHAT DO WE KNOW ABOUT THAT, RIGHT? I BARELY WENT INTO MANHATTAN GROWING UP.
BUT HERE'S THE THING: I'VE SEEN ANOTHER UNIVERSE. SHOOT, I EVEN ROBBED IT.
IT'S DONE THINGS TO MY MIND, PROWLER. I'VE FORGOTTEN LOTS OF WHAT I'VE SEEN ALREADY...
...BUT SOME THINGS STIC OUT.

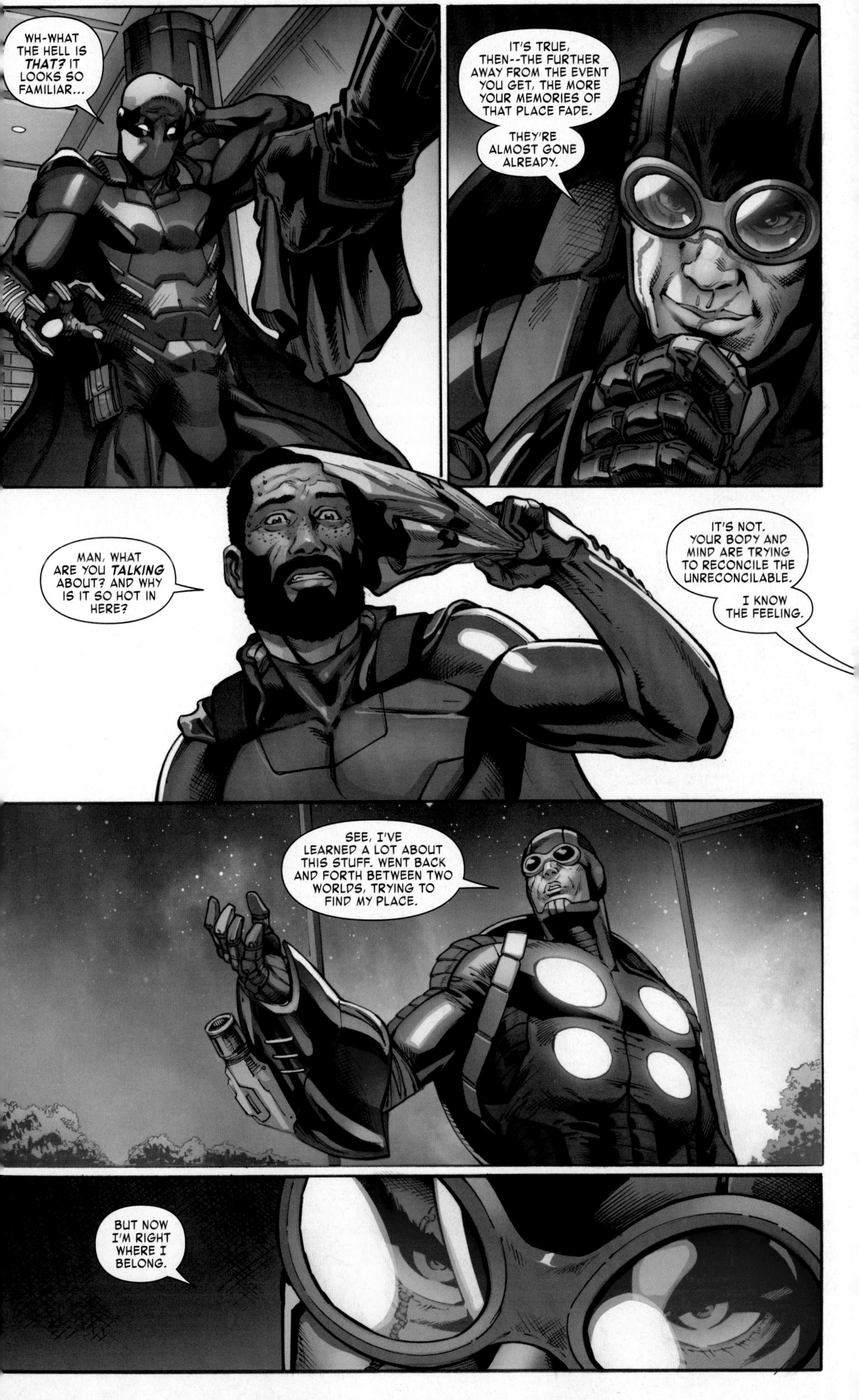
WH-WHAT THE HELL IS *THAT?* IT LOOKS SO FAMILIAR...
IT'S TRUE, THEN--THE FURTHER AWAY FROM THE EVENT YOU GET, THE MORE YOUR MEMORIES OF THAT PLACE FADE.
THEY'RE ALMOST GONE ALREADY.
MAN, WHAT ARE YOU *TALKING* ABOUT? AND WHY IS IT SO HOT IN HERE?
IT'S NOT. YOUR BODY AND MIND ARE TRYING TO RECONCILE THE UNRECONCILABLE.
I KNOW THE FEELING.
SEE, I'VE LEARNED A LOT ABOUT THIS STUFF. WENT BACK AND FORTH BETWEEN TWO WORLDS, TRYING TO FIND MY PLACE.
BUT NOW I'M RIGHT WHERE I BELONG.

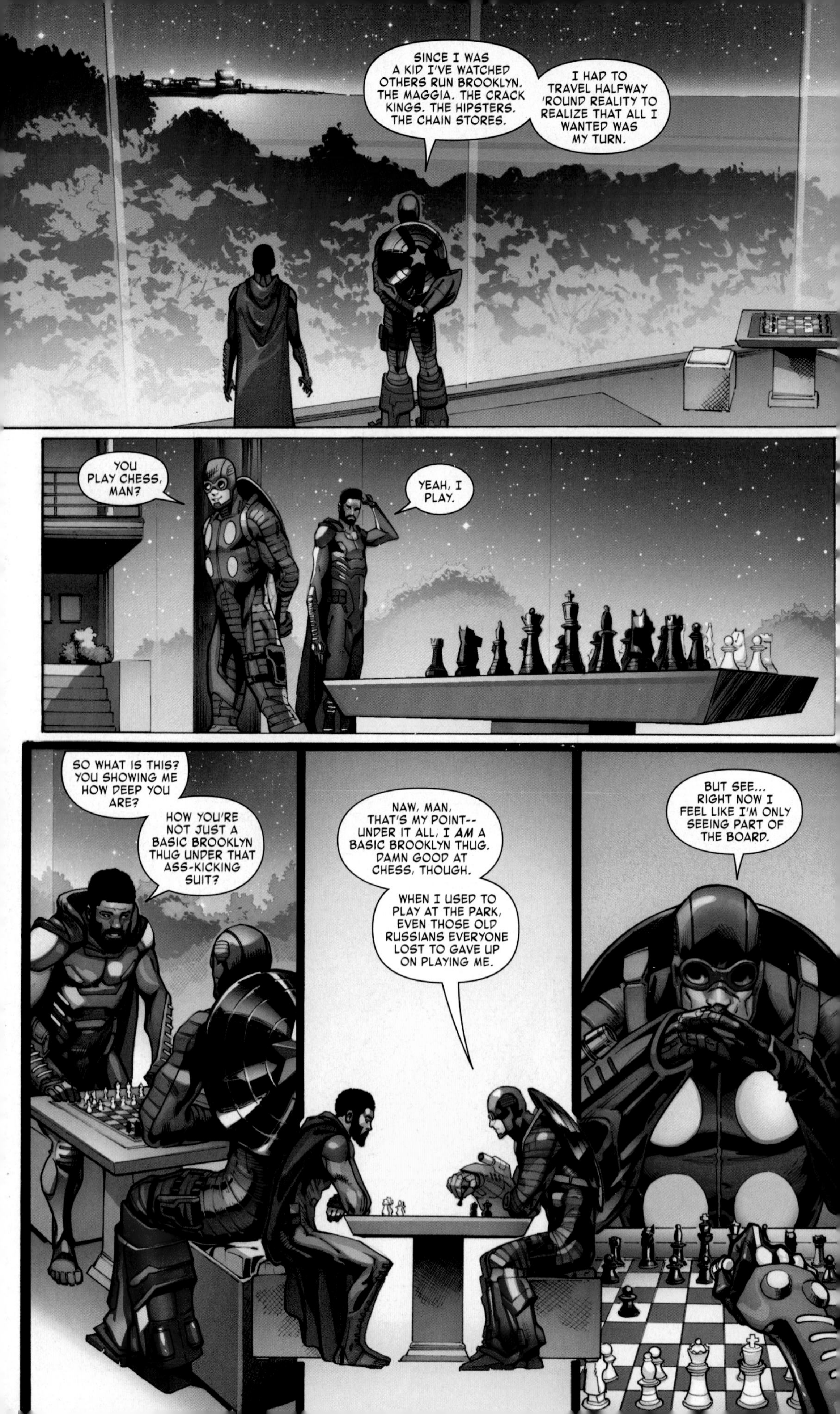
SINCE I WAS A KID I'VE WATCHED OTHERS RUN BROOKLYN. THE MAGGIA. THE CRACK KINGS. THE HIPSTERS. THE CHAIN STORES.
I HAD TO TRAVEL HALFWAY 'ROUND REALITY TO REALIZE THAT ALL I WANTED WAS MY TURN.
YOU PLAY CHESS, MAN?
YEAH, I PLAY.
SO WHAT IS THIS? YOU SHOWING ME HOW DEEP YOU ARE?
HOW YOU'RE NOT JUST A BASIC BROOKLYN THUG UNDER THAT ASS-KICKING SUIT?
NAW, MAN, THAT'S MY POINT-- UNDER IT ALL, I *AM* A BASIC BROOKLYN THUG. DAMN GOOD AT CHESS, THOUGH.
WHEN I USED TO PLAY AT THE PARK, EVEN THOSE OLD RUSSIANS EVERYONE LOST TO GAVE UP ON PLAYING ME.
BUT SEE... RIGHT NOW I FEEL LIKE I'M ONLY SEEING PART OF THE BOARD.

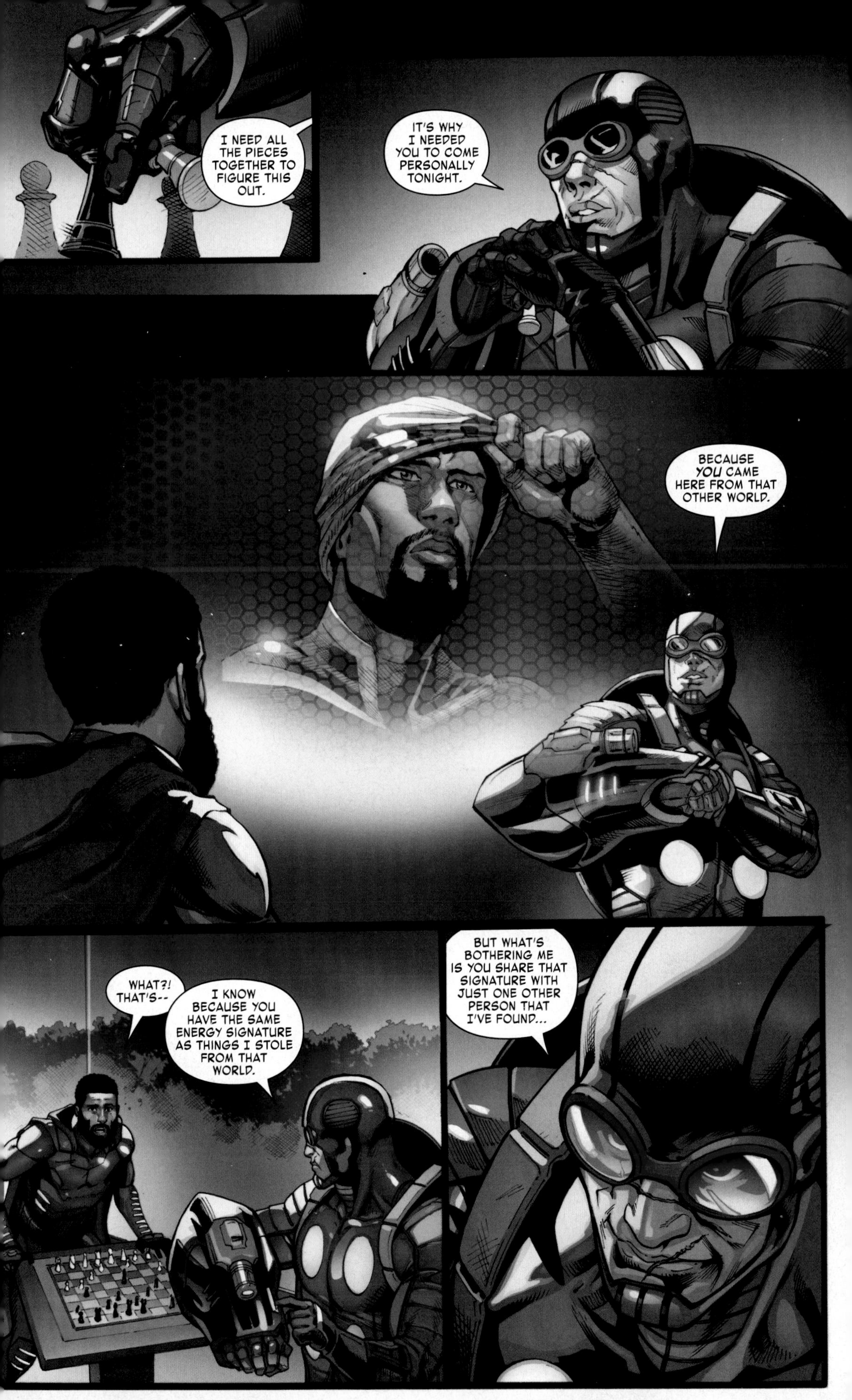
I NEED ALL THE PIECES TOGETHER TO FIGURE THIS OUT.
IT'S WHY I NEEDED YOU TO COME PERSONALLY TONIGHT.
BECAUSE *YOU* CAME HERE FROM THAT OTHER WORLD.
WHAT?! THAT'S--
I KNOW BECAUSE YOU HAVE THE SAME ENERGY SIGNATURE AS THINGS I STOLE FROM THAT WORLD.
BUT WHAT'S BOTHERING ME IS YOU SHARE THAT SIGNATURE WITH JUST ONE OTHER PERSON THAT I'VE FOUND...

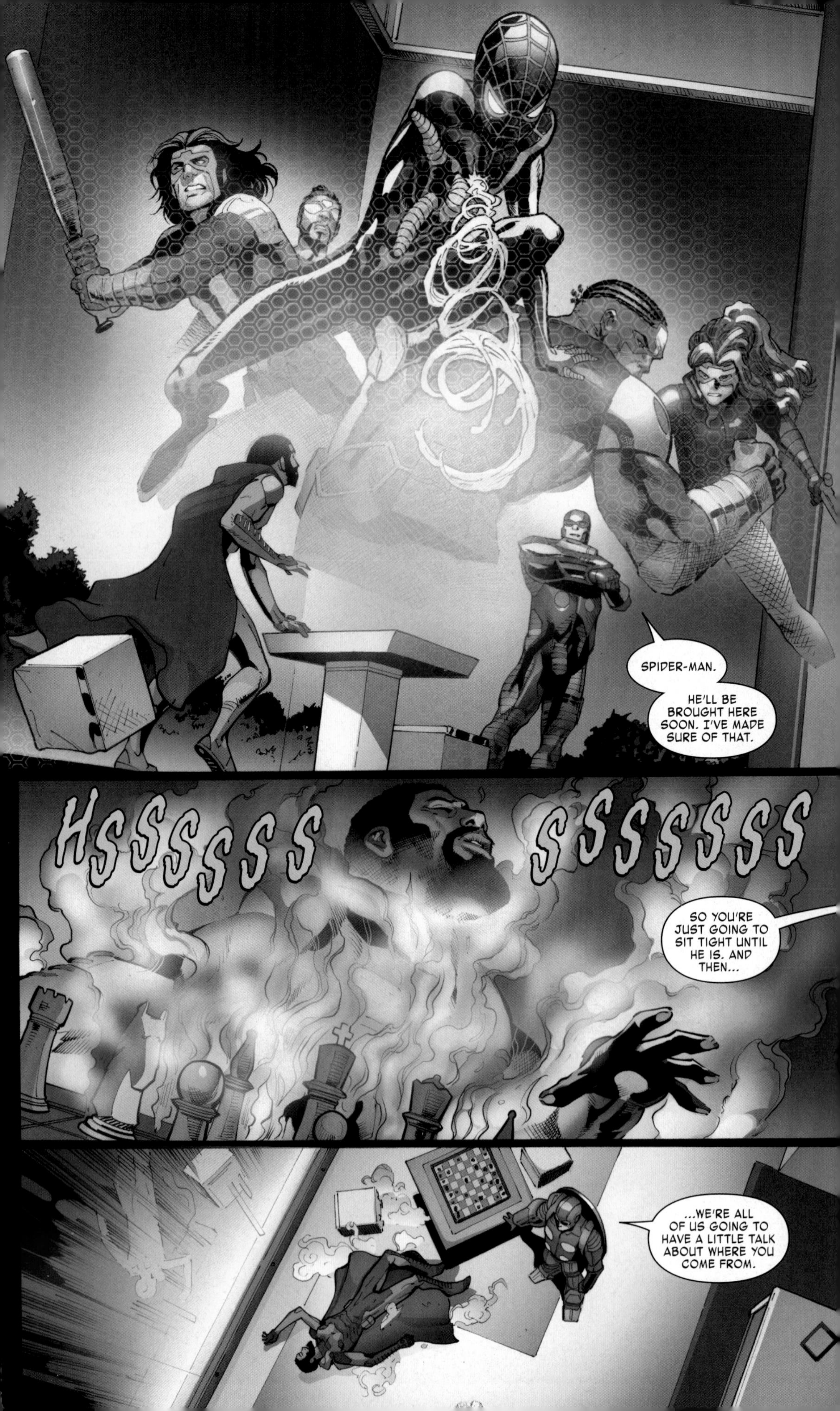
SPIDER-MAN.
HE'LL BE BROUGHT HERE SOON. I'VE MADE SURE OF THAT.
HSSSSSSS SSSSSSS
SO YOU'RE JUST GOING TO SIT TIGHT UNTIL HE IS. AND THEN...
...WE'RE ALL OF US GOING TO HAVE A LITTLE TALK ABOUT WHERE YOU COME FROM.

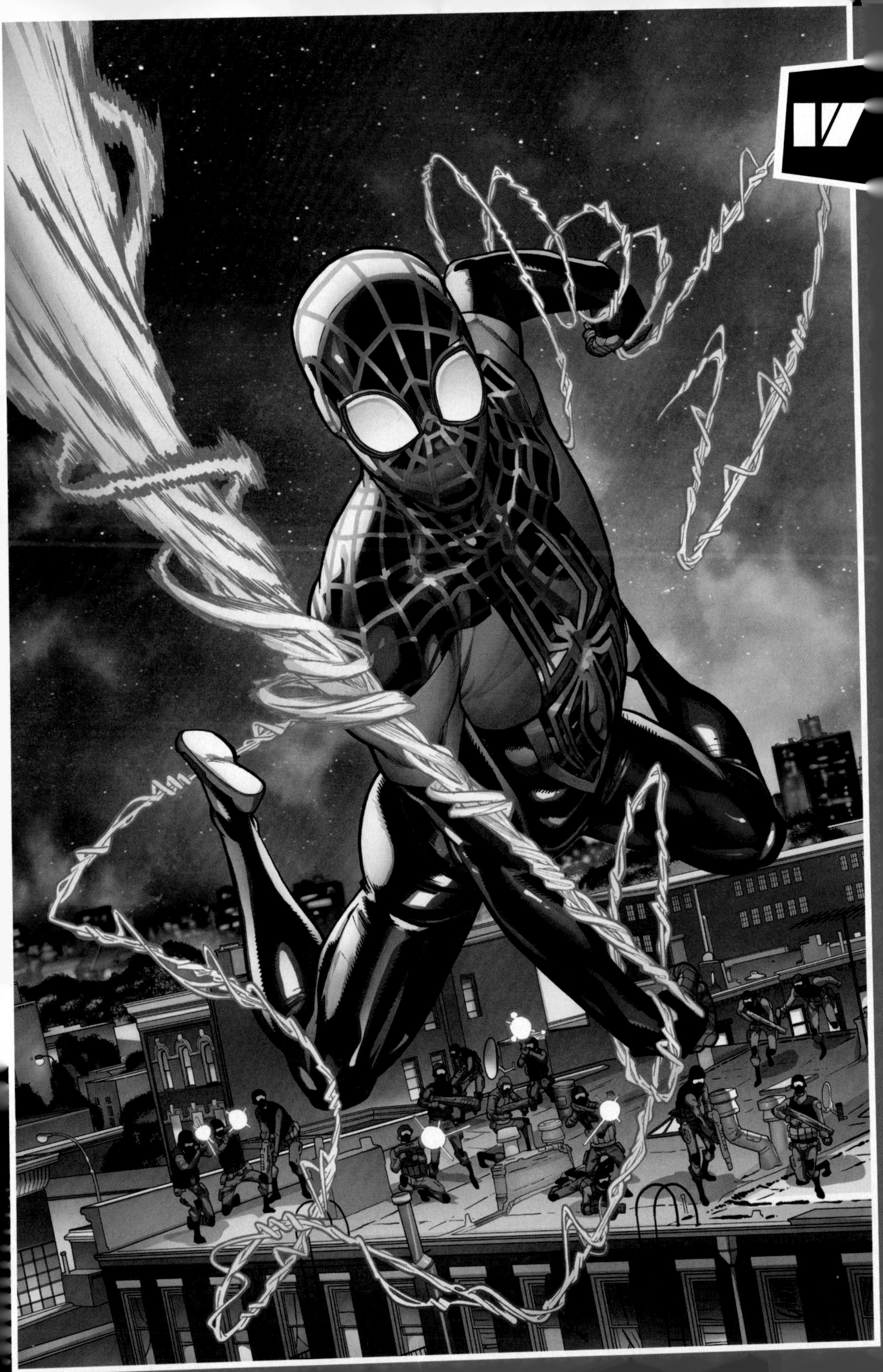

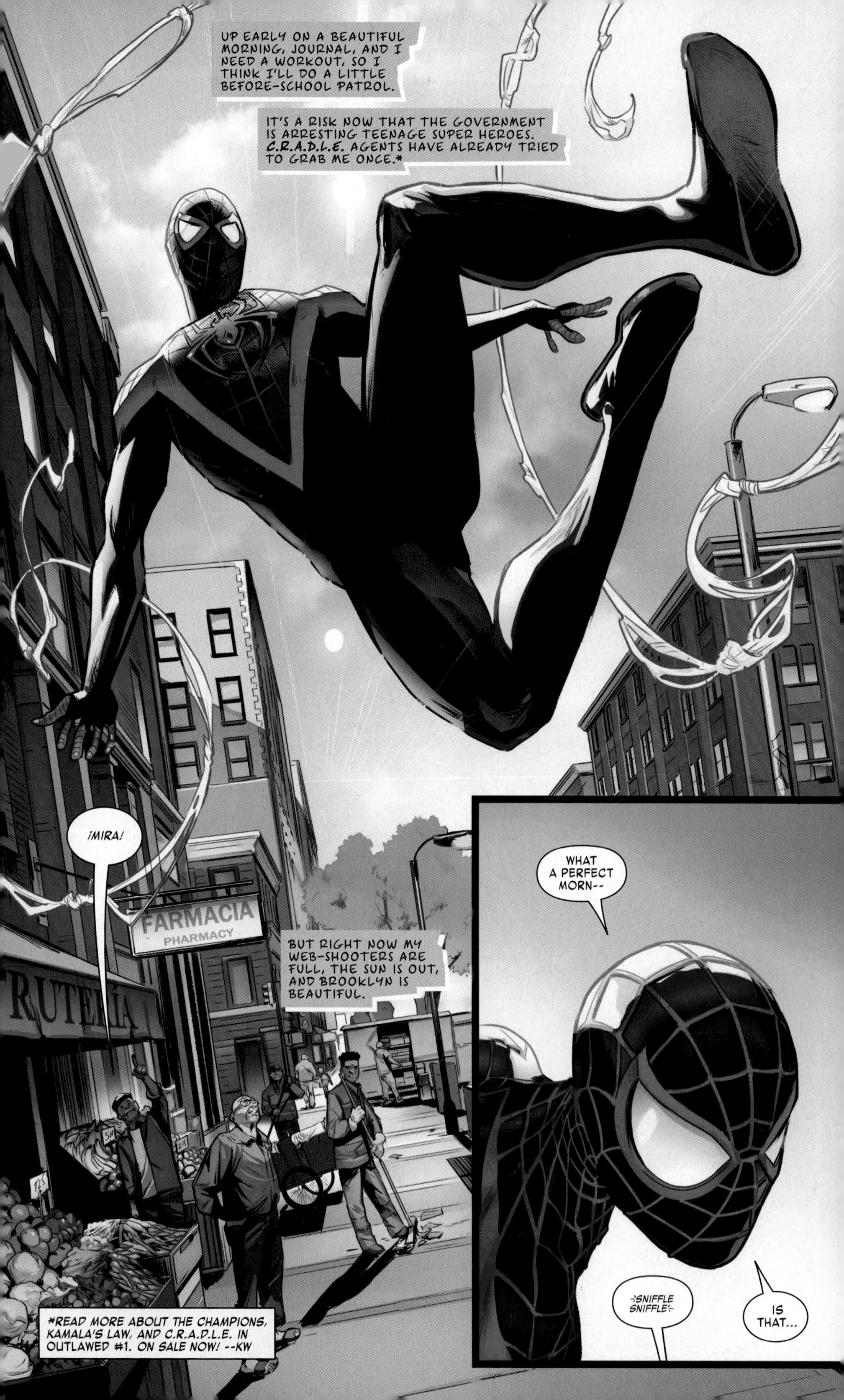

UP EARLY ON A BEAUTIFUL MORNING, JOURNAL, AND I NEED A WORKOUT, SO I THINK I'LL DO A LITTLE BEFORE-SCHOOL PATROL.
IT'S A RISK NOW THAT THE GOVERNMENT IS ARRESTING TEENAGE SUPER HEROES. C.R.A.D.L.E. AGENTS HAVE ALREADY TRIED TO GRAB ME ONCE.*
¡MIRA!
FARMACIA
PHARMACY
RUTERÍA
BUT RIGHT NOW MY WEB-SHOOTERS ARE FULL, THE SUN IS OUT, AND BROOKLYN IS BEAUTIFUL.
*READ MORE ABOUT THE CHAMPIONS, KAMALA'S LAW, AND C.R.A.D.L.E. IN OUTLAWED #1. ON SALE NOW! --KW
WHAT A PERFECT MORN--
SNIFFLE SNIFFLE
IS THAT...

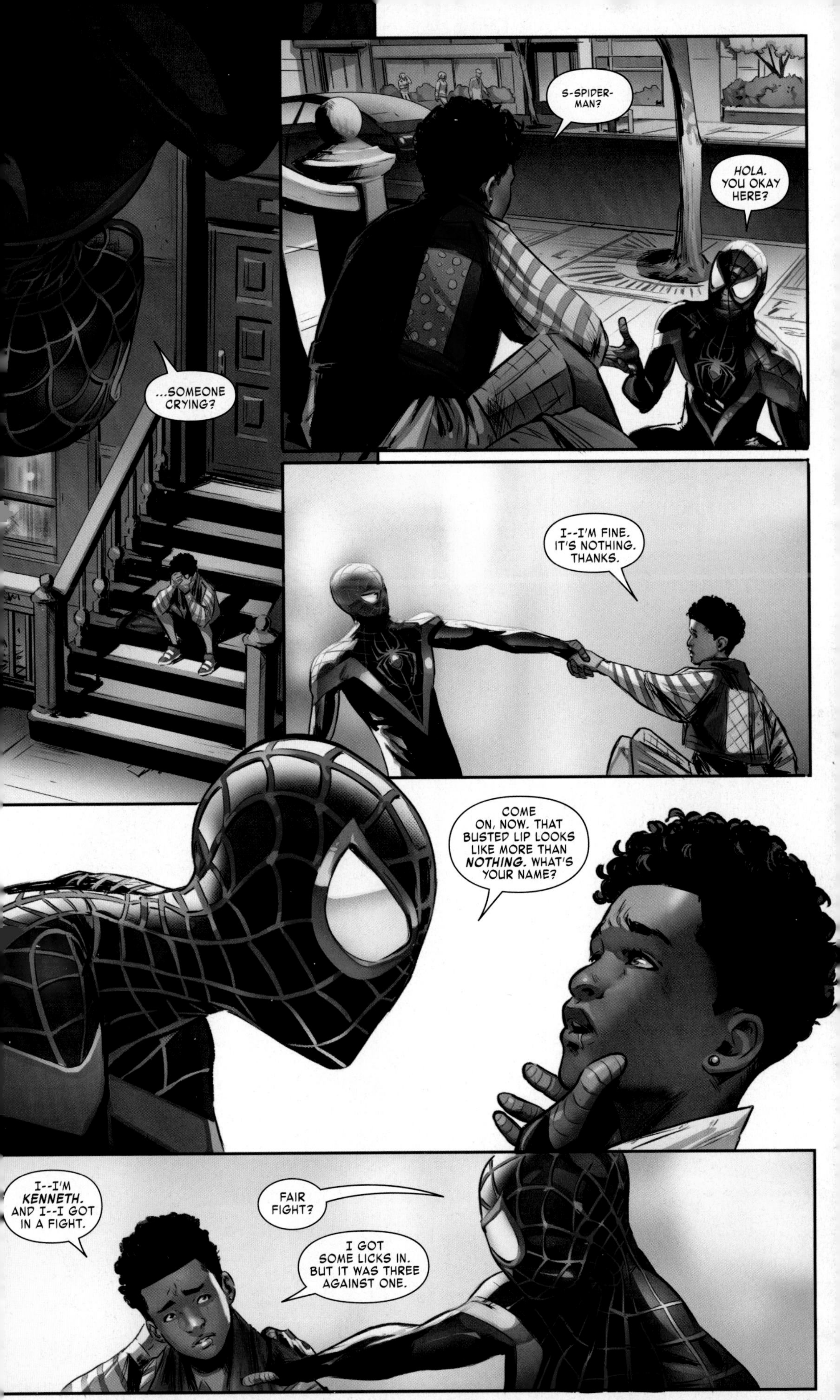
...SOMEONE CRYING?
S-SPIDER-MAN?
HOLA. YOU OKAY HERE?
I--I'M FINE. IT'S NOTHING. THANKS.
COME ON, NOW. THAT BUSTED LIP LOOKS LIKE MORE THAN NOTHING. WHAT'S YOUR NAME?
I--I'M KENNETH. AND I--I GOT IN A FIGHT.
FAIR FIGHT?
I GOT SOME LICKS IN. BUT IT WAS THREE AGAINST ONE.

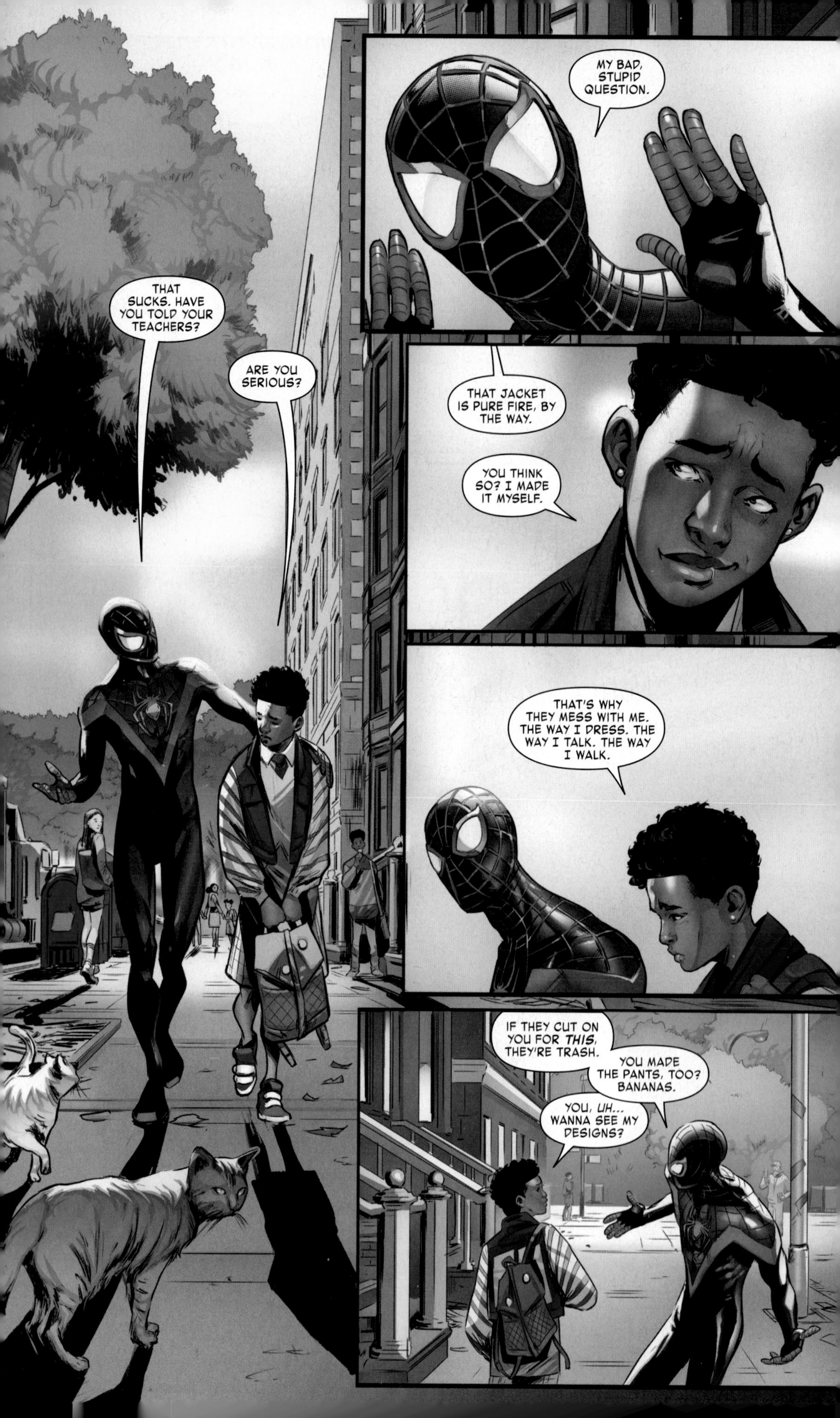
THAT SUCKS. HAVE YOU TOLD YOUR TEACHERS?
ARE YOU SERIOUS?
MY BAD, STUPID QUESTION.
THAT JACKET IS PURE FIRE, BY THE WAY.
YOU THINK SO? I MADE IT MYSELF.
THAT'S WHY THEY MESS WITH ME. THE WAY I DRESS. THE WAY I TALK. THE WAY I WALK.
IF THEY CUT ON YOU FOR *THIS*, THEY'RE TRASH.
YOU MADE THE PANTS, TOO? BANANAS.
YOU, *UH*... WANNA SEE MY DESIGNS?

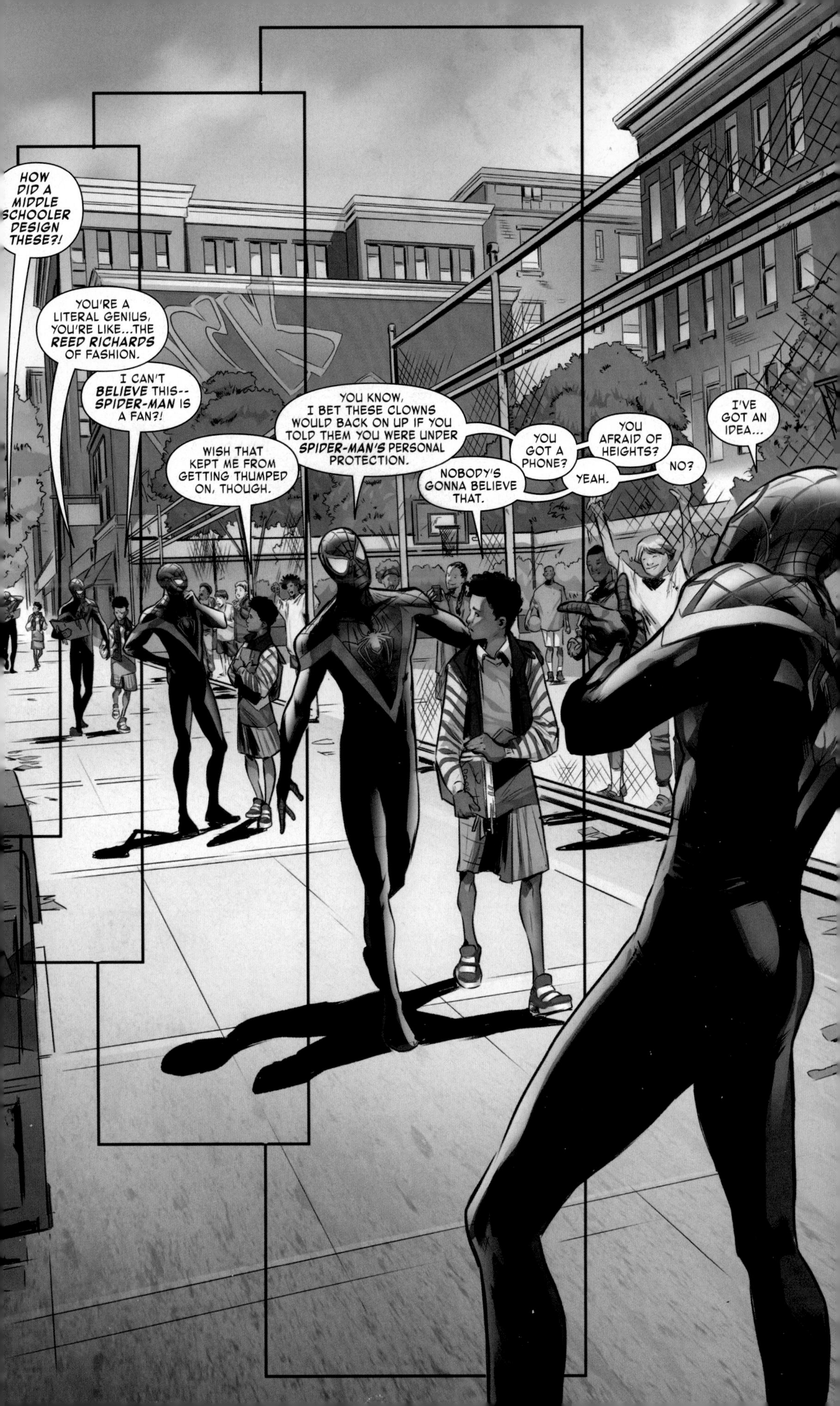

HOW DID A MIDDLE SCHOOLER DESIGN THESE?!
YOU'RE A LITERAL GENIUS, YOU'RE LIKE...THE REED RICHARDS OF FASHION.
I CAN'T BELIEVE THIS-- SPIDER-MAN IS A FAN?!
WISH THAT KEPT ME FROM GETTING THUMPED ON, THOUGH.
YOU KNOW, I BET THESE CLOWNS WOULD BACK ON UP IF YOU TOLD THEM YOU WERE UNDER SPIDER-MAN'S PERSONAL PROTECTION.
NOBODY'S GONNA BELIEVE THAT.
YOU GOT A PHONE?
YEAH.
YOU AFRAID OF HEIGHTS?
NO?
I'VE GOT AN IDEA...

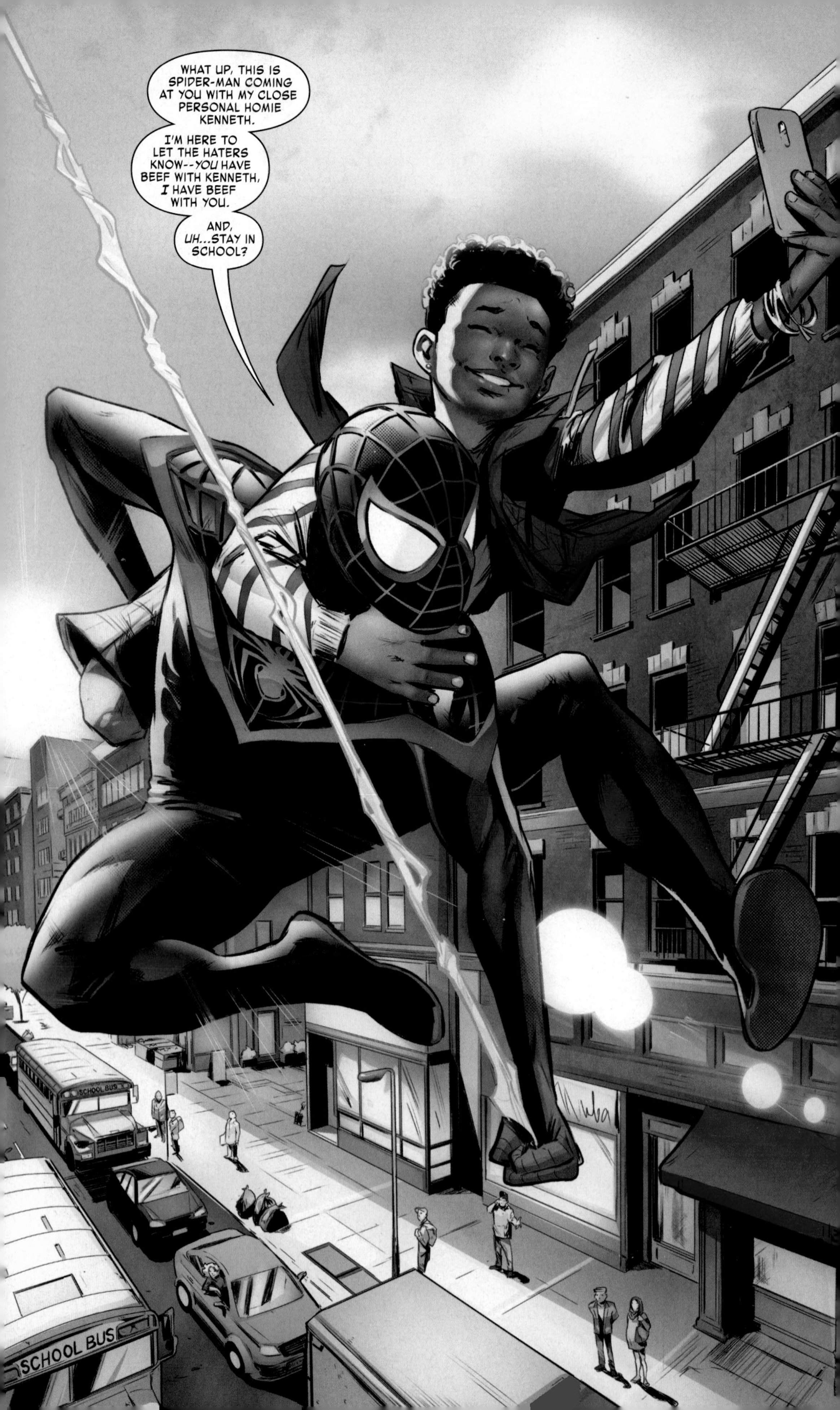

WHAT UP, THIS IS SPIDER-MAN COMING AT YOU WITH MY CLOSE PERSONAL HOMIE KENNETH.
I'M HERE TO LET THE HATERS KNOW--*YOU* HAVE BEEF WITH KENNETH, *I* HAVE BEEF WITH YOU.
AND, *UH*...STAY IN SCHOOL?
SCHOOL BUS
SCHOOL BUS

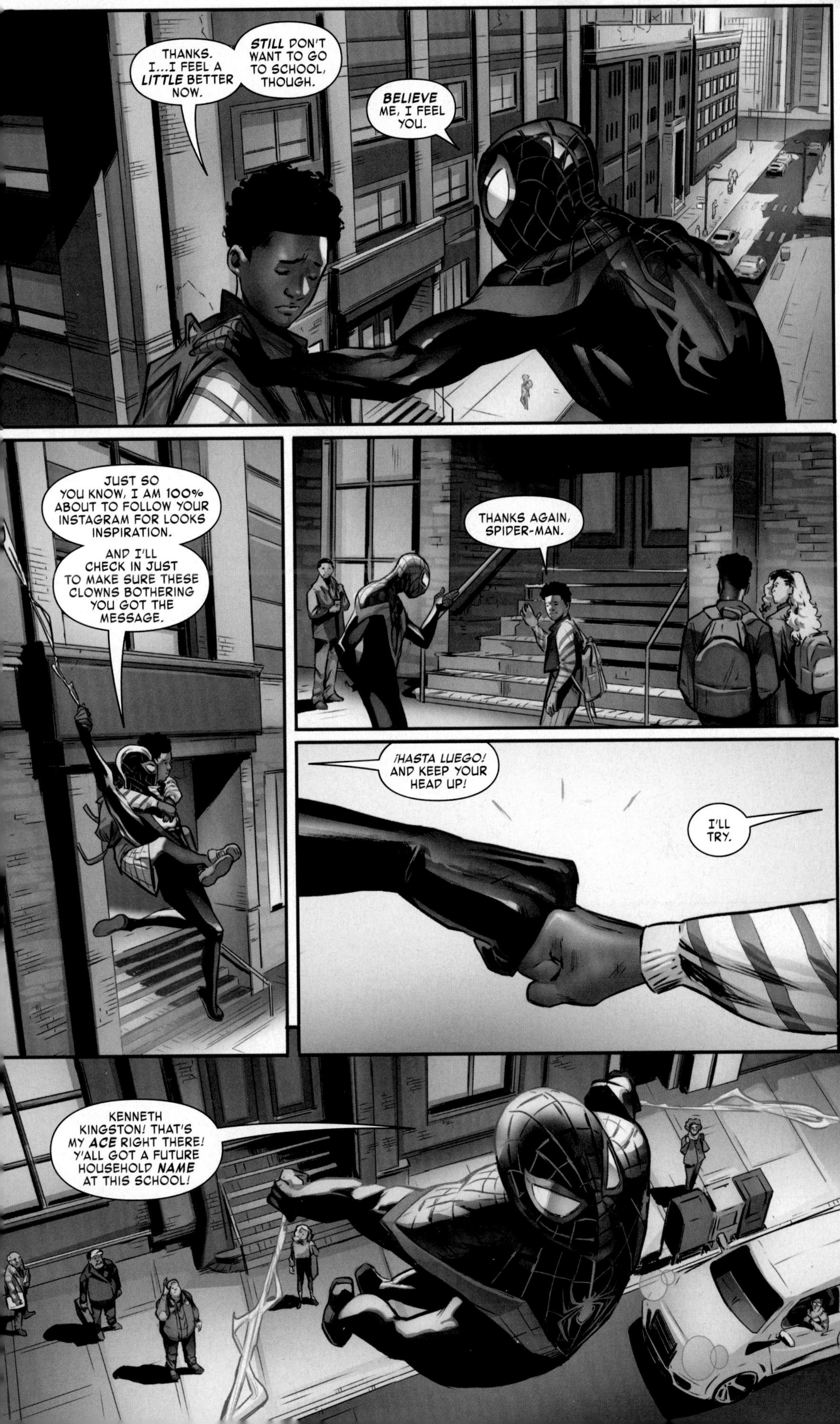
THANKS. I...I FEEL A LITTLE BETTER NOW.
STILL DON'T WANT TO GO TO SCHOOL, THOUGH.
BELIEVE ME, I FEEL YOU.
JUST SO YOU KNOW, I AM 100% ABOUT TO FOLLOW YOUR INSTAGRAM FOR LOOKS INSPIRATION.
AND I'LL CHECK IN JUST TO MAKE SURE THESE CLOWNS BOTHERING YOU GOT THE MESSAGE.
THANKS AGAIN, SPIDER-MAN.
¡HASTA LUEGO! AND KEEP YOUR HEAD UP!
I'LL TRY.
KENNETH KINGSTON! THAT'S MY ACE RIGHT THERE! Y'ALL GOT A FUTURE HOUSEHOLD NAME AT THIS SCHOOL!

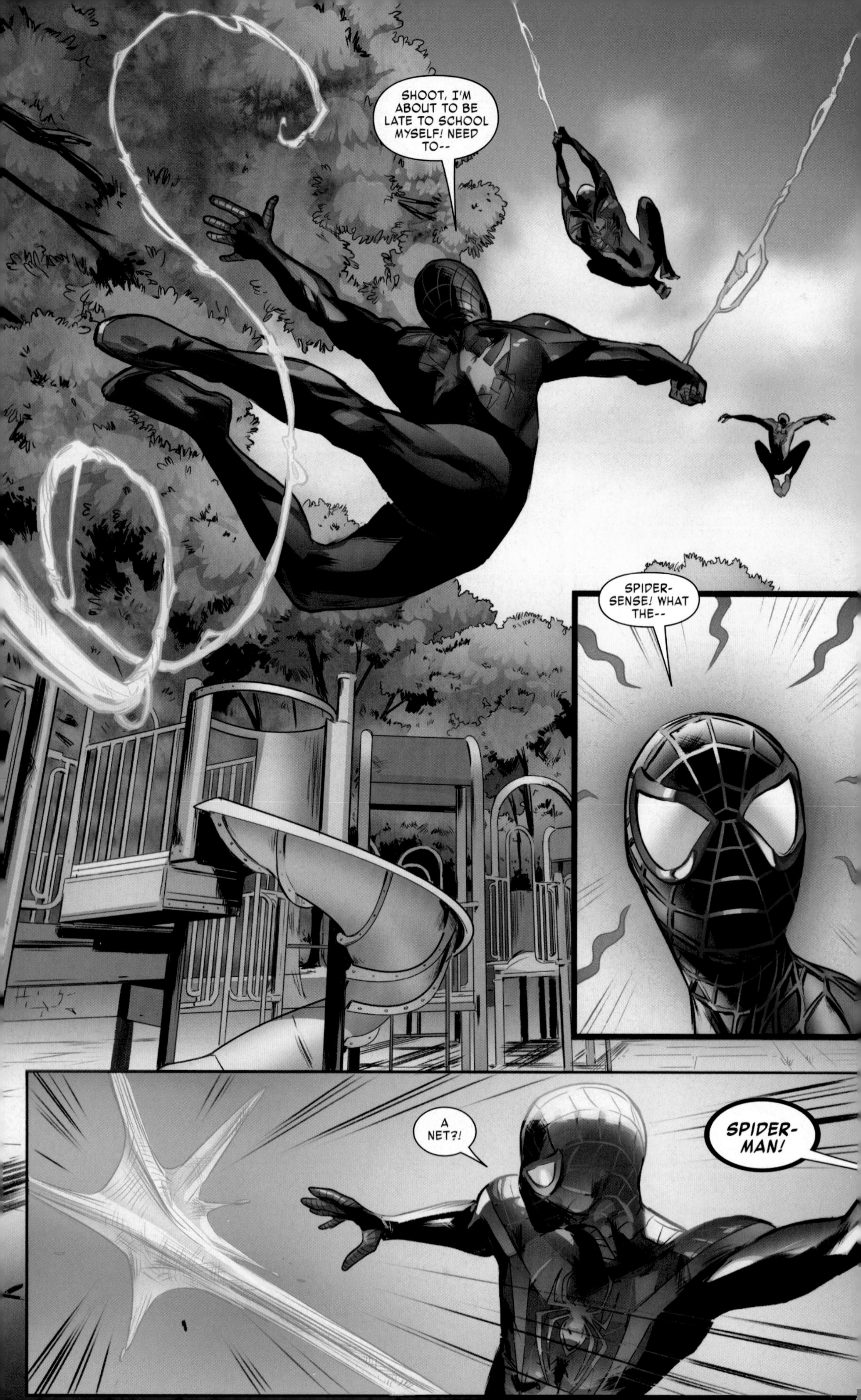
SHOOT, I'M ABOUT TO BE LATE TO SCHOOL MYSELF! NEED TO--
SPIDER-SENSE! WHAT THE--
A NET?!
SPIDER-MAN!

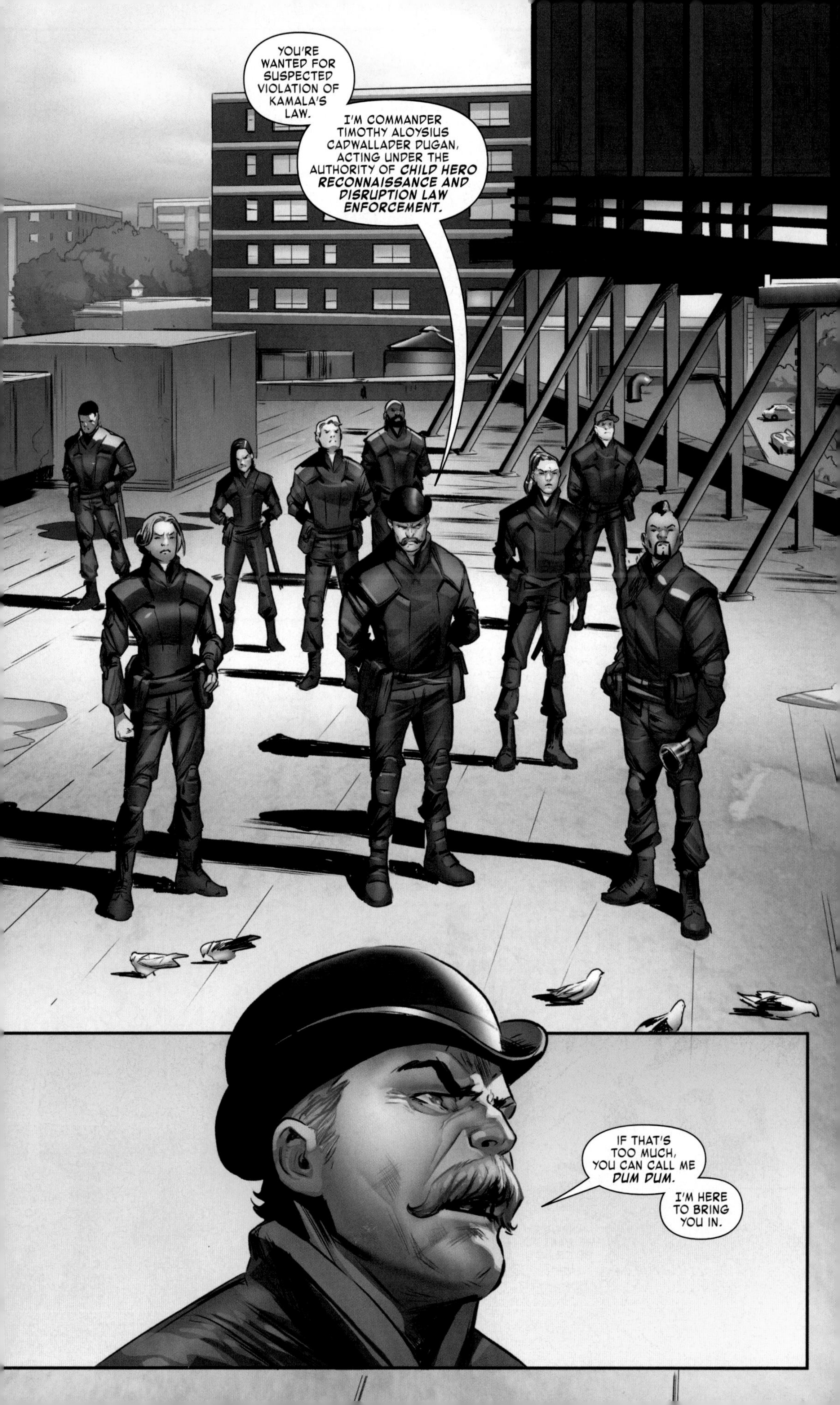
YOU'RE WANTED FOR SUSPECTED VIOLATION OF KAMALA'S LAW.
I'M COMMANDER TIMOTHY ALOYSIUS CADWALLADER DUGAN, ACTING UNDER THE AUTHORITY OF CHILD HERO RECONNAISSANCE AND DISRUPTION LAW ENFORCEMENT.
IF THAT'S TOO MUCH, YOU CAN CALL ME DUM DUM.
I'M HERE TO BRING YOU IN.

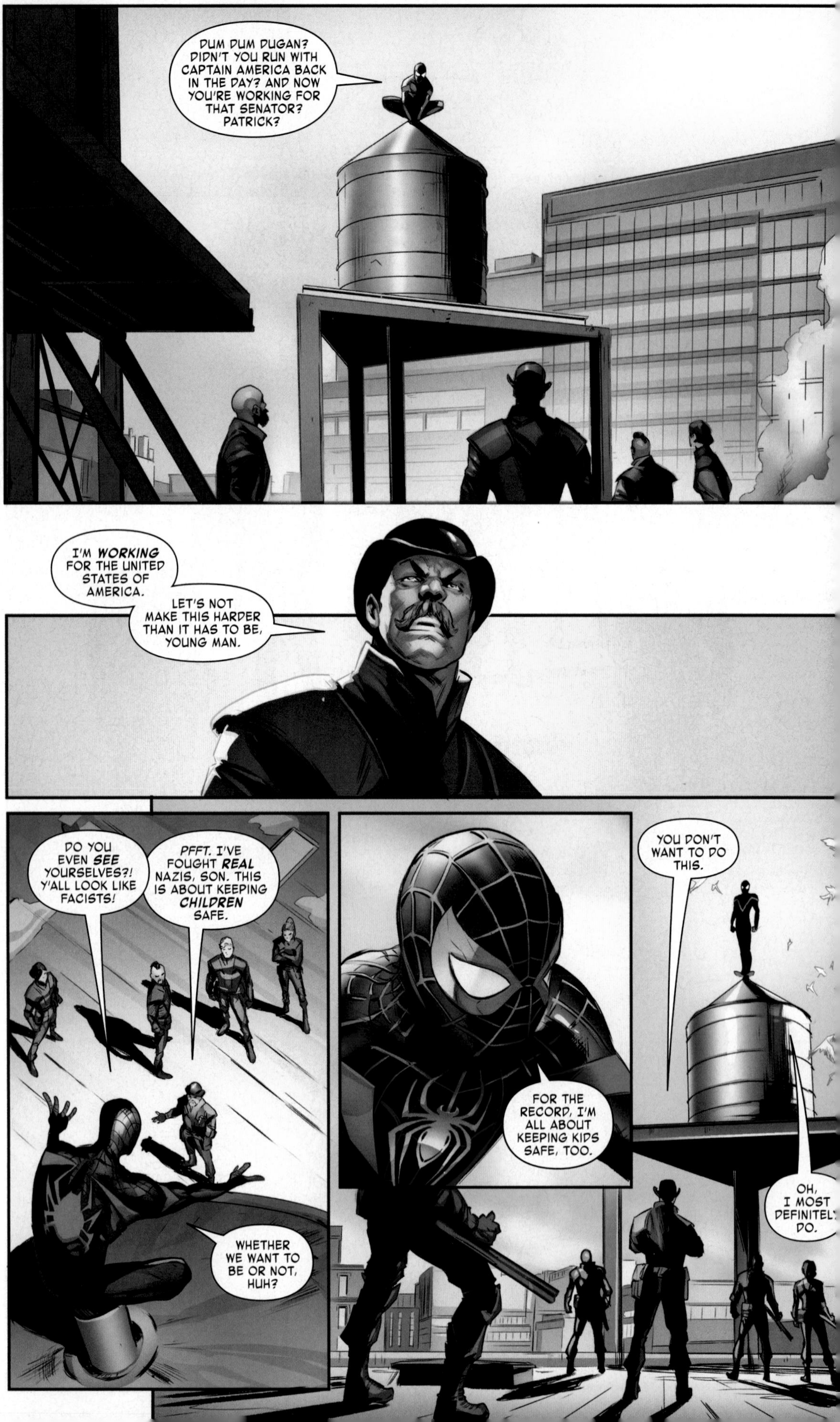

DUM DUM DUGAN? DIDN'T YOU RUN WITH CAPTAIN AMERICA BACK IN THE DAY? AND NOW YOU'RE WORKING FOR THAT SENATOR? PATRICK?
I'M *WORKING* FOR THE UNITED STATES OF AMERICA.
LET'S NOT MAKE THIS HARDER THAN IT HAS TO BE, YOUNG MAN.
DO YOU EVEN *SEE* YOURSELVES?! Y'ALL LOOK LIKE FACISTS!
PFFT. I'VE FOUGHT *REAL* NAZIS, SON. THIS IS ABOUT KEEPING *CHILDREN* SAFE.
WHETHER WE WANT TO BE OR NOT, HUH?
FOR THE RECORD, I'M ALL ABOUT KEEPING KIDS SAFE, TOO.
YOU DON'T WANT TO DO THIS.
OH, I MOST DEFINITEL DO.

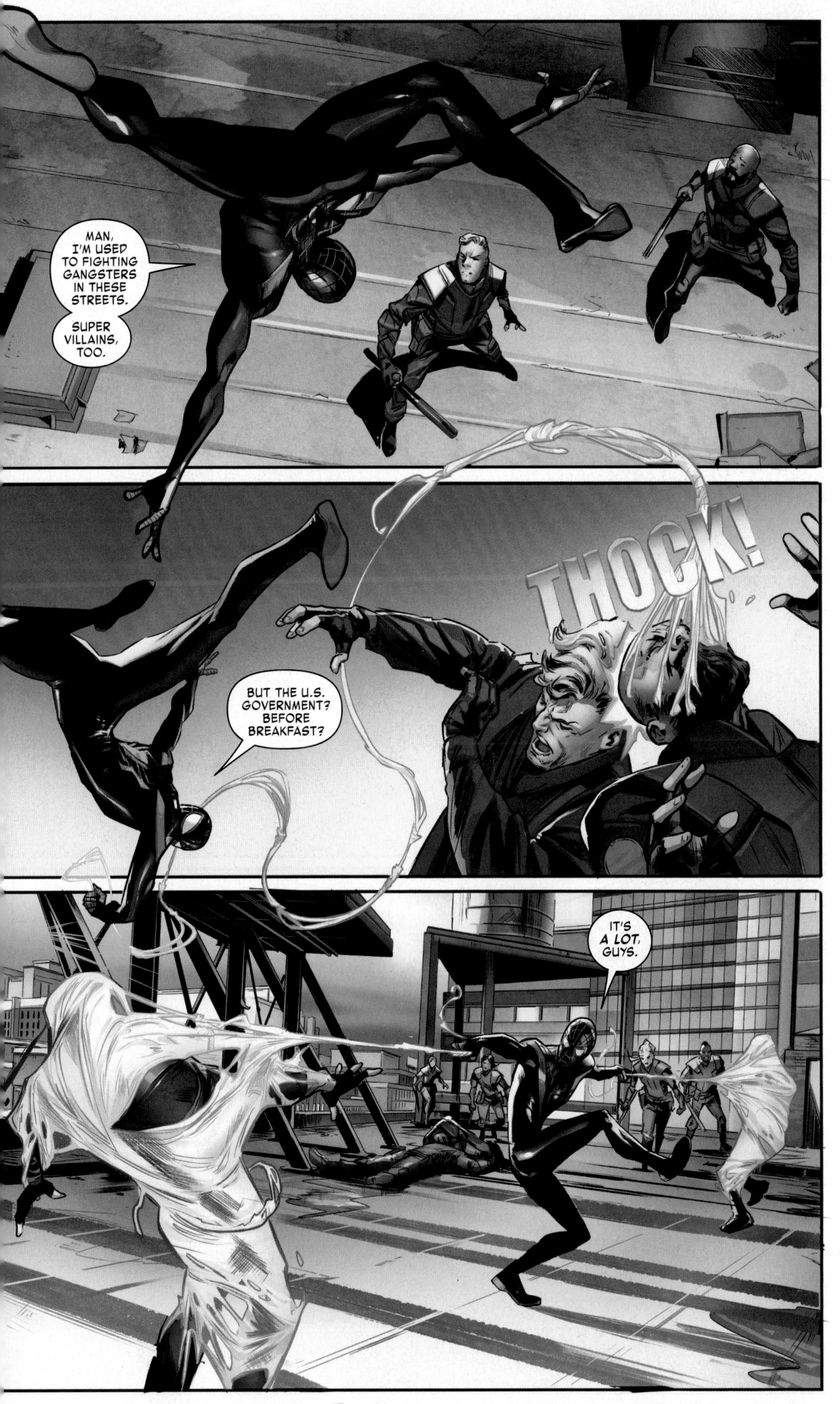
MAN, I'M USED TO FIGHTING GANGSTERS IN THESE STREETS.
SUPER VILLAINS, TOO.
THOCK!
BUT THE U.S. GOVERNMENT? BEFORE BREAKFAST?
IT'S A LOT, GUYS.

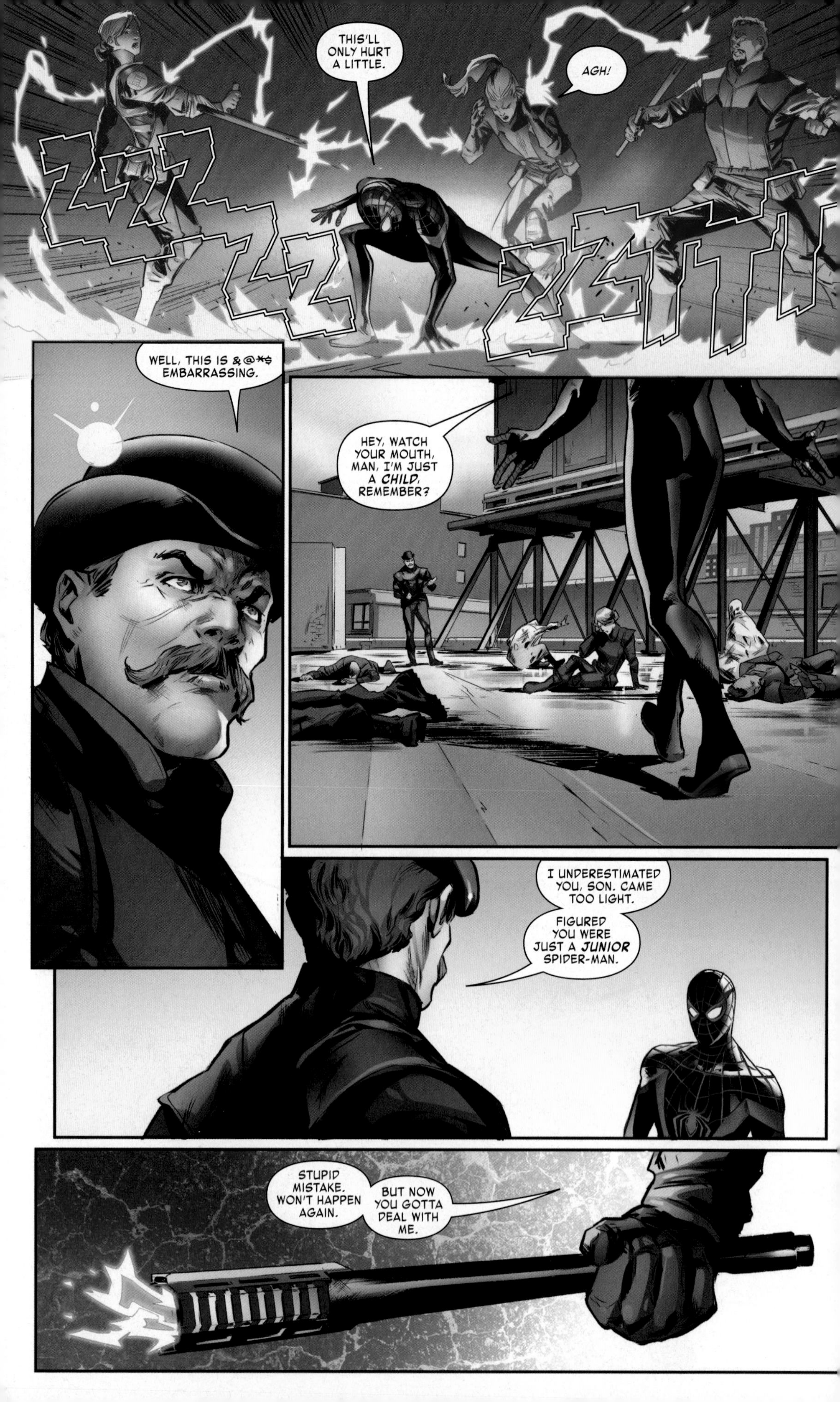
THIS'LL ONLY HURT A LITTLE.
AGH!
ZZZZZZZAK
ZZZZRTTT
WELL, THIS IS &@*$ EMBARRASSING.
HEY, WATCH YOUR MOUTH, MAN, I'M JUST A CHILD, REMEMBER?
I UNDERESTIMATED YOU, SON. CAME TOO LIGHT.
FIGURED YOU WERE JUST A JUNIOR SPIDER-MAN.
STUPID MISTAKE. WON'T HAPPEN AGAIN.
BUT NOW YOU GOTTA DEAL WITH ME.

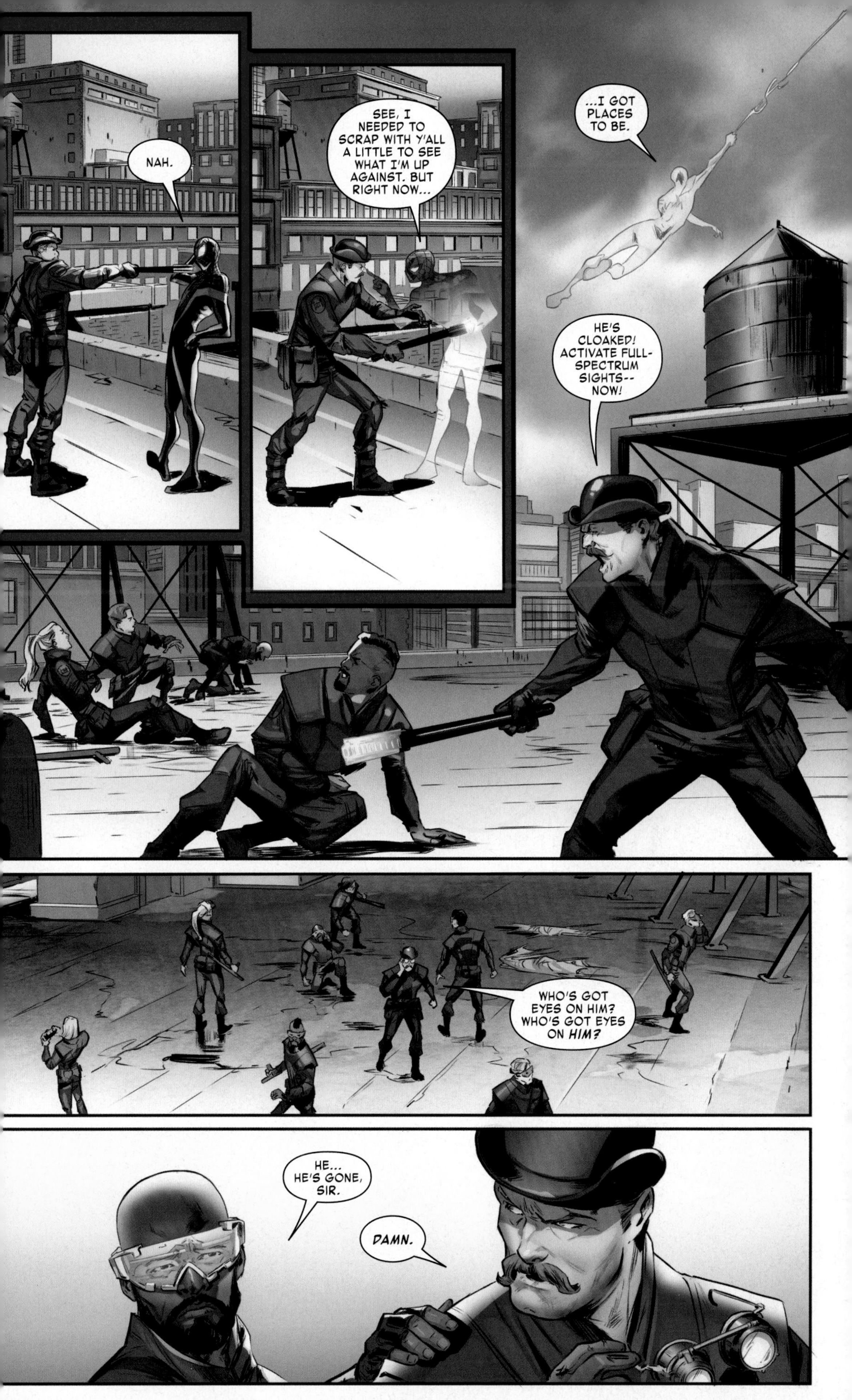
NAH.
SEE, I NEEDED TO SCRAP WITH Y'ALL A LITTLE TO SEE WHAT I'M UP AGAINST. BUT RIGHT NOW...
...I GOT PLACES TO BE.
HE'S CLOAKED! ACTIVATE FULL-SPECTRUM SIGHTS--NOW!
WHO'S GOT EYES ON HIM? WHO'S GOT EYES ON *HIM?*
HE... HE'S GONE, SIR.
DAMN.

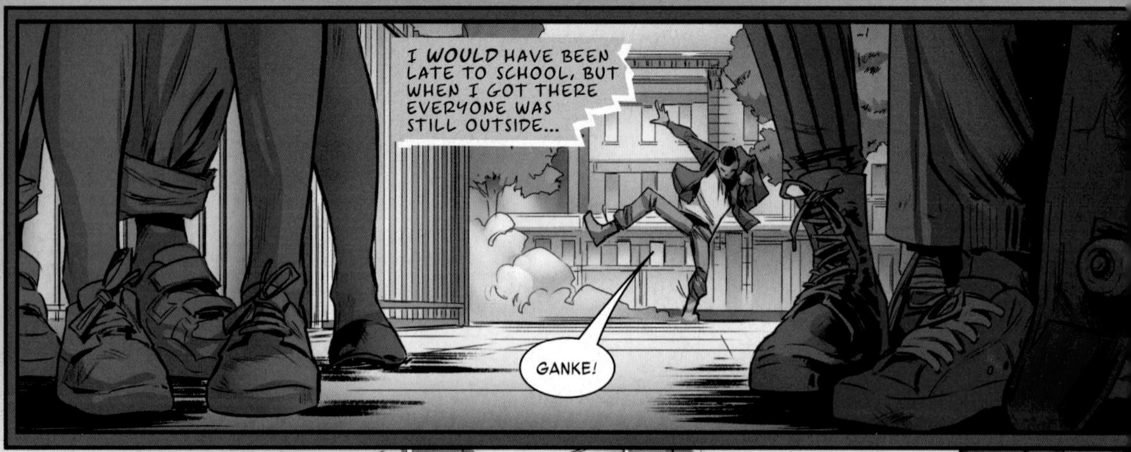
I WOULD HAVE BEEN LATE TO SCHOOL, BUT WHEN I GOT THERE EVERYONE WAS STILL OUTSIDE...
GANKE!

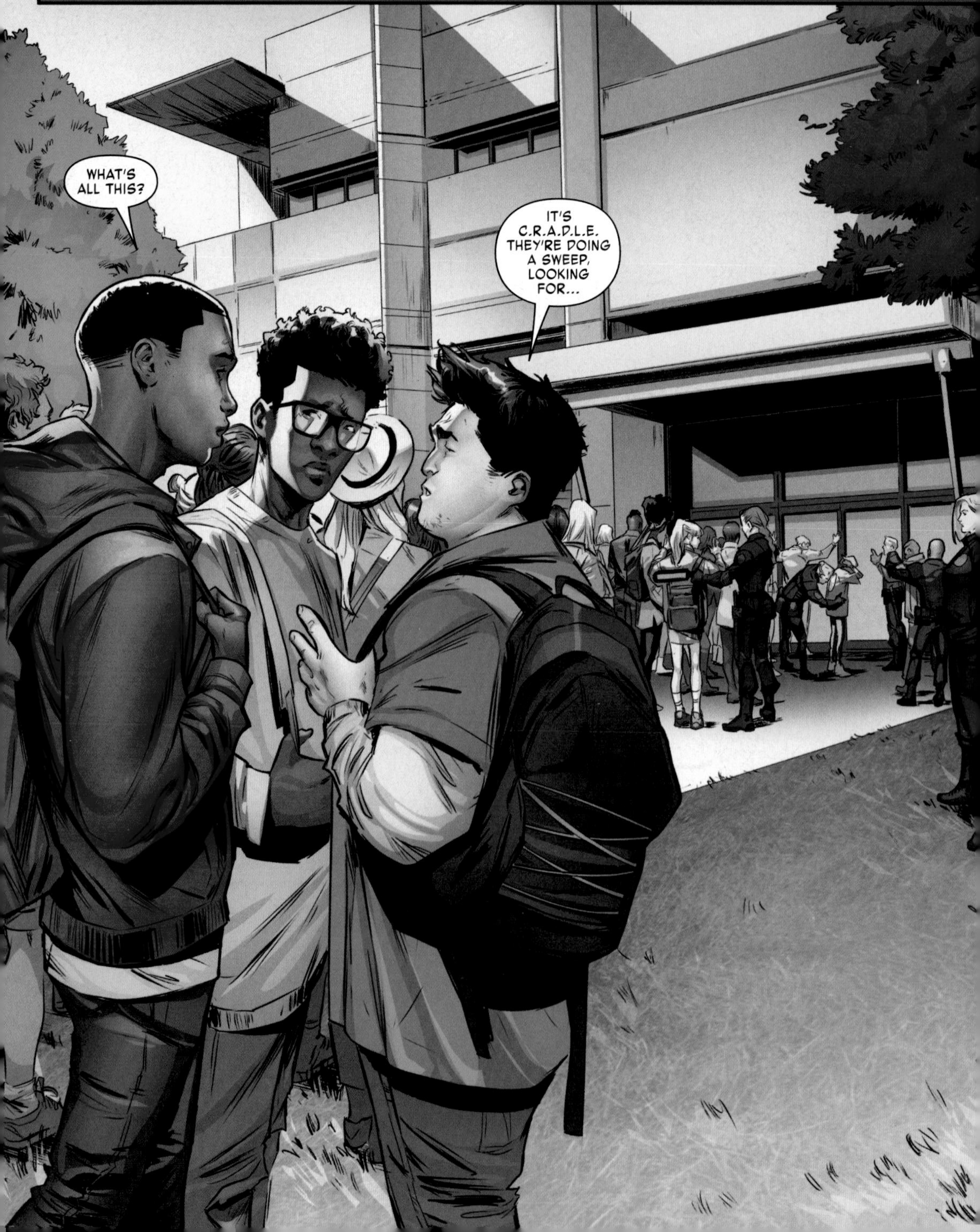
WHAT'S ALL THIS?
IT'S C.R.A.D.L.E. THEY'RE DOING A SWEEP, LOOKING FOR...

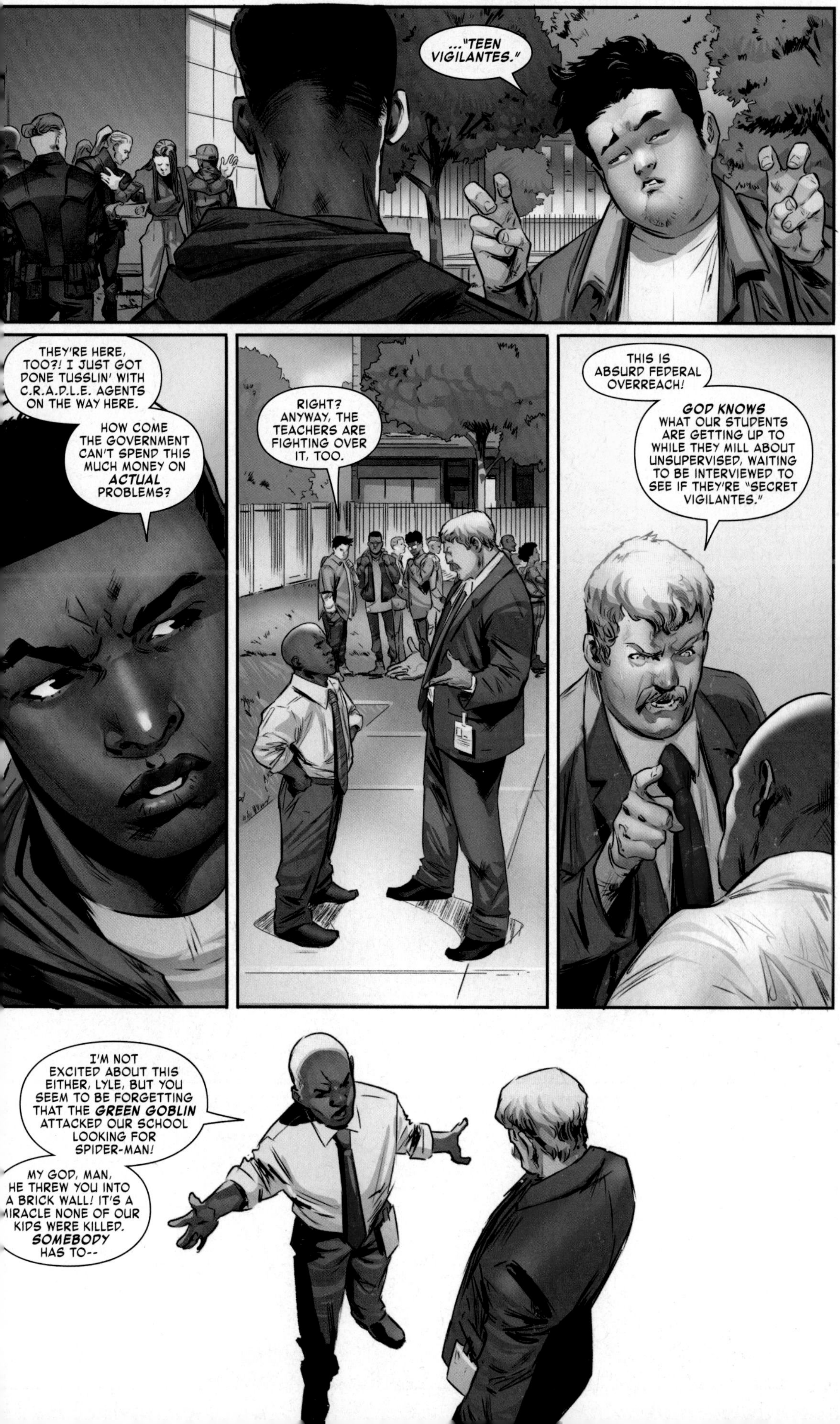
..."TEEN VIGILANTES."
THEY'RE HERE, TOO?! I JUST GOT DONE TUSSLIN' WITH C.R.A.D.L.E. AGENTS ON THE WAY HERE.
HOW COME THE GOVERNMENT CAN'T SPEND THIS MUCH MONEY ON ACTUAL PROBLEMS?
RIGHT? ANYWAY, THE TEACHERS ARE FIGHTING OVER IT, TOO.
THIS IS ABSURD FEDERAL OVERREACH!
GOD KNOWS WHAT OUR STUDENTS ARE GETTING UP TO WHILE THEY MILL ABOUT UNSUPERVISED, WAITING TO BE INTERVIEWED TO SEE IF THEY'RE "SECRET VIGILANTES."
I'M NOT EXCITED ABOUT THIS EITHER, LYLE, BUT YOU SEEM TO BE FORGETTING THAT THE GREEN GOBLIN ATTACKED OUR SCHOOL LOOKING FOR SPIDER-MAN!
MY GOD, MAN, HE THREW YOU INTO A BRICK WALL! IT'S A MIRACLE NONE OF OUR KIDS WERE KILLED. SOMEBODY HAS TO--

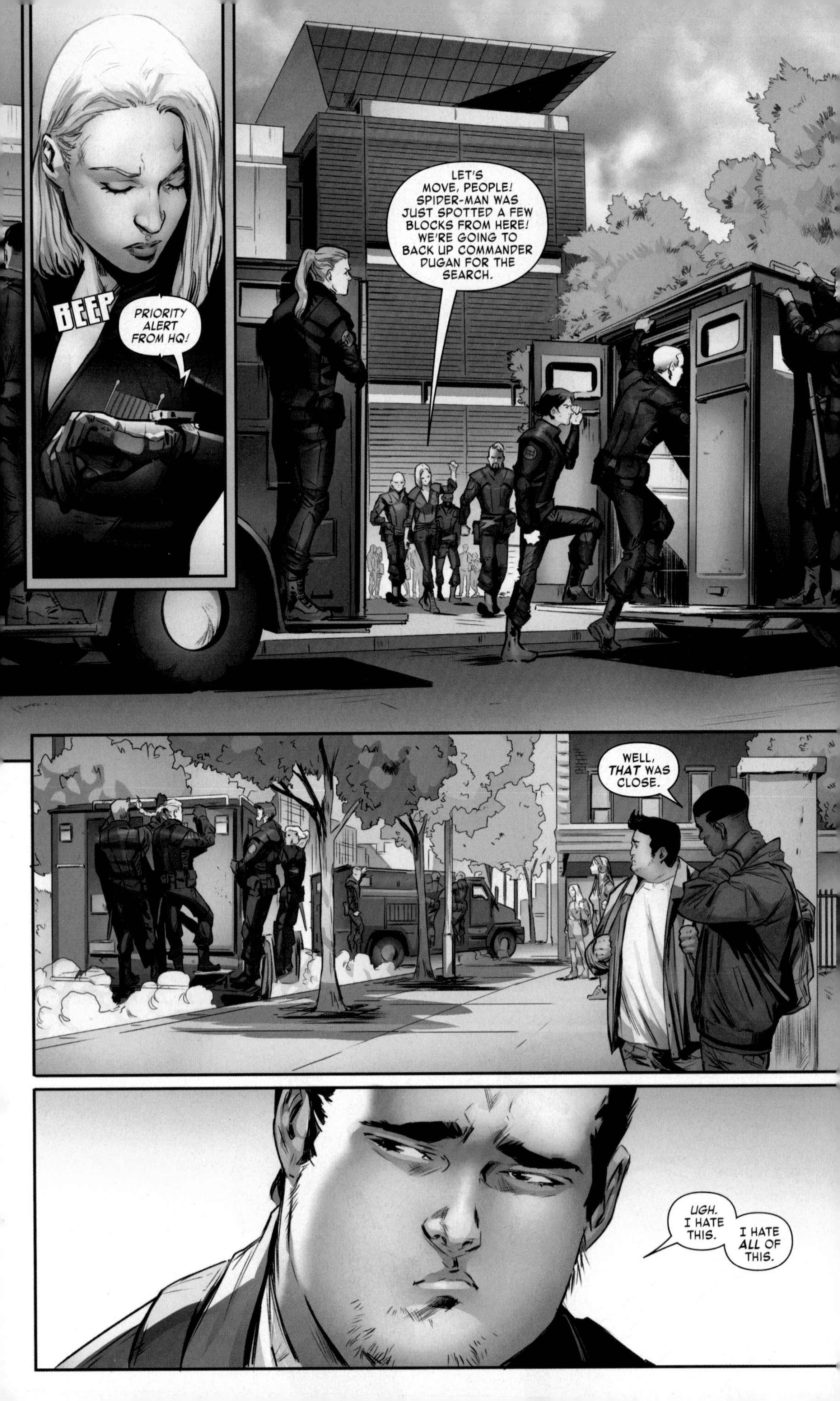
BEEP
PRIORITY ALERT FROM HQ!
LET'S MOVE, PEOPLE! SPIDER-MAN WAS JUST SPOTTED A FEW BLOCKS FROM HERE! WE'RE GOING TO BACK UP COMMANDER DUGAN FOR THE SEARCH.
WELL, THAT WAS CLOSE.
UGH. I HATE THIS.
I HATE ALL OF THIS.

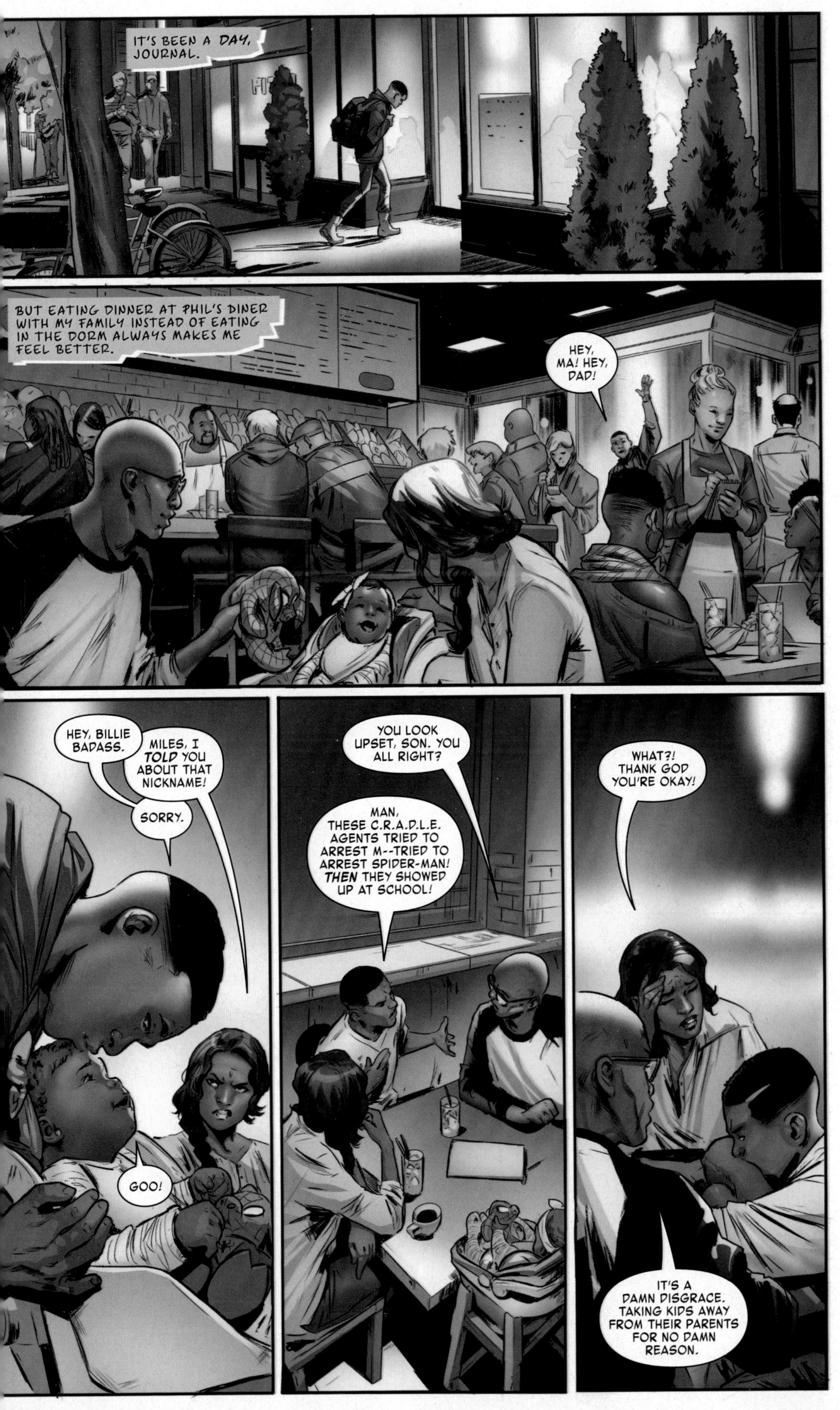

IT'S BEEN A DAY, JOURNAL.
BUT EATING DINNER AT PHIL'S DINER WITH MY FAMILY INSTEAD OF EATING IN THE DORM ALWAYS MAKES ME FEEL BETTER.
HEY, MA! HEY, DAD!
HEY, BILLIE BADASS.
MILES, I TOLD YOU ABOUT THAT NICKNAME!
SORRY.
GOO!
YOU LOOK UPSET, SON. YOU ALL RIGHT?
MAN, THESE C.R.A.D.L.E. AGENTS TRIED TO ARREST M--TRIED TO ARREST SPIDER-MAN! THEN THEY SHOWED UP AT SCHOOL!
WHAT?! THANK GOD YOU'RE OKAY!
IT'S A DAMN DISGRACE. TAKING KIDS AWAY FROM THEIR PARENTS FOR NO DAMN REASON.

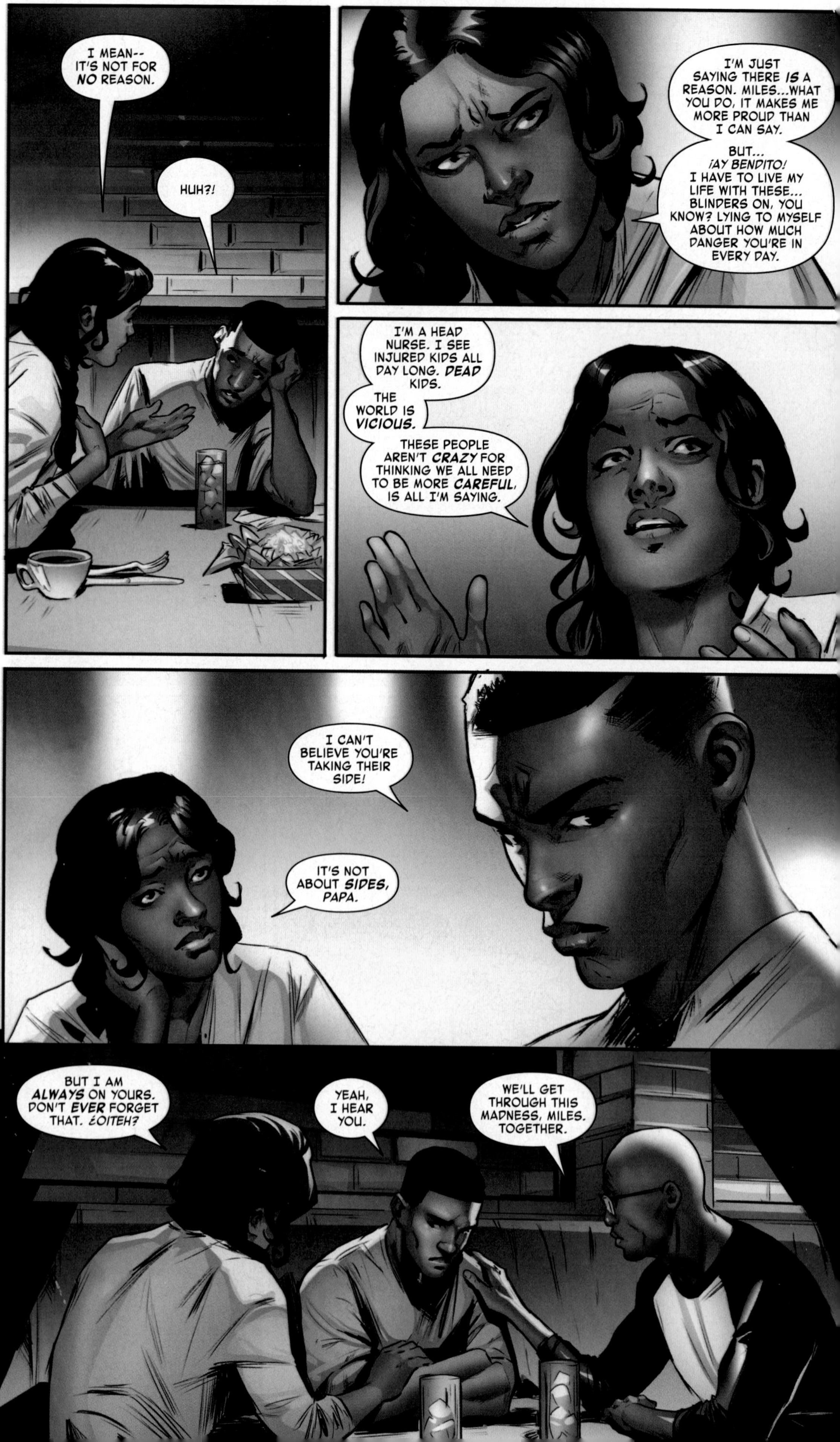

I MEAN-- IT'S NOT FOR NO REASON.
HUH?!
I'M JUST SAYING THERE IS A REASON. MILES...WHAT YOU DO, IT MAKES ME MORE PROUD THAN I CAN SAY.
BUT... ¡AY BENDITO! I HAVE TO LIVE MY LIFE WITH THESE... BLINDERS ON, YOU KNOW? LYING TO MYSELF ABOUT HOW MUCH DANGER YOU'RE IN EVERY DAY.
I'M A HEAD NURSE. I SEE INJURED KIDS ALL DAY LONG. DEAD KIDS.
THE WORLD IS VICIOUS.
THESE PEOPLE AREN'T CRAZY FOR THINKING WE ALL NEED TO BE MORE CAREFUL, IS ALL I'M SAYING.
I CAN'T BELIEVE YOU'RE TAKING THEIR SIDE!
IT'S NOT ABOUT SIDES, PAPA.
BUT I AM ALWAYS ON YOURS. DON'T EVER FORGET THAT. ¿OITEH?
YEAH, I HEAR YOU.
WE'LL GET THROUGH THIS MADNESS, MILES. TOGETHER.

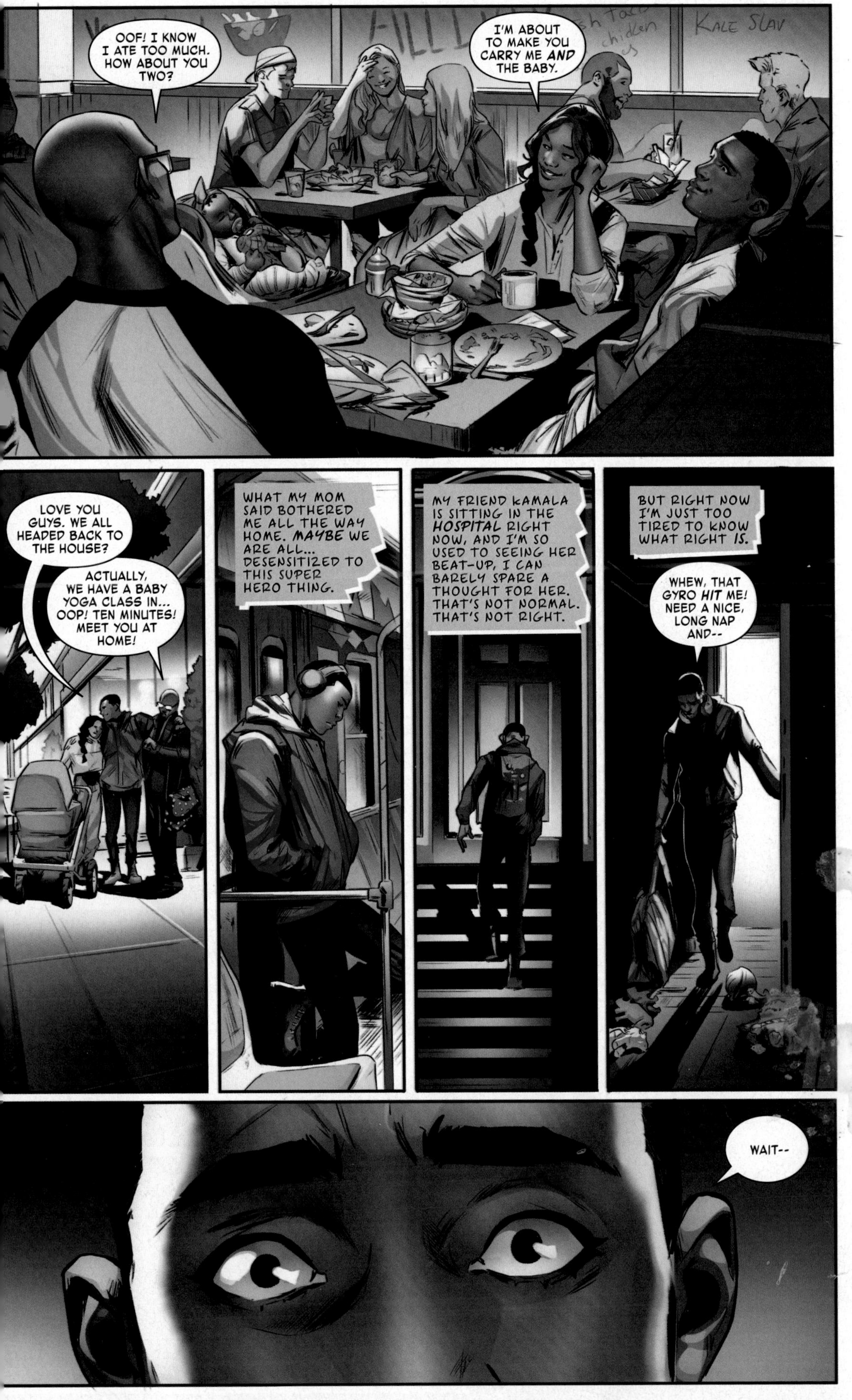
HALL
Kale Slav
OOF! I KNOW I ATE TOO MUCH. HOW ABOUT YOU TWO?
I'M ABOUT TO MAKE YOU CARRY ME AND THE BABY.
LOVE YOU GUYS. WE ALL HEADED BACK TO THE HOUSE?
ACTUALLY, WE HAVE A BABY YOGA CLASS IN... OOP! TEN MINUTES! MEET YOU AT HOME!
WHAT MY MOM SAID BOTHERED ME ALL THE WAY HOME. MAYBE WE ARE ALL... DESENSITIZED TO THIS SUPER HERO THING.
MY FRIEND KAMALA IS SITTING IN THE HOSPITAL RIGHT NOW, AND I'M SO USED TO SEEING HER BEAT-UP, I CAN BARELY SPARE A THOUGHT FOR HER. THAT'S NOT NORMAL. THAT'S NOT RIGHT.
BUT RIGHT NOW I'M JUST TOO TIRED TO KNOW WHAT RIGHT IS.
WHEW, THAT GYRO HIT ME! NEED A NICE, LONG NAP AND--
WAIT--

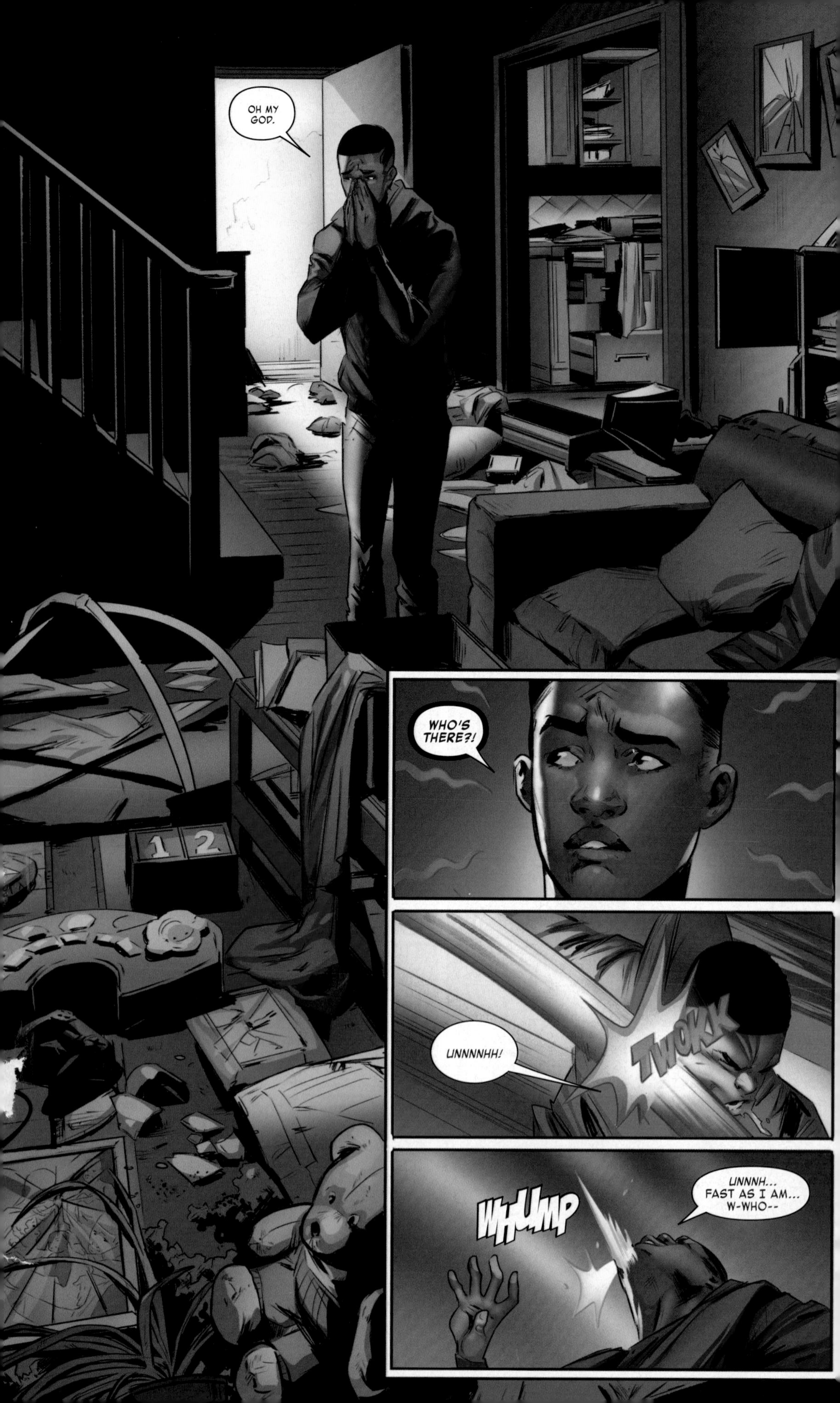
OH MY GOD.
WHO'S THERE?!
UNNNNHH!
TWOKK
WHUMP
UNNNH... FAST AS I AM... W-WHO--

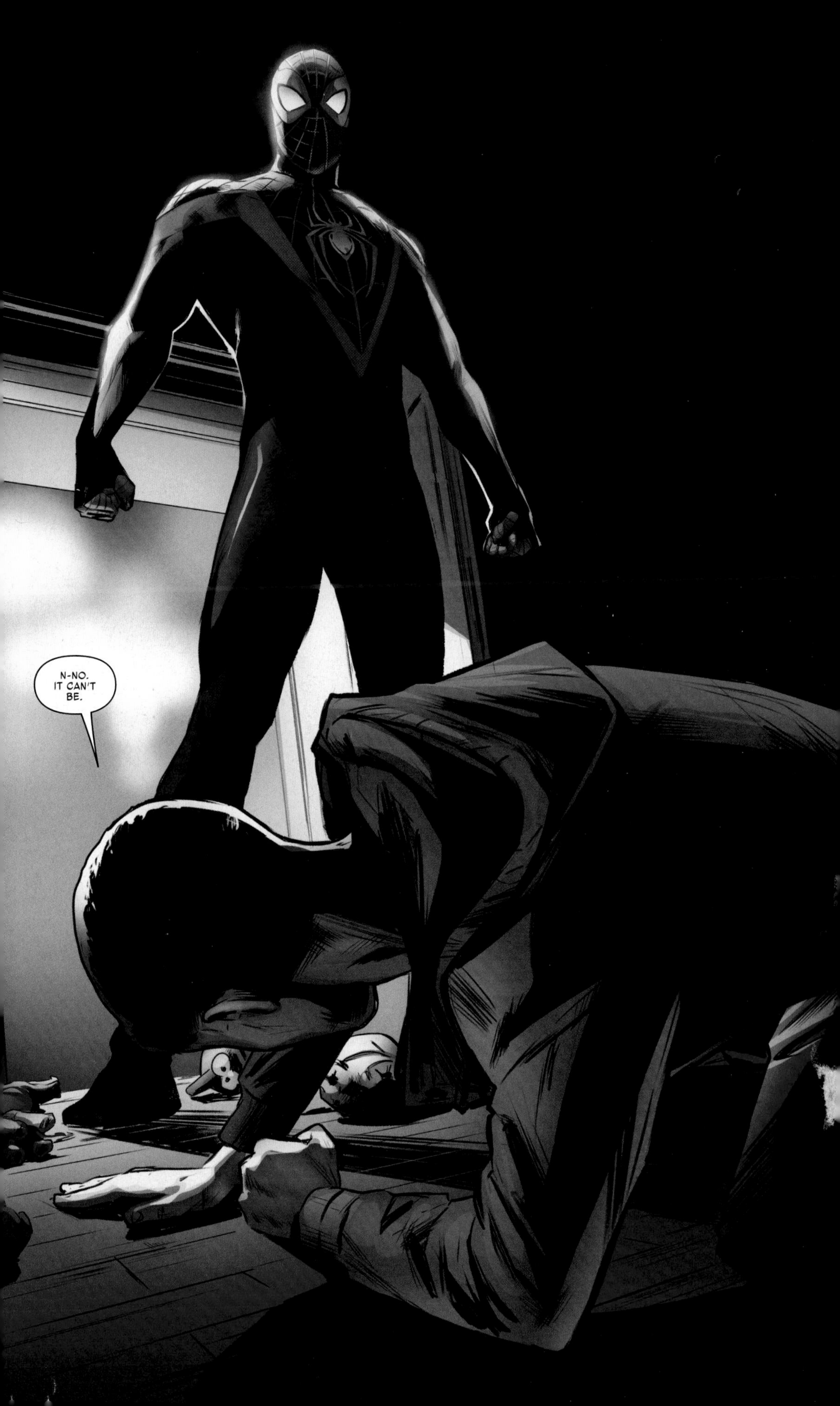
N-NO. IT CAN'T BE.

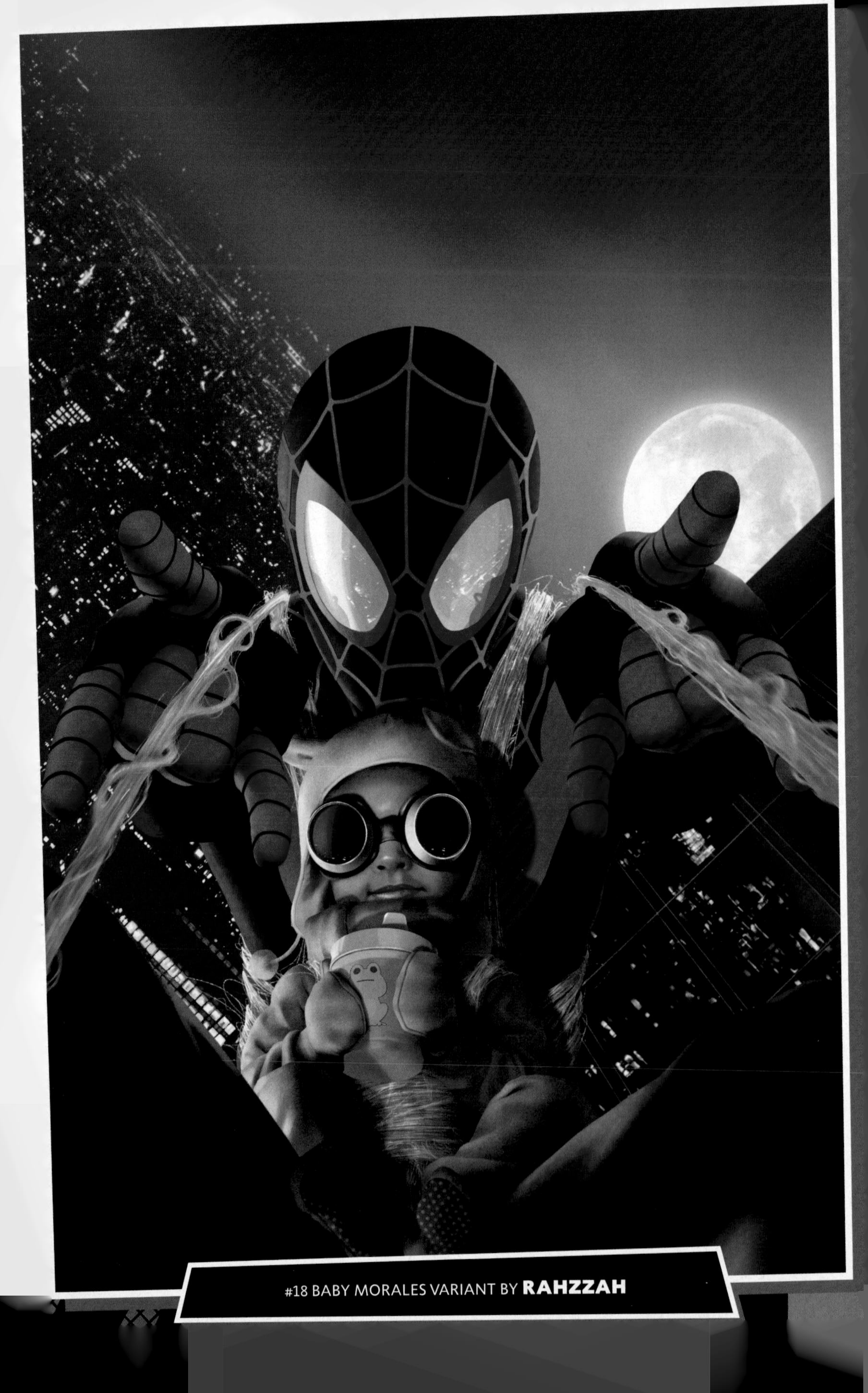

#18 BABY MORALES VARIANT BY **RAHZZAH**

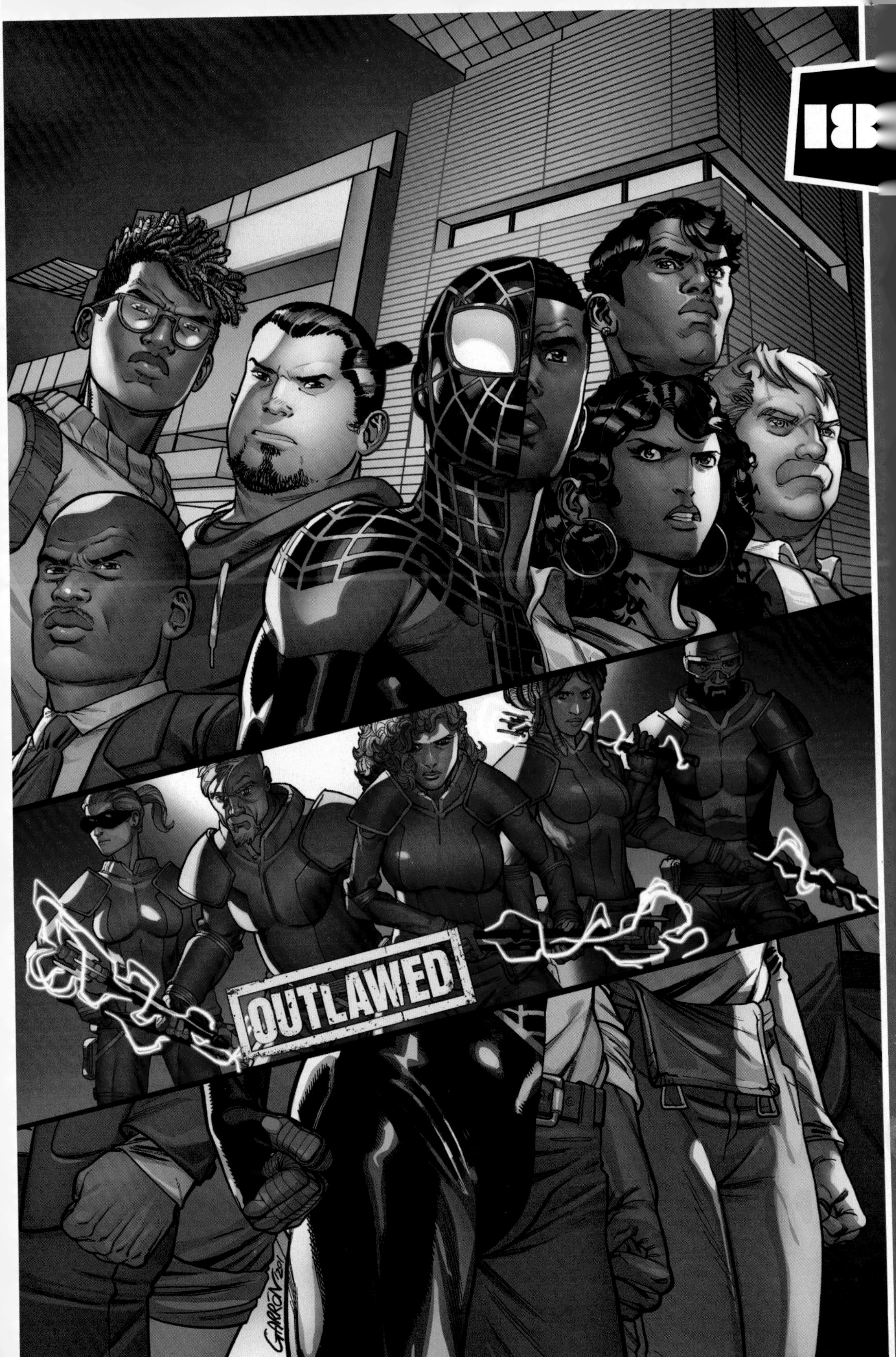
18
OUTLAWED
GARRÓN '20

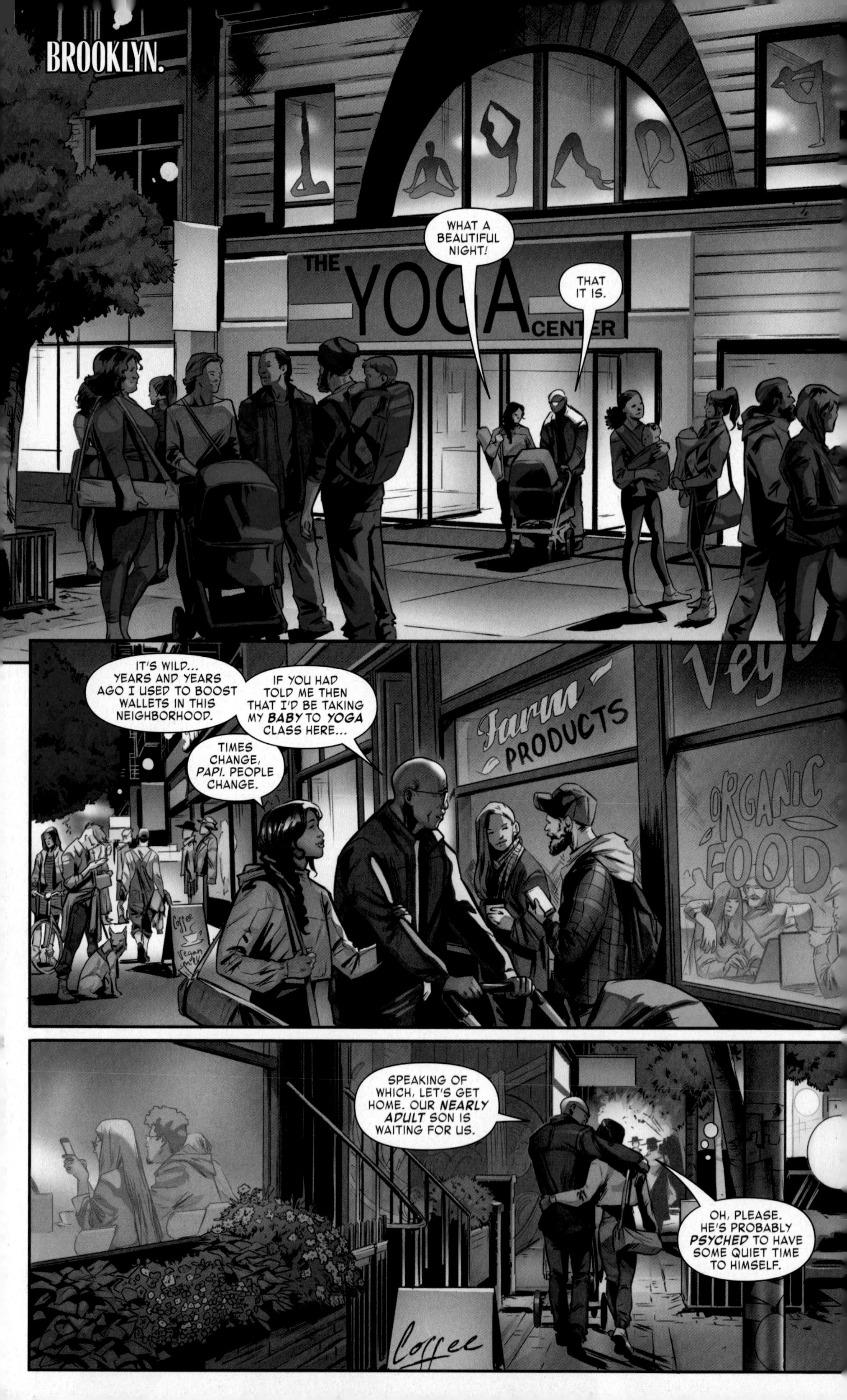
BROOKLYN.
WHAT A BEAUTIFUL NIGHT!
THAT IT IS.
THE YOGA CENTER
IT'S WILD... YEARS AND YEARS AGO I USED TO BOOST WALLETS IN THIS NEIGHBORHOOD.
IF YOU HAD TOLD ME THEN THAT I'D BE TAKING MY *BABY* TO *YOGA* CLASS HERE...
TIMES CHANGE, *PAPI*. PEOPLE CHANGE.
Farm PRODUCTS
ORGANIC FOOD
SPEAKING OF WHICH, LET'S GET HOME. OUR *NEARLY ADULT* SON IS WAITING FOR US.
OH, PLEASE. HE'S PROBABLY *PSYCHED* TO HAVE SOME QUIET TIME TO HIMSELF.
Coffee

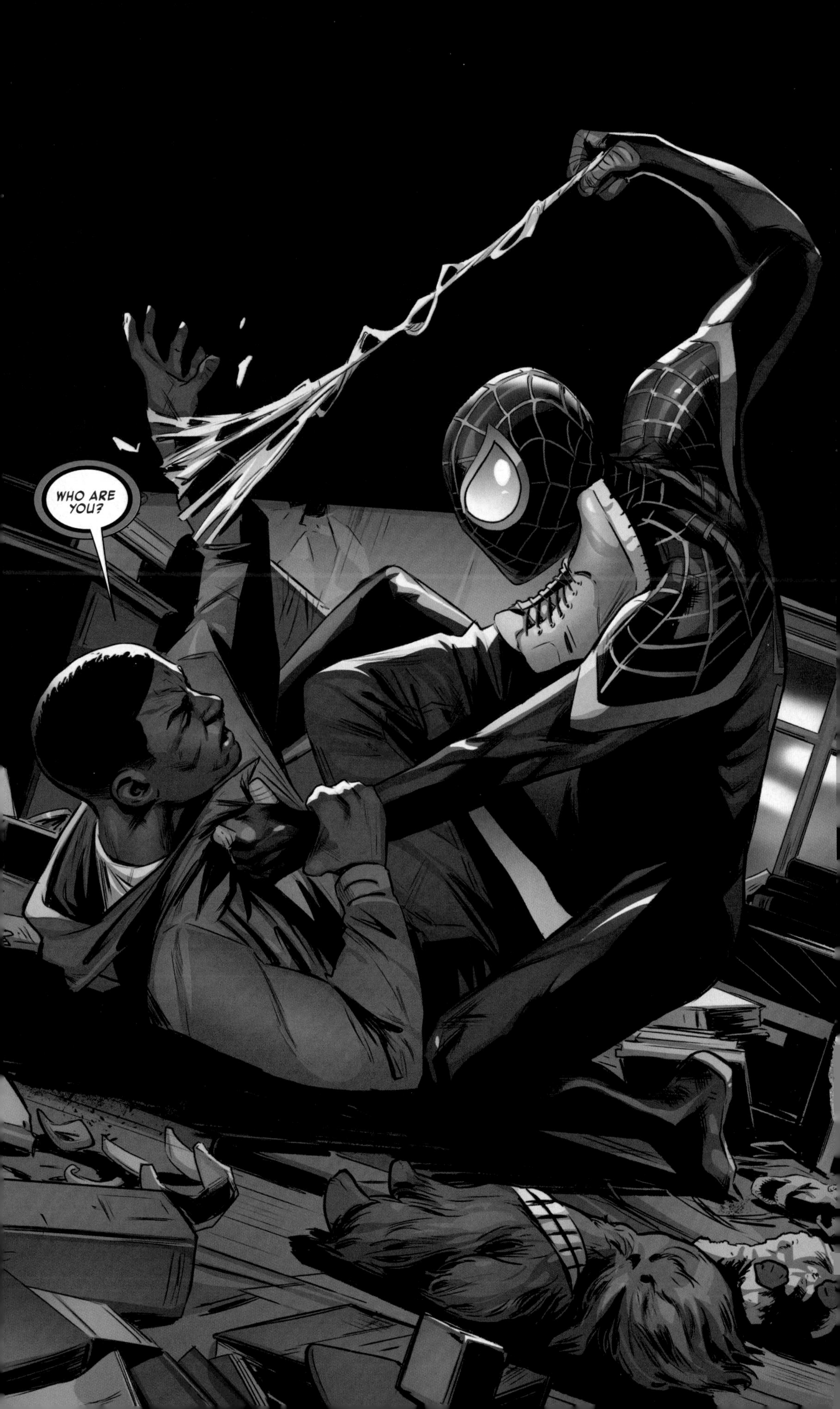
WHO ARE YOU?

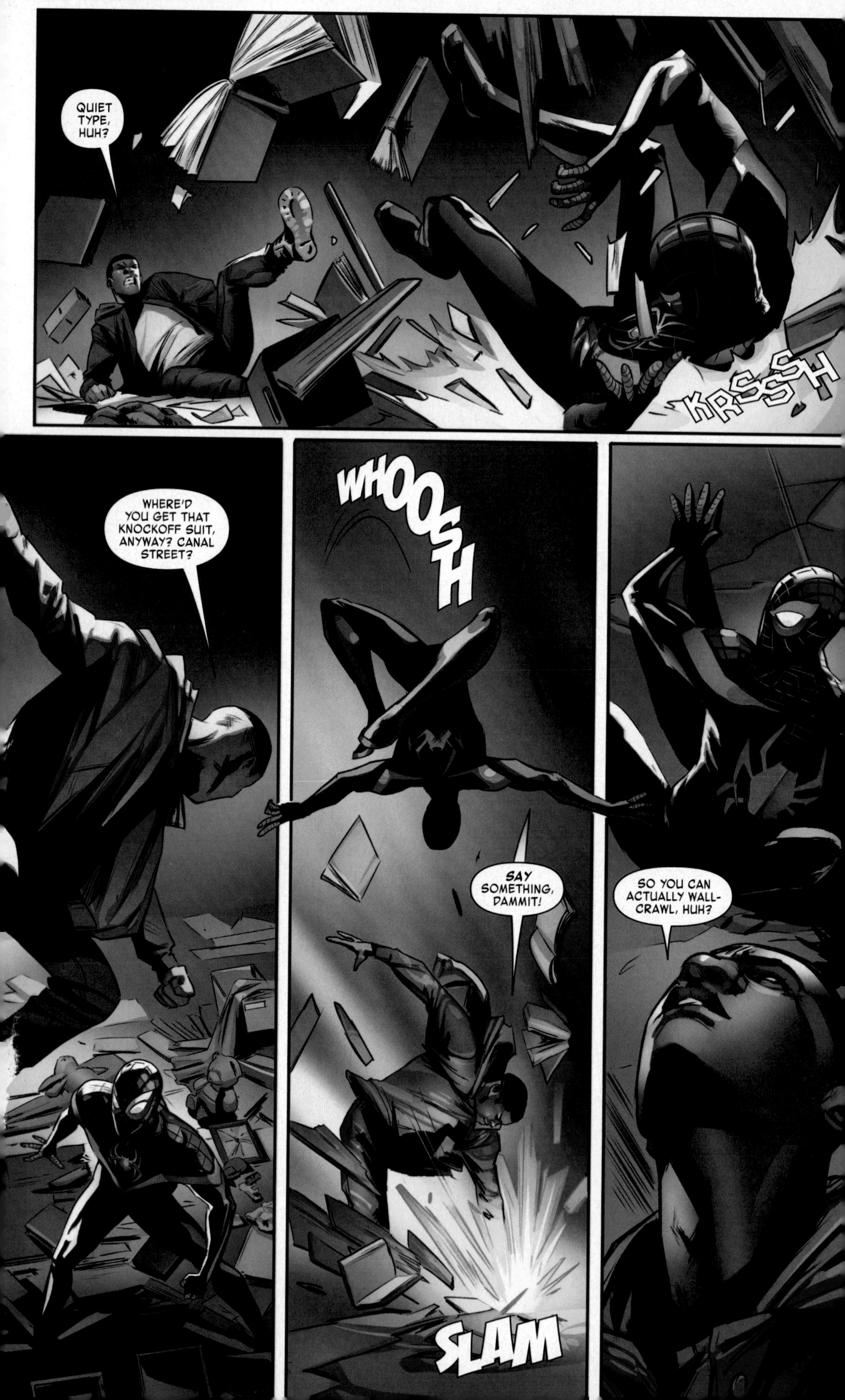
QUIET TYPE, HUH?
KRSSSH
WHERE'D YOU GET THAT KNOCKOFF SUIT, ANYWAY? CANAL STREET?
WHOOSH
SAY SOMETHING, DAMMIT!
SLAM
SO YOU CAN ACTUALLY WALL-CRAWL, HUH?

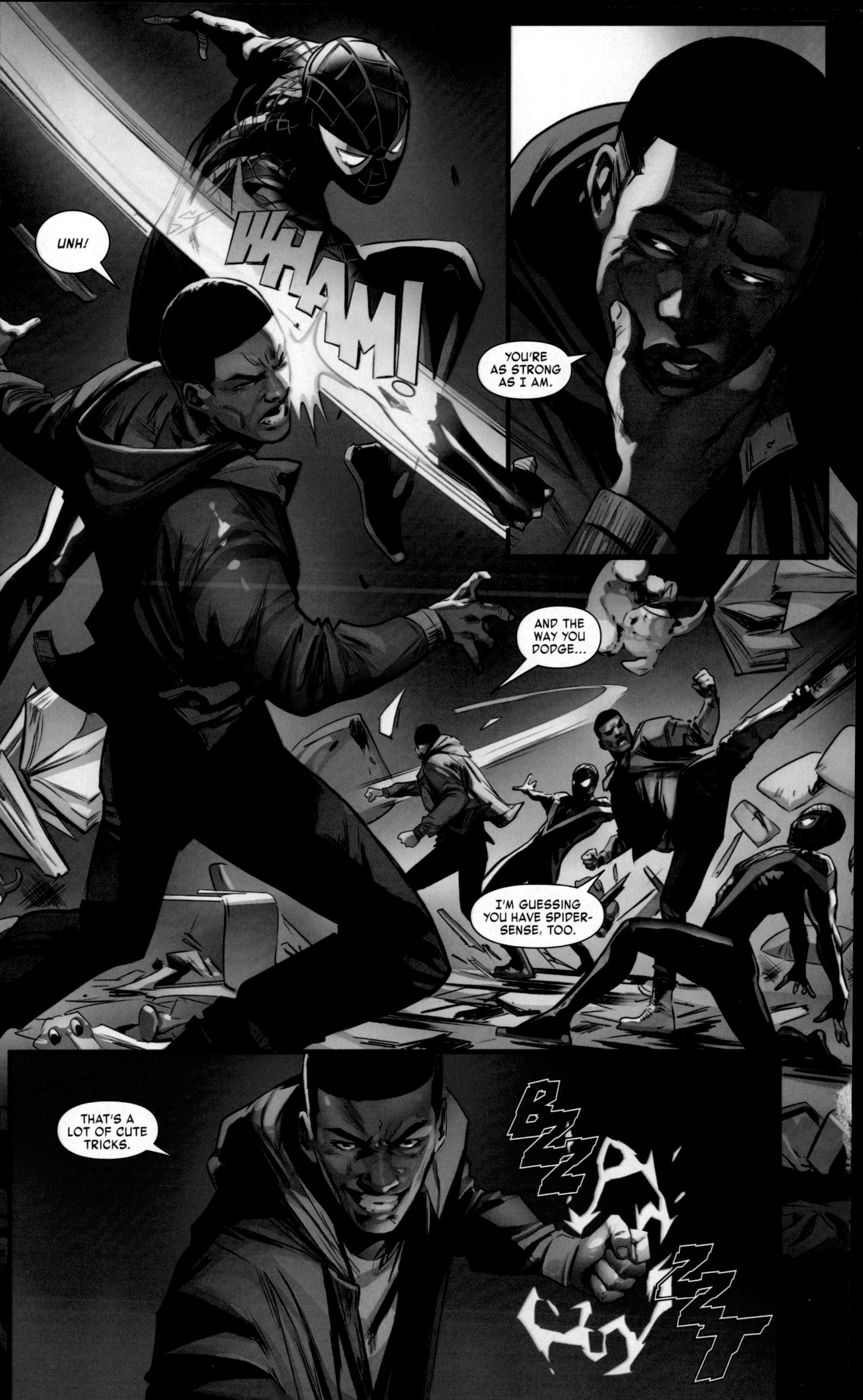
UNH!
WHAM!
YOU'RE AS STRONG AS I AM.
AND THE WAY YOU DODGE...
I'M GUESSING YOU HAVE SPIDER-SENSE, TOO.
THAT'S A LOT OF CUTE TRICKS.
BZZAAZZT

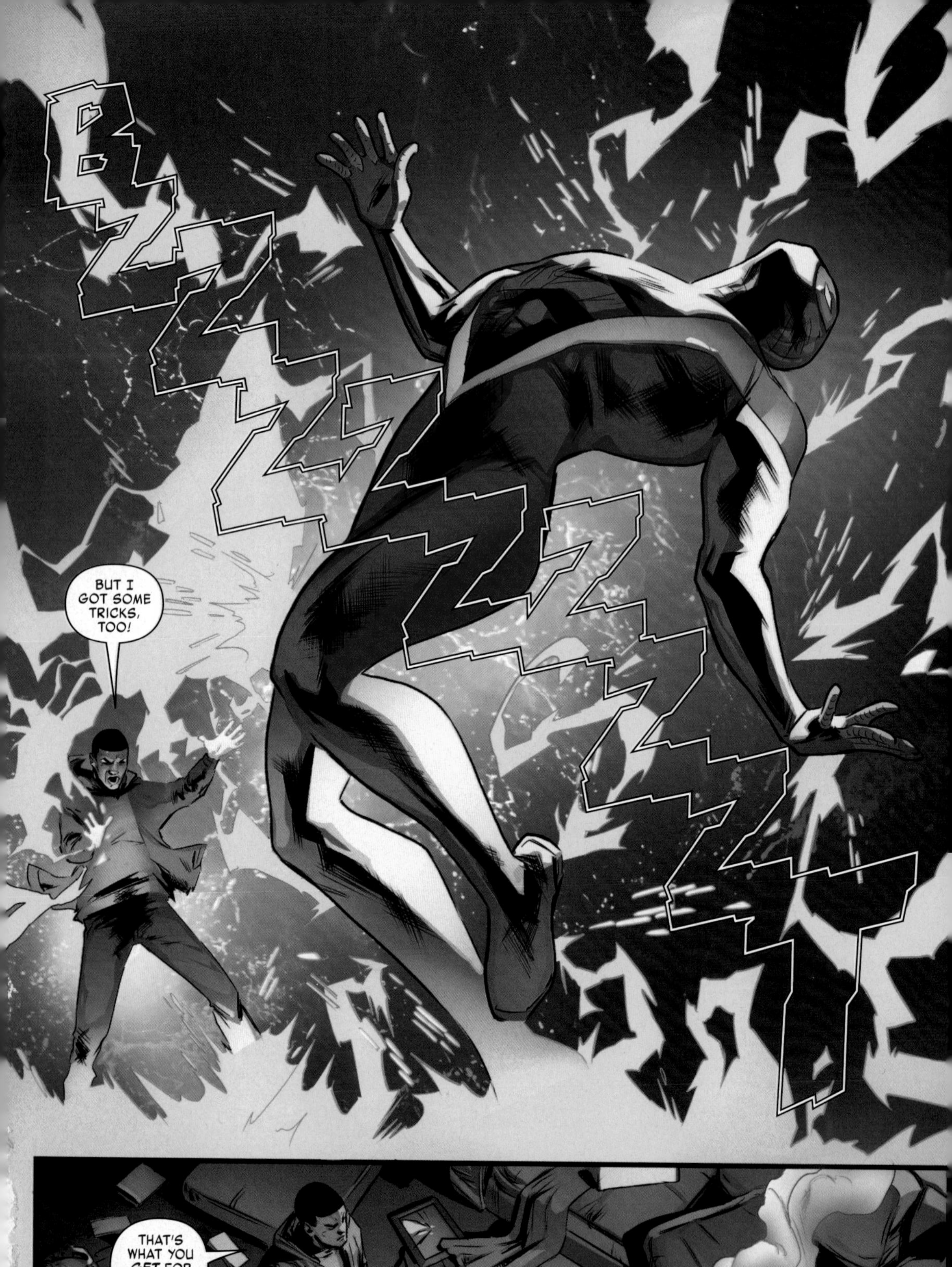
BZZZZZZZT
BUT I GOT SOME TRICKS, TOO!

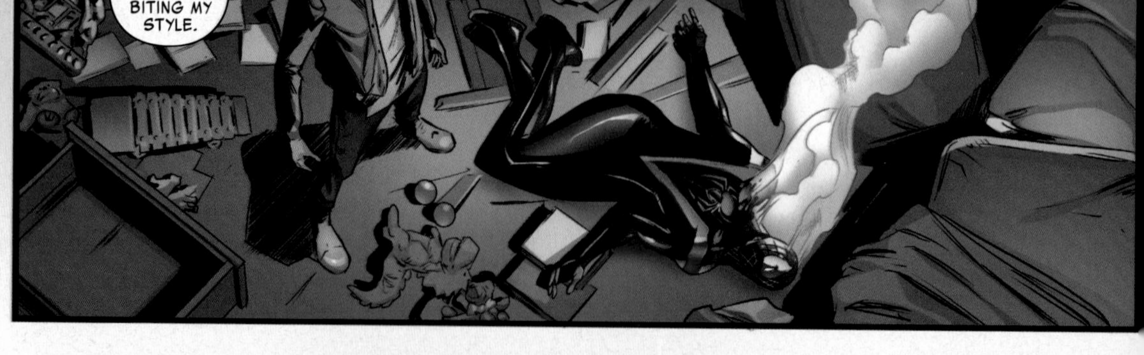
THAT'S WHAT YOU *GET* FOR BITING MY STYLE.

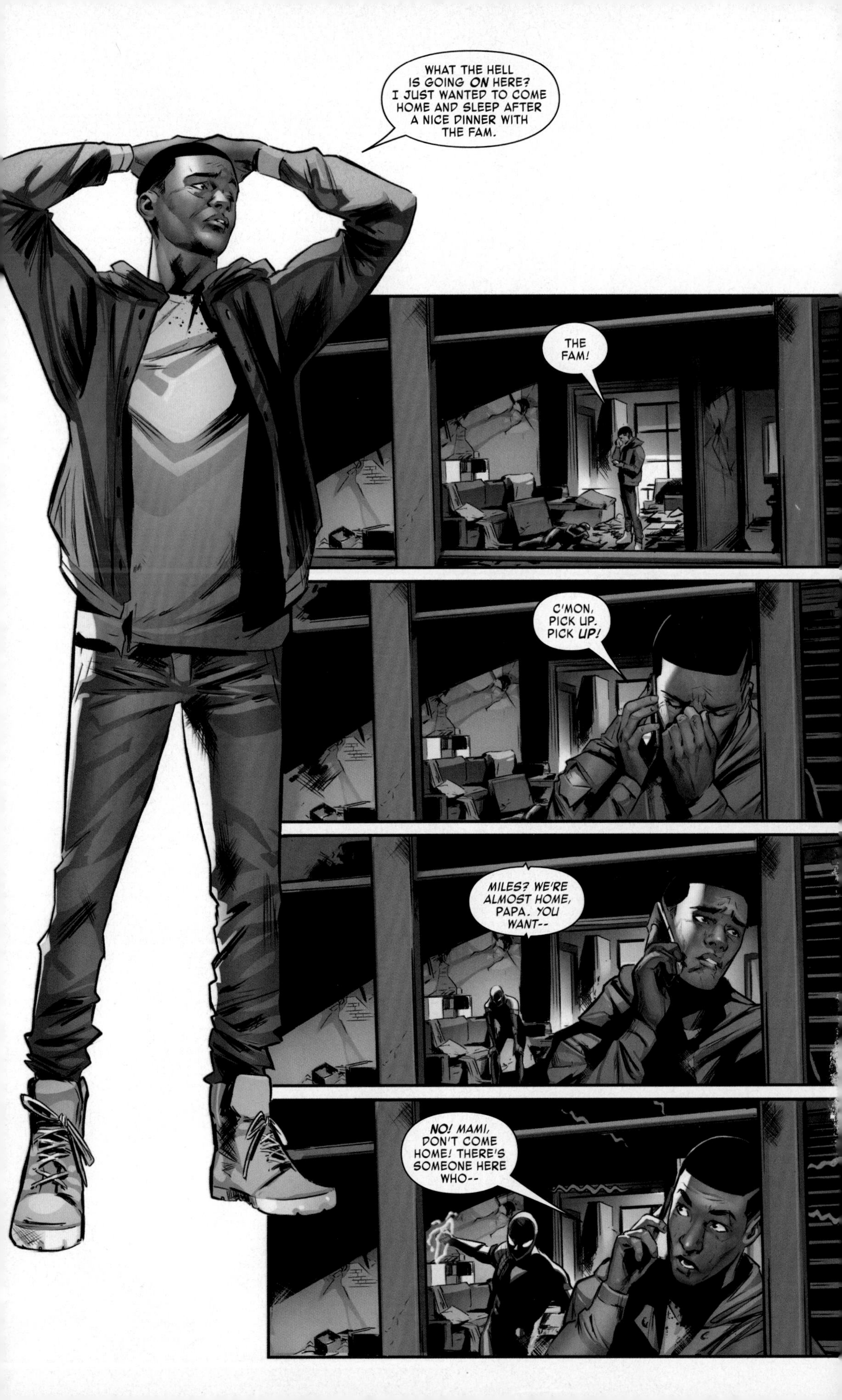

WHAT THE HELL IS GOING ON HERE? I JUST WANTED TO COME HOME AND SLEEP AFTER A NICE DINNER WITH THE FAM.
THE FAM!
C'MON, PICK UP. PICK UP!
MILES? WE'RE ALMOST HOME, PAPA. YOU WANT--
NO! MAMI, DON'T COME HOME! THERE'S SOMEONE HERE WHO--

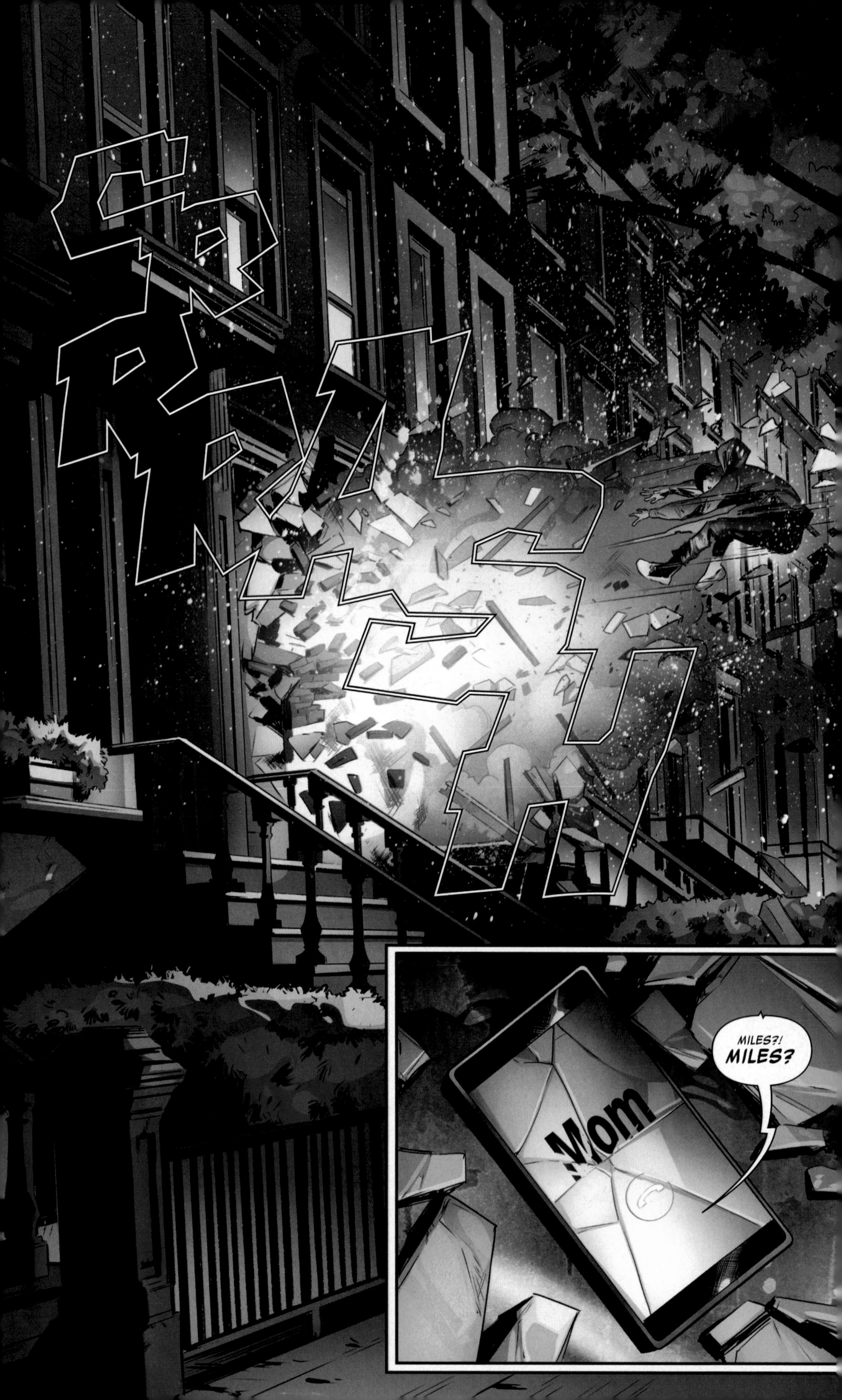
CRASH
Mom
MILES?!
MILES?

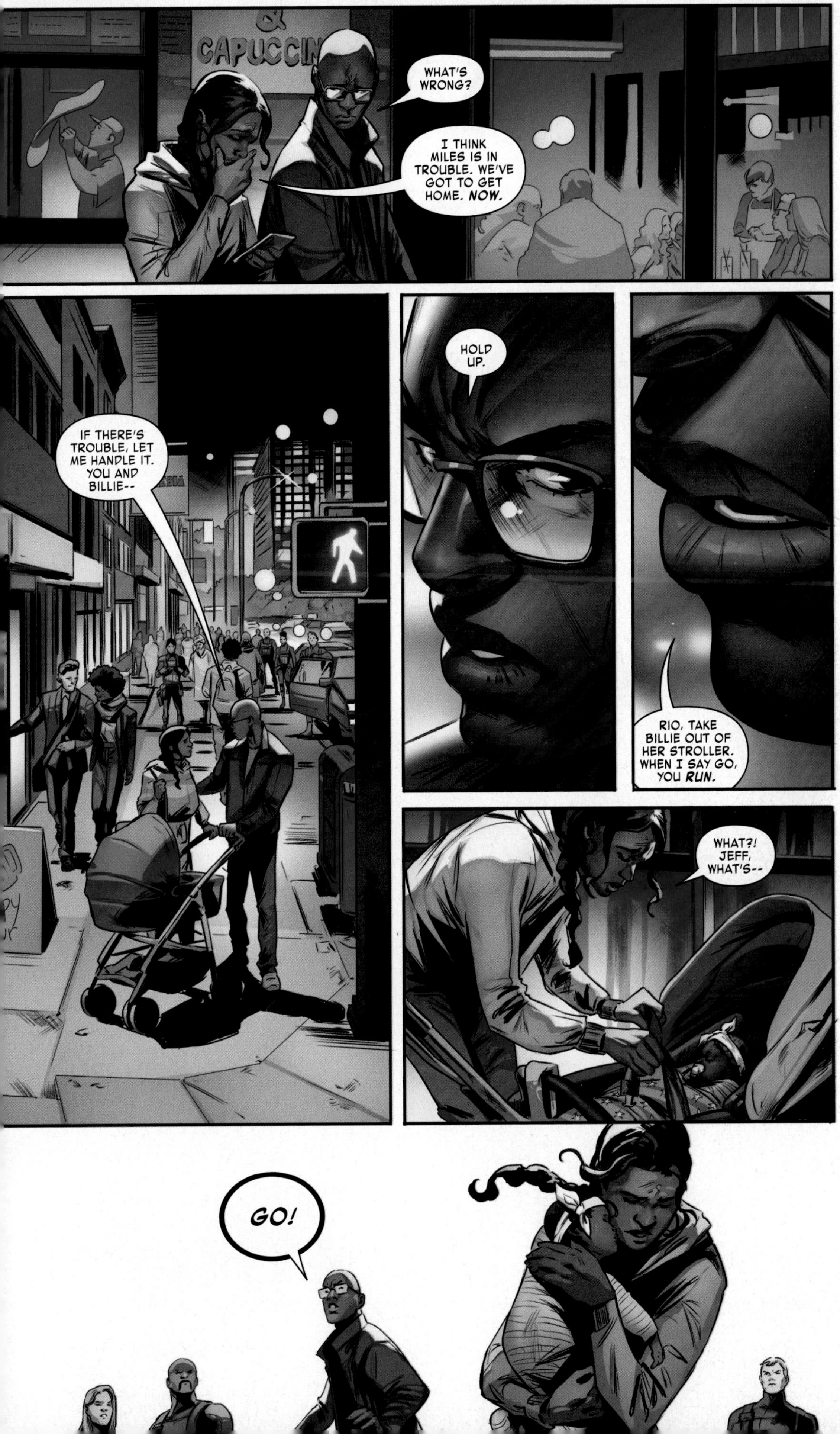

& CAPUCCIN
WHAT'S WRONG?
I THINK MILES IS IN TROUBLE. WE'VE GOT TO GET HOME. *NOW.*
IF THERE'S TROUBLE, LET ME HANDLE IT. YOU AND BILLIE--
HOLD UP.
RIO, TAKE BILLIE OUT OF HER STROLLER. WHEN I SAY GO, YOU *RUN.*
WHAT?! JEFF, WHAT'S--
GO!

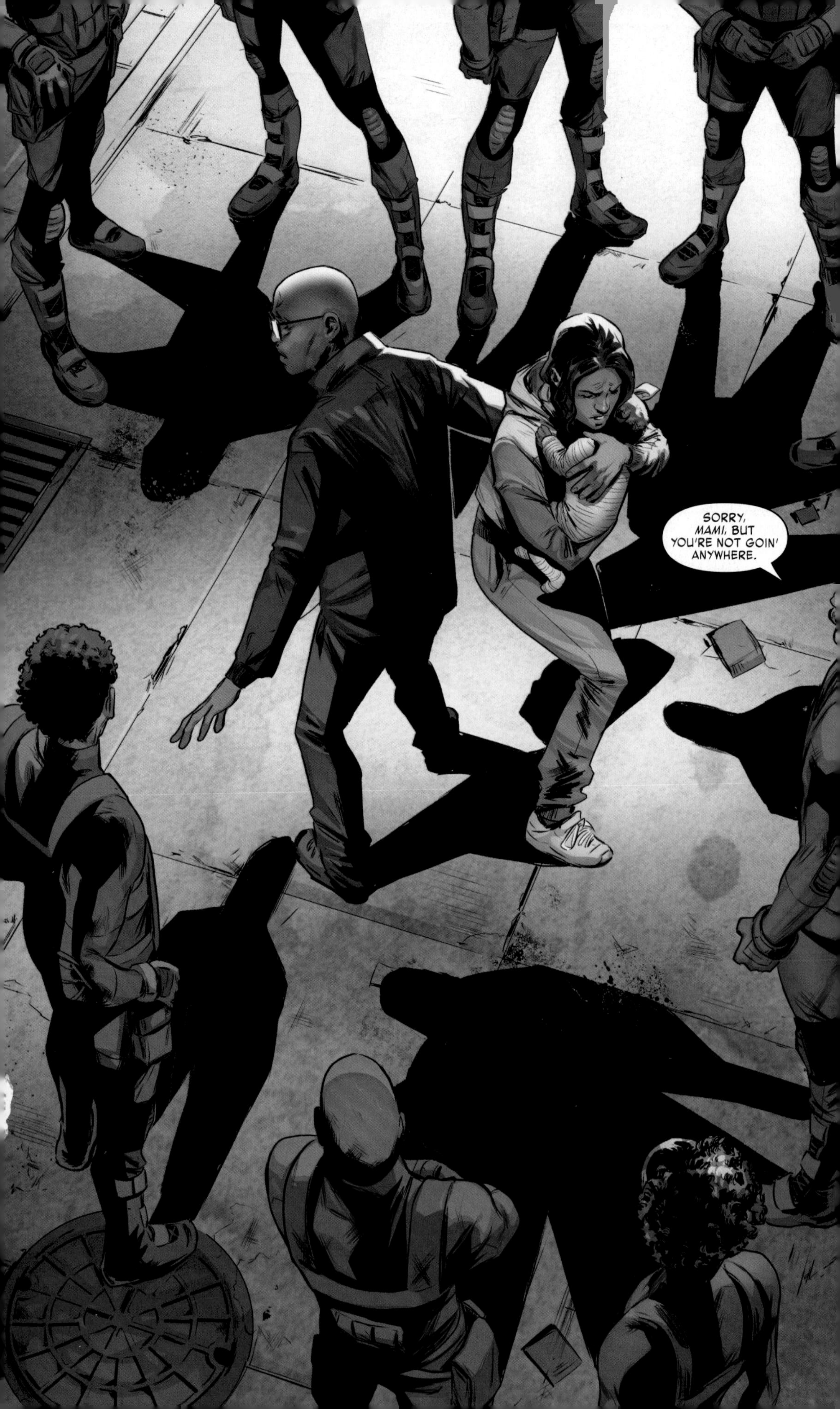
SORRY, *MAMI*, BUT YOU'RE NOT GOIN' ANYWHERE.

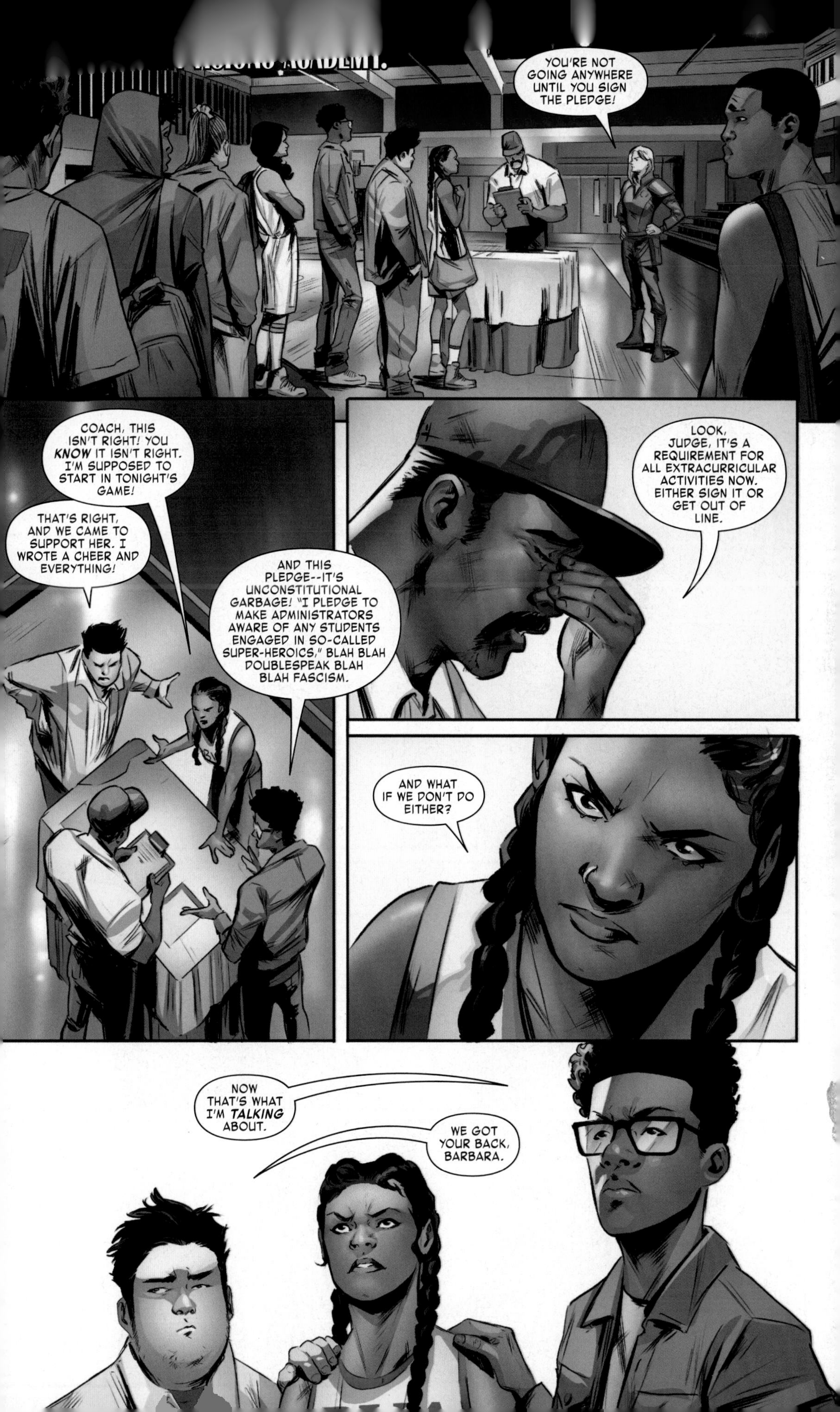

YOU'RE NOT GOING ANYWHERE UNTIL YOU SIGN THE PLEDGE!
COACH, THIS ISN'T RIGHT! YOU *KNOW* IT ISN'T RIGHT. I'M SUPPOSED TO START IN TONIGHT'S GAME!
THAT'S RIGHT, AND WE CAME TO SUPPORT HER. I WROTE A CHEER AND EVERYTHING!
AND THIS PLEDGE--IT'S UNCONSTITUTIONAL GARBAGE! "I PLEDGE TO MAKE ADMINISTRATORS AWARE OF ANY STUDENTS ENGAGED IN SO-CALLED SUPER-HEROICS," BLAH BLAH DOUBLESPEAK BLAH BLAH FASCISM.
LOOK, JUDGE, IT'S A REQUIREMENT FOR ALL EXTRACURRICULAR ACTIVITIES NOW. EITHER SIGN IT OR GET OUT OF LINE.
AND WHAT IF WE DON'T DO EITHER?
NOW THAT'S WHAT I'M *TALKING* ABOUT.
WE GOT YOUR BACK, BARBARA.

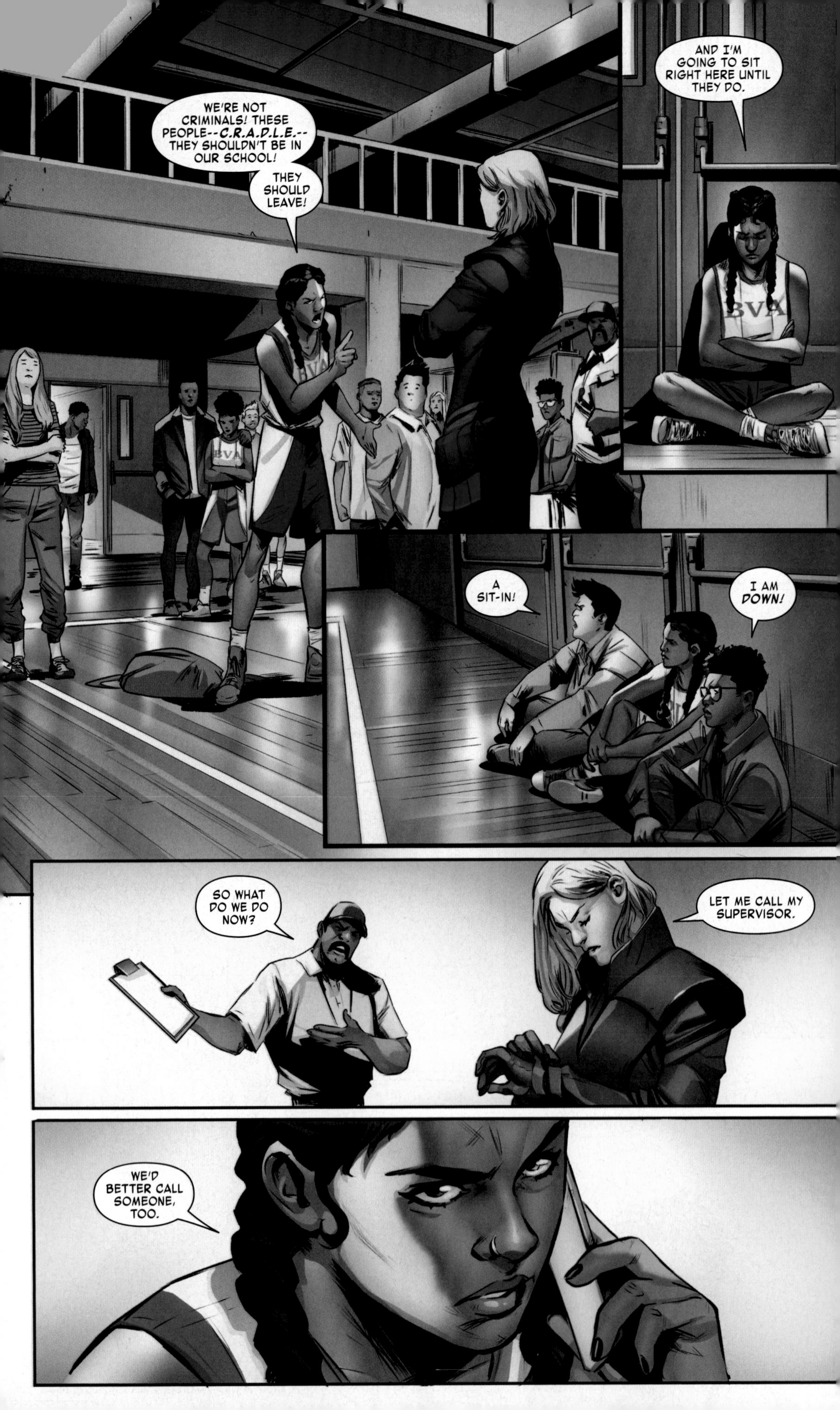
WE'RE NOT CRIMINALS! THESE PEOPLE--C.R.A.D.L.E.--THEY SHOULDN'T BE IN OUR SCHOOL!
THEY SHOULD LEAVE!
AND I'M GOING TO SIT RIGHT HERE UNTIL THEY DO.
A SIT-IN!
I AM DOWN!
SO WHAT DO WE DO NOW?
LET ME CALL MY SUPERVISOR.
WE'D BETTER CALL SOMEONE, TOO.

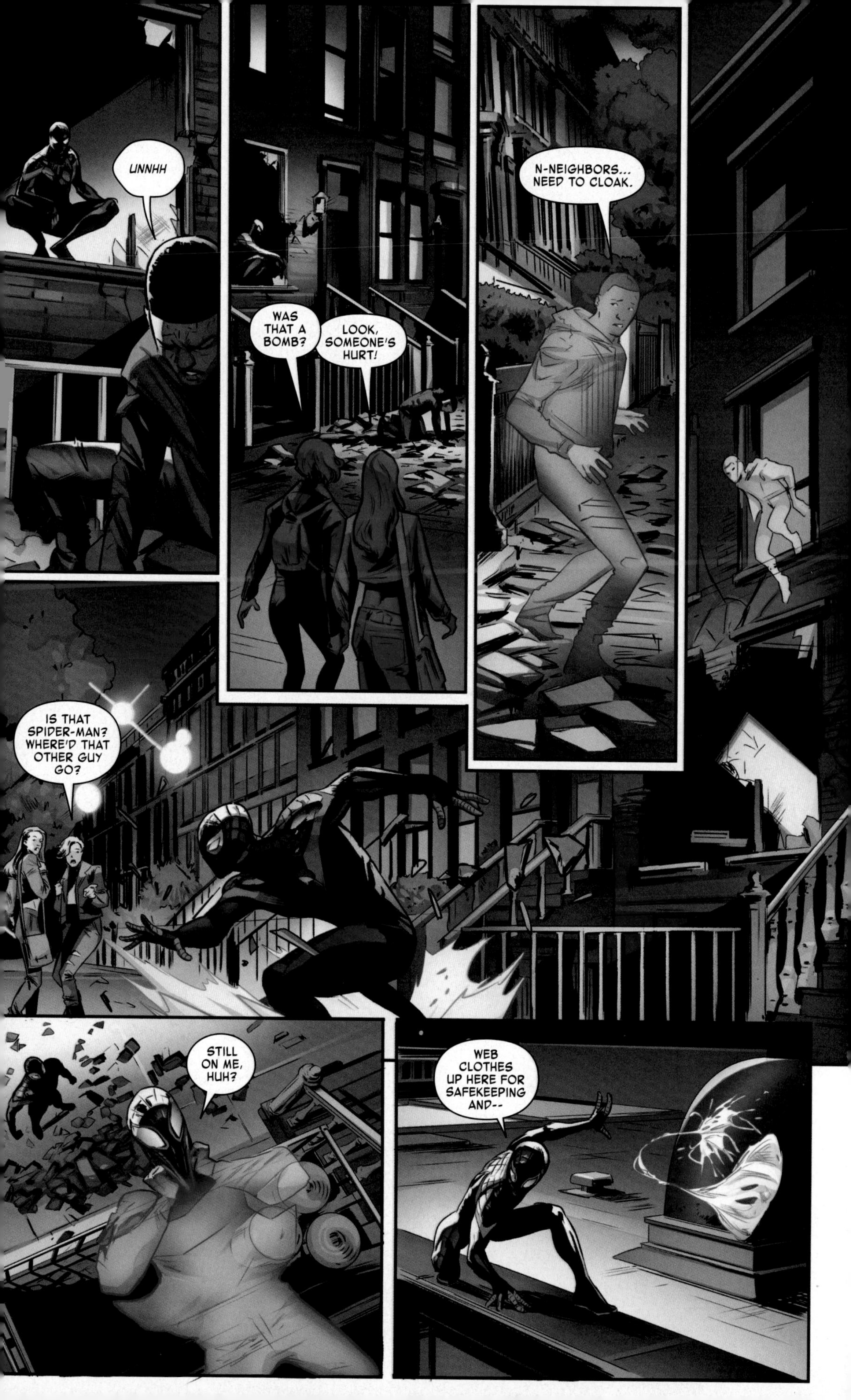
UNNHH
WAS THAT A BOMB?
LOOK, SOMEONE'S HURT!
N-NEIGHBORS... NEED TO CLOAK.
IS THAT SPIDER-MAN? WHERE'D THAT OTHER GUY GO?
STILL ON ME, HUH?
WEB CLOTHES UP HERE FOR SAFEKEEPING AND--

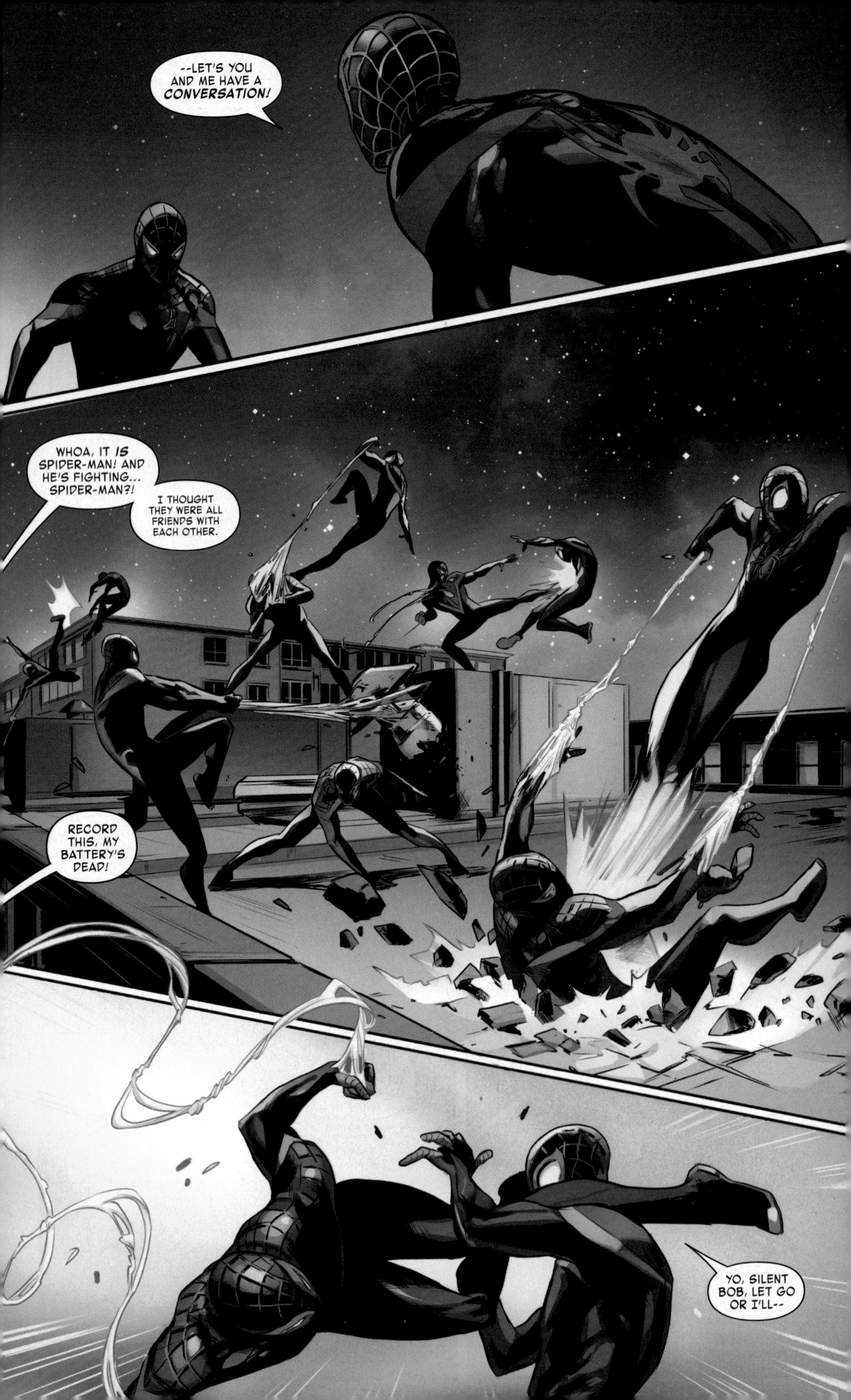
--LET'S YOU AND ME HAVE A *CONVERSATION!*
WHOA, IT *IS* SPIDER-MAN! AND HE'S FIGHTING... SPIDER-MAN?!
I THOUGHT THEY WERE ALL FRIENDS WITH EACH OTHER.
RECORD THIS, MY BATTERY'S DEAD!
YO, SILENT BOB, LET GO OR I'LL--

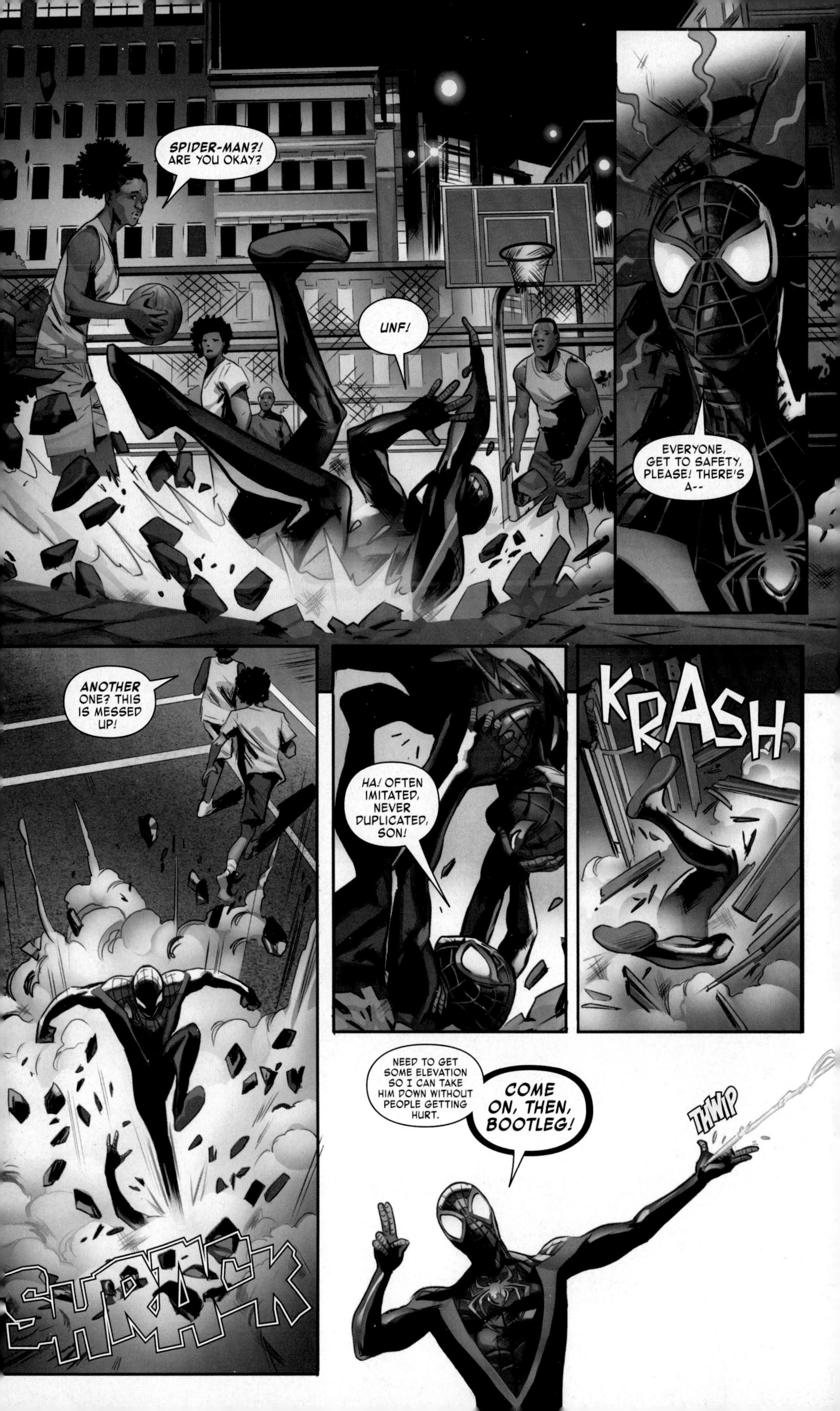

SPIDER-MAN?! ARE YOU OKAY?
UNF!
EVERYONE, GET TO SAFETY, PLEASE! THERE'S A--
ANOTHER ONE? THIS IS MESSED UP!
HA! OFTEN IMITATED, NEVER DUPLICATED, SON!
KRASH
NEED TO GET SOME ELEVATION SO I CAN TAKE HIM DOWN WITHOUT PEOPLE GETTING HURT.
COME ON, THEN, BOOTLEG!
THWIP

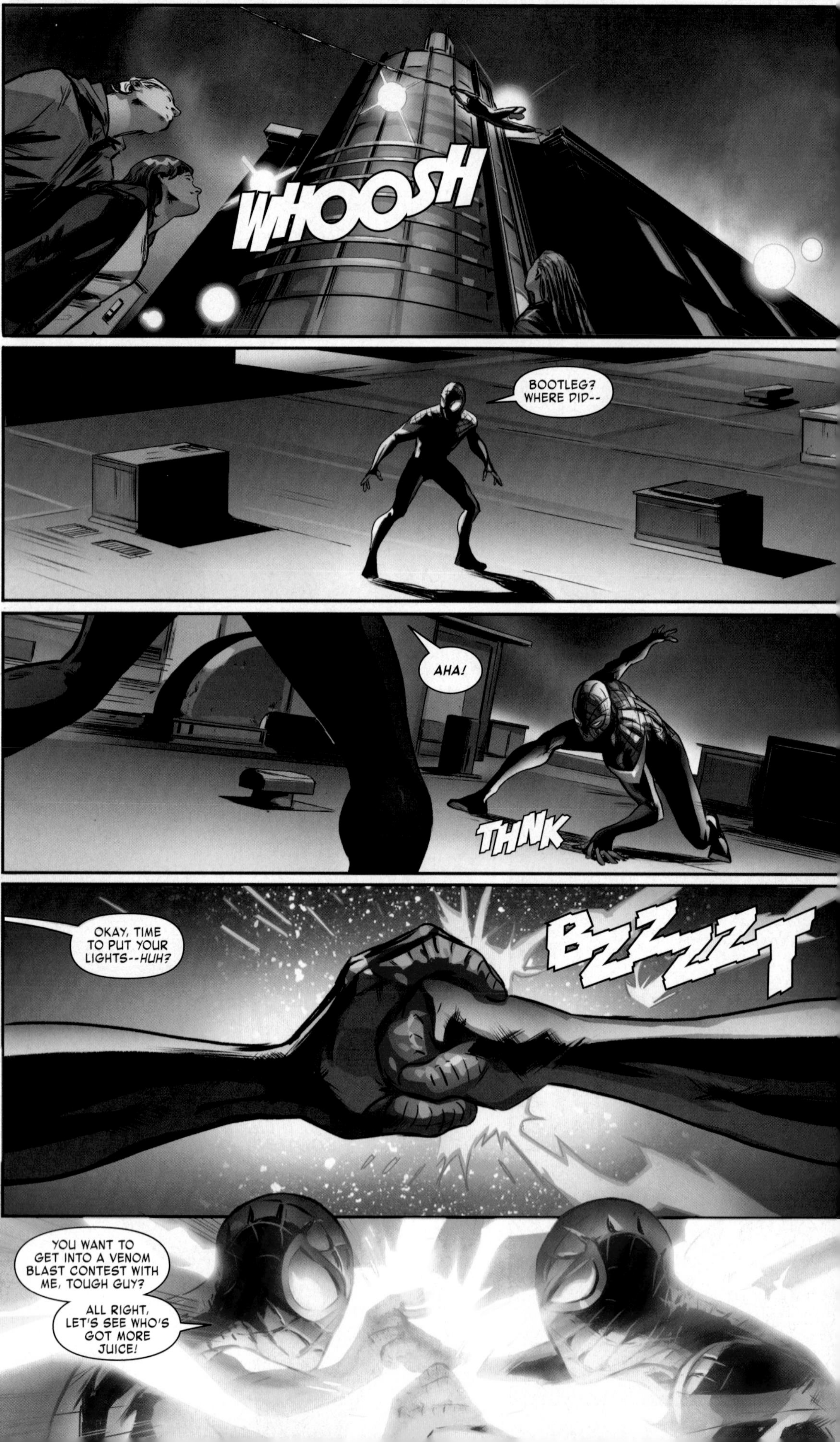
WHOOSH
BOOTLEG? WHERE DID--
AHA!
THNK
OKAY, TIME TO PUT YOUR LIGHTS--HUH?
BZZZZT
YOU WANT TO GET INTO A VENOM BLAST CONTEST WITH ME, TOUGH GUY?
ALL RIGHT, LET'S SEE WHO'S GOT MORE JUICE!

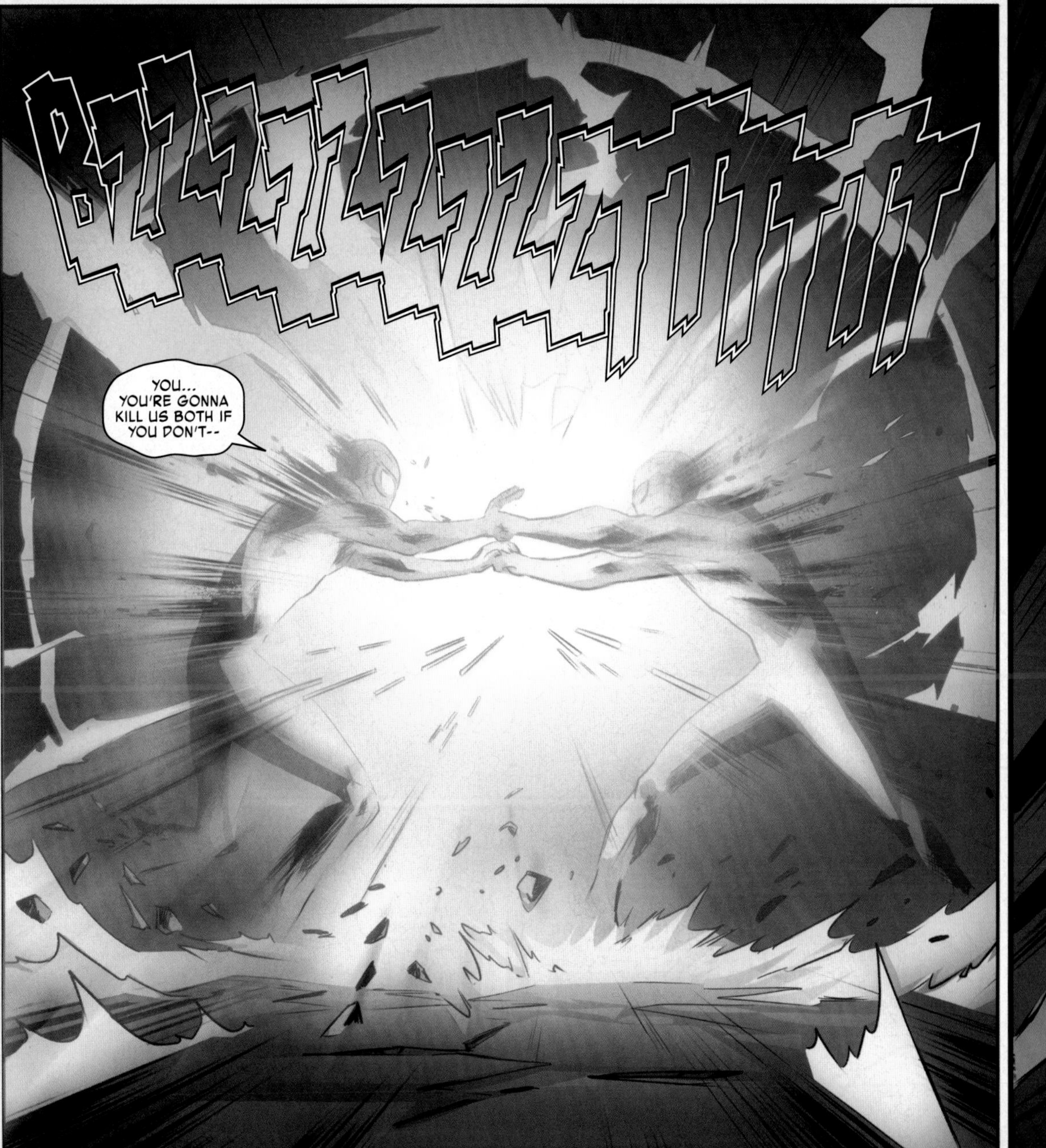
YOU...
YOU'RE GONNA KILL US BOTH IF YOU DON'T--

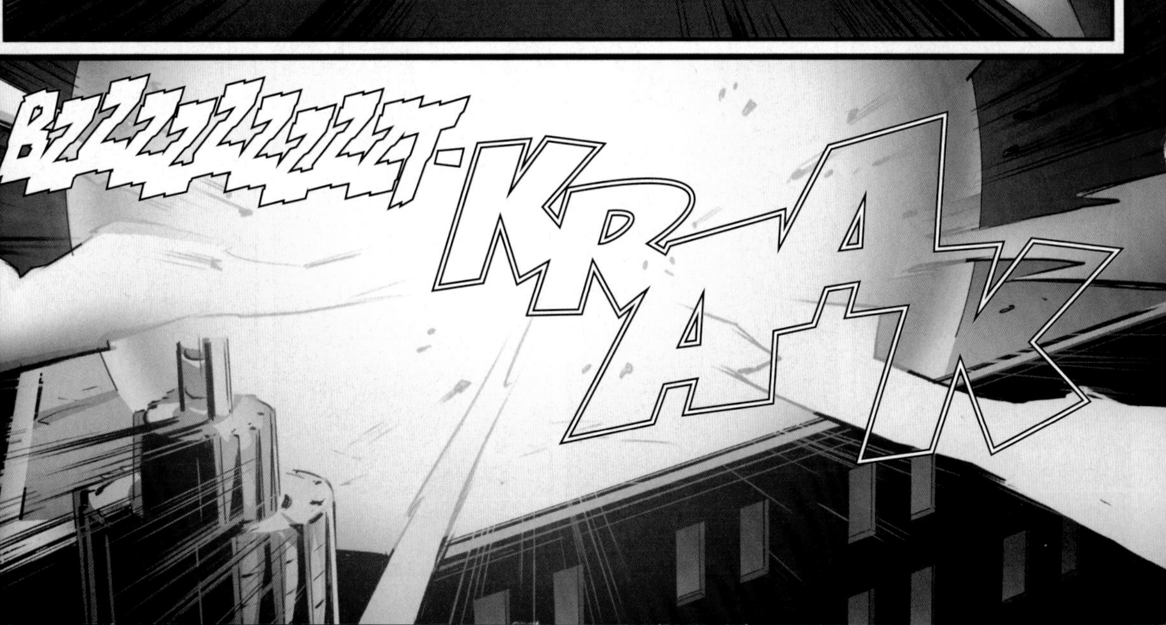
KRAK

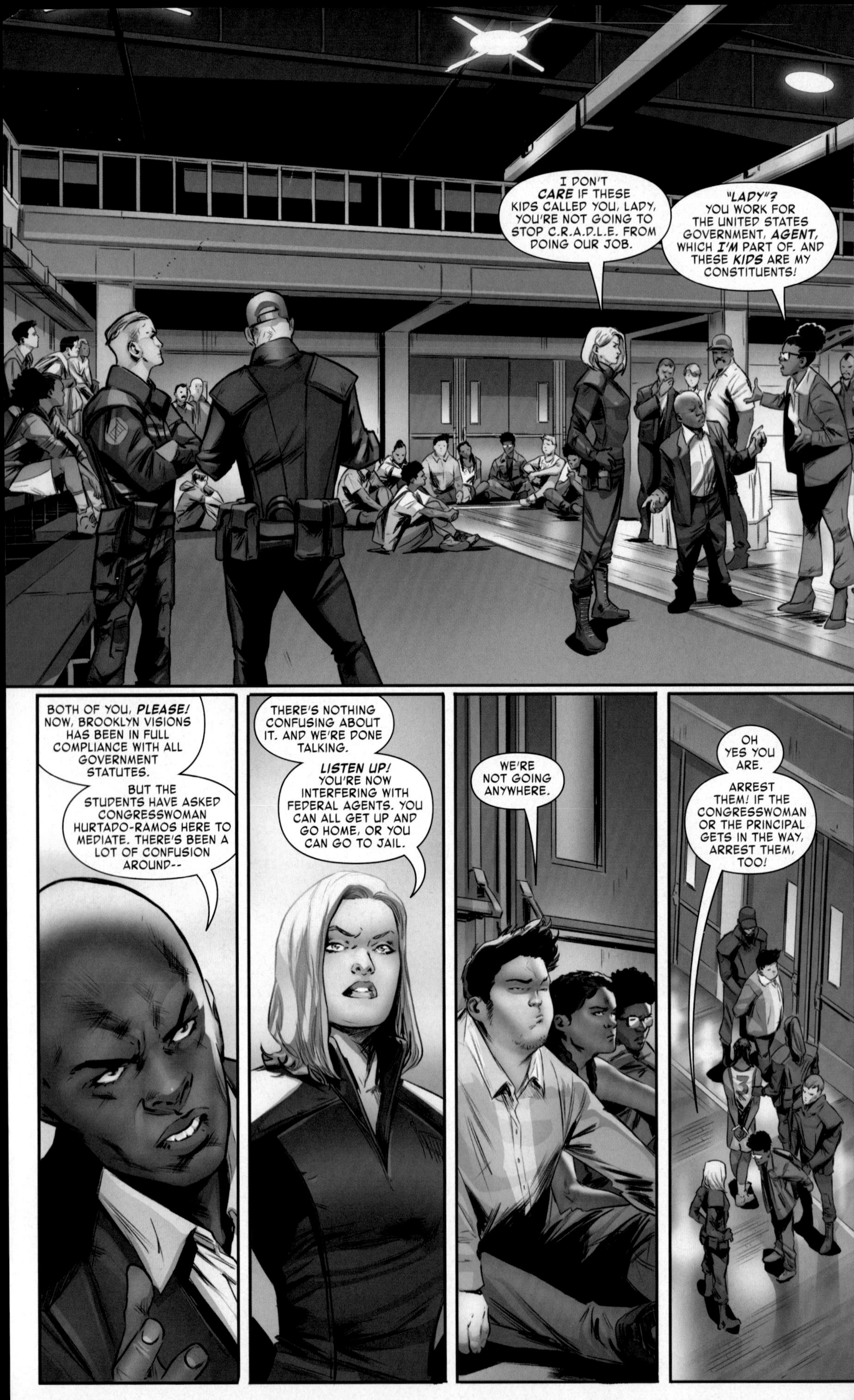
I DON'T CARE IF THESE KIDS CALLED YOU, LADY, YOU'RE NOT GOING TO STOP C.R.A.D.L.E. FROM DOING OUR JOB.
"LADY"? YOU WORK FOR THE UNITED STATES GOVERNMENT, AGENT, WHICH I'M PART OF. AND THESE KIDS ARE MY CONSTITUENTS!
BOTH OF YOU, PLEASE! NOW, BROOKLYN VISIONS HAS BEEN IN FULL COMPLIANCE WITH ALL GOVERNMENT STATUTES.
BUT THE STUDENTS HAVE ASKED CONGRESSWOMAN HURTADO-RAMOS HERE TO MEDIATE. THERE'S BEEN A LOT OF CONFUSION AROUND--
THERE'S NOTHING CONFUSING ABOUT IT. AND WE'RE DONE TALKING.
LISTEN UP! YOU'RE NOW INTERFERING WITH FEDERAL AGENTS. YOU CAN ALL GET UP AND GO HOME, OR YOU CAN GO TO JAIL.
WE'RE NOT GOING ANYWHERE.
OH YES YOU ARE.
ARREST THEM! IF THE CONGRESSWOMAN OR THE PRINCIPAL GETS IN THE WAY, ARREST THEM, TOO!

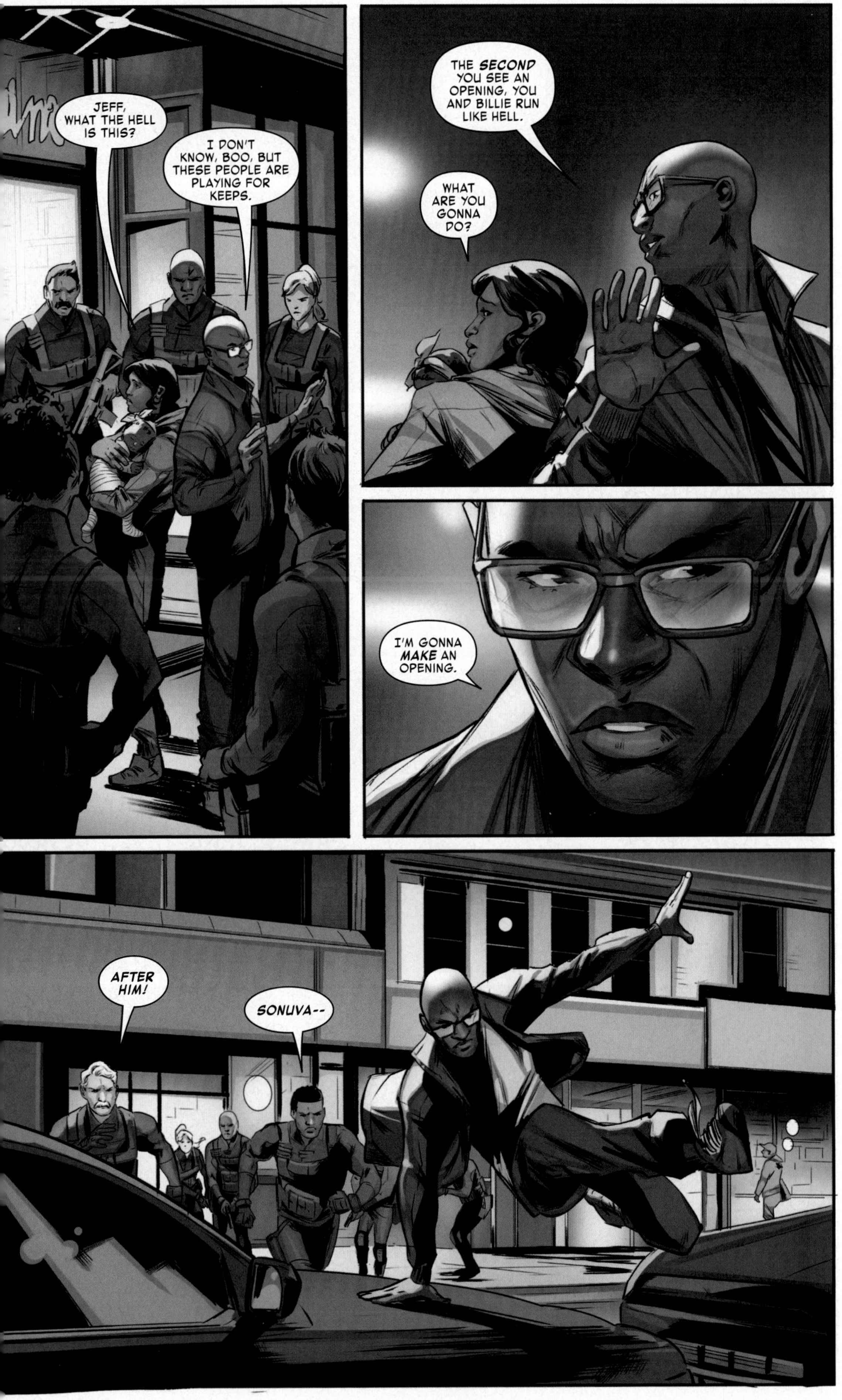
JEFF, WHAT THE HELL IS THIS?
I DON'T KNOW, BOO, BUT THESE PEOPLE ARE PLAYING FOR KEEPS.
THE SECOND YOU SEE AN OPENING, YOU AND BILLIE RUN LIKE HELL.
WHAT ARE YOU GONNA DO?
I'M GONNA MAKE AN OPENING.
AFTER HIM!
SONUVA--

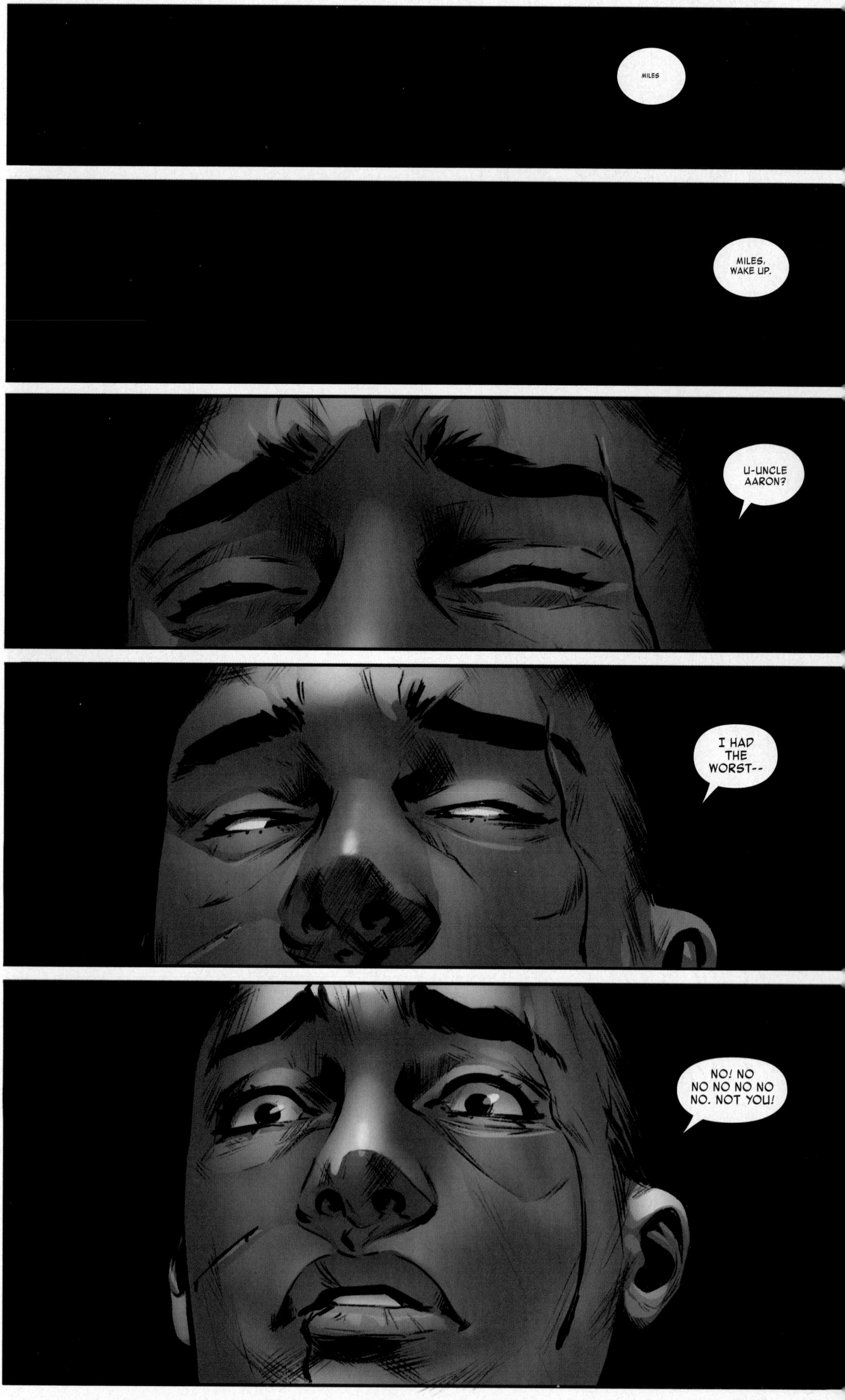
MILES
MILES, WAKE UP.
U-UNCLE AARON?
I HAD THE WORST--
NO! NO NO NO NO NO NO. NOT YOU!

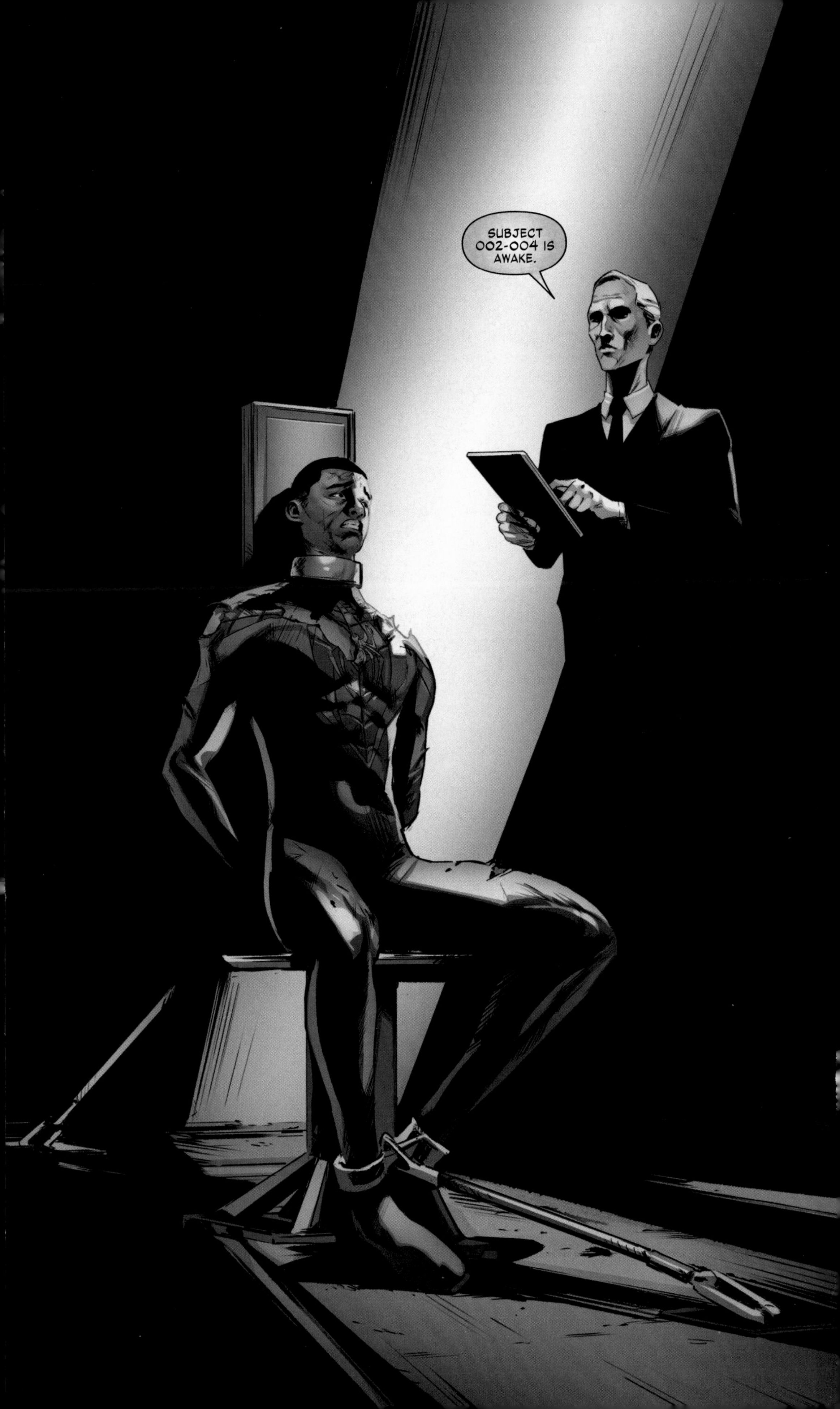
SUBJECT 002-004 IS AWAKE.

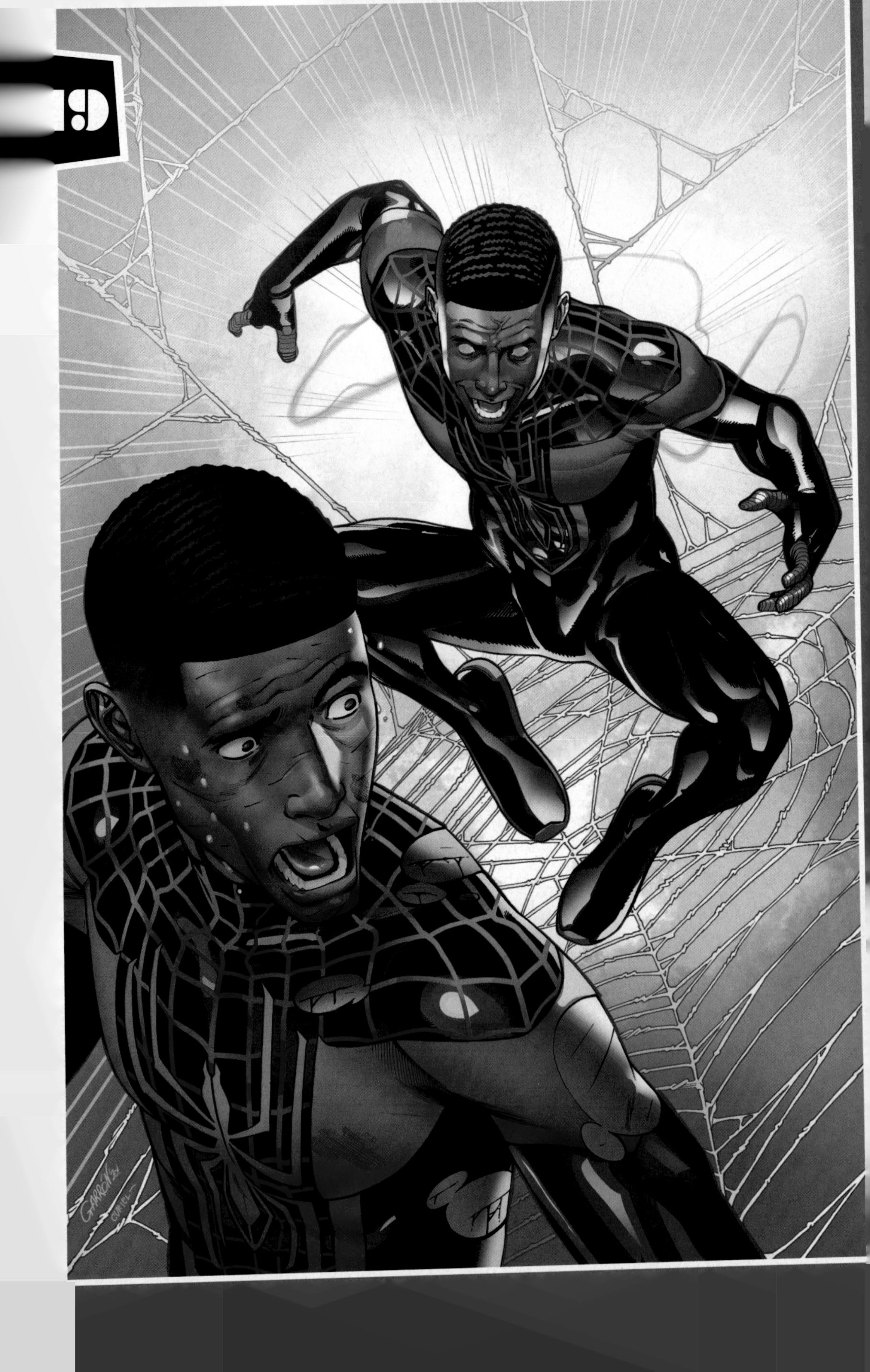

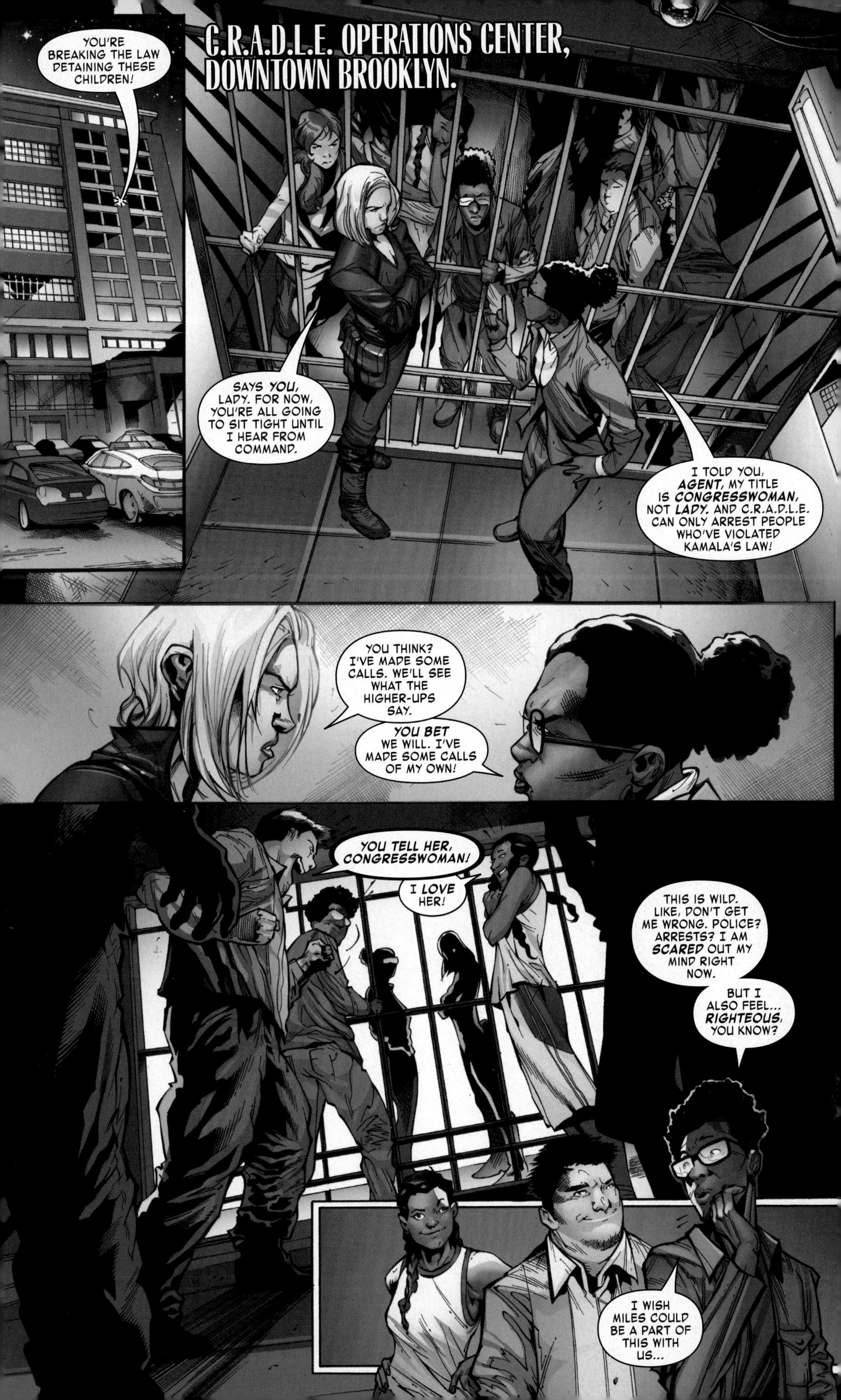
C.R.A.D.L.E. OPERATIONS CENTER, DOWNTOWN BROOKLYN.
YOU'RE BREAKING THE LAW DETAINING THESE CHILDREN!
SAYS YOU, LADY. FOR NOW, YOU'RE ALL GOING TO SIT TIGHT UNTIL I HEAR FROM COMMAND.
I TOLD YOU, AGENT, MY TITLE IS CONGRESSWOMAN, NOT LADY. AND C.R.A.D.L.E. CAN ONLY ARREST PEOPLE WHO'VE VIOLATED KAMALA'S LAW!
YOU THINK? I'VE MADE SOME CALLS. WE'LL SEE WHAT THE HIGHER-UPS SAY.
YOU BET WE WILL. I'VE MADE SOME CALLS OF MY OWN!
YOU TELL HER, CONGRESSWOMAN!
I LOVE HER!
THIS IS WILD. LIKE, DON'T GET ME WRONG. POLICE? ARRESTS? I AM SCARED OUT MY MIND RIGHT NOW.
BUT I ALSO FEEL... RIGHTEOUS, YOU KNOW?
I WISH MILES COULD BE A PART OF THIS WITH US...

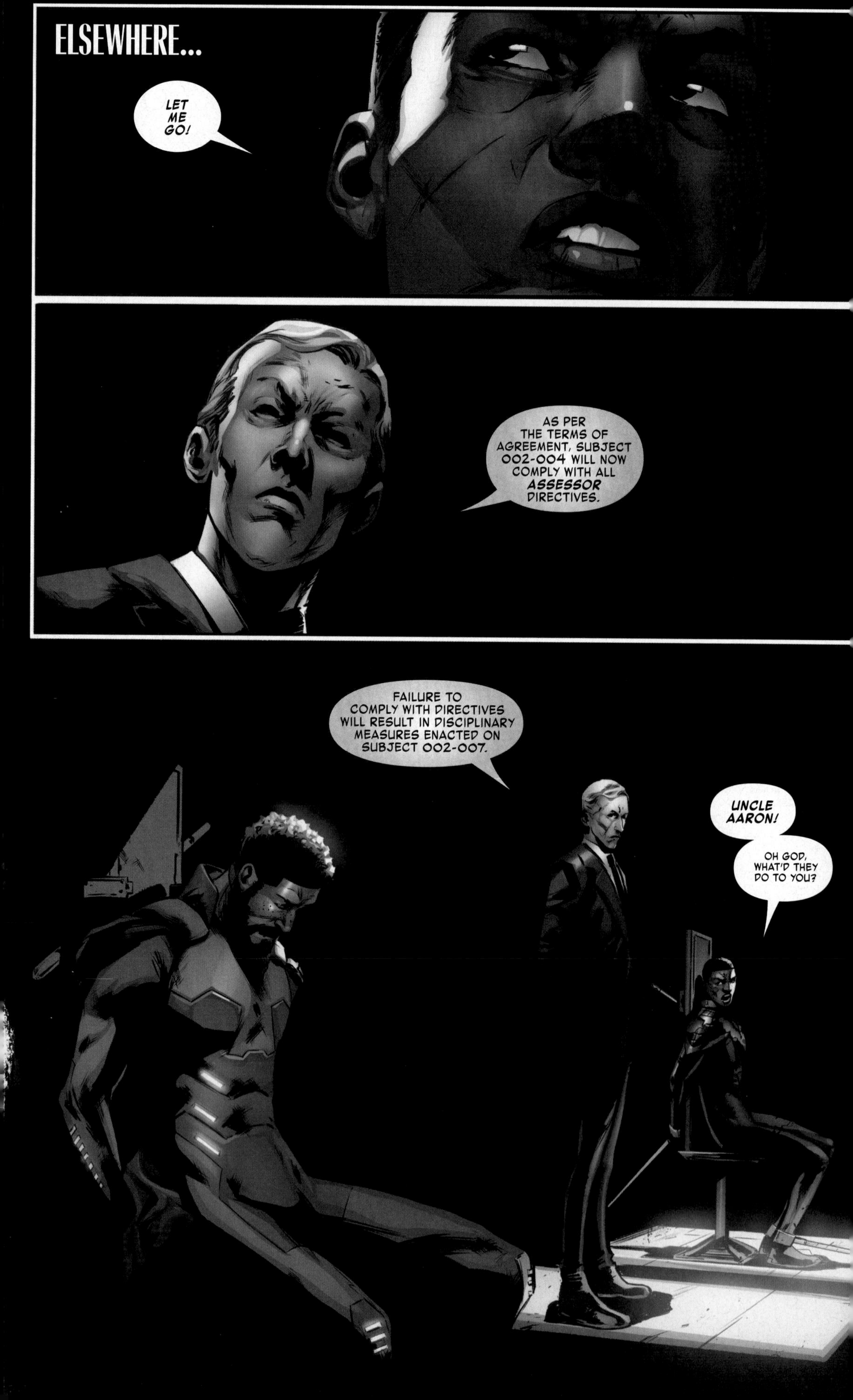
ELSEWHERE...
LET ME GO!
AS PER THE TERMS OF AGREEMENT, SUBJECT 002-004 WILL NOW COMPLY WITH ALL ASSESSOR DIRECTIVES.
FAILURE TO COMPLY WITH DIRECTIVES WILL RESULT IN DISCIPLINARY MEASURES ENACTED ON SUBJECT 002-007.
UNCLE AARON!
OH GOD, WHAT'D THEY DO TO YOU?

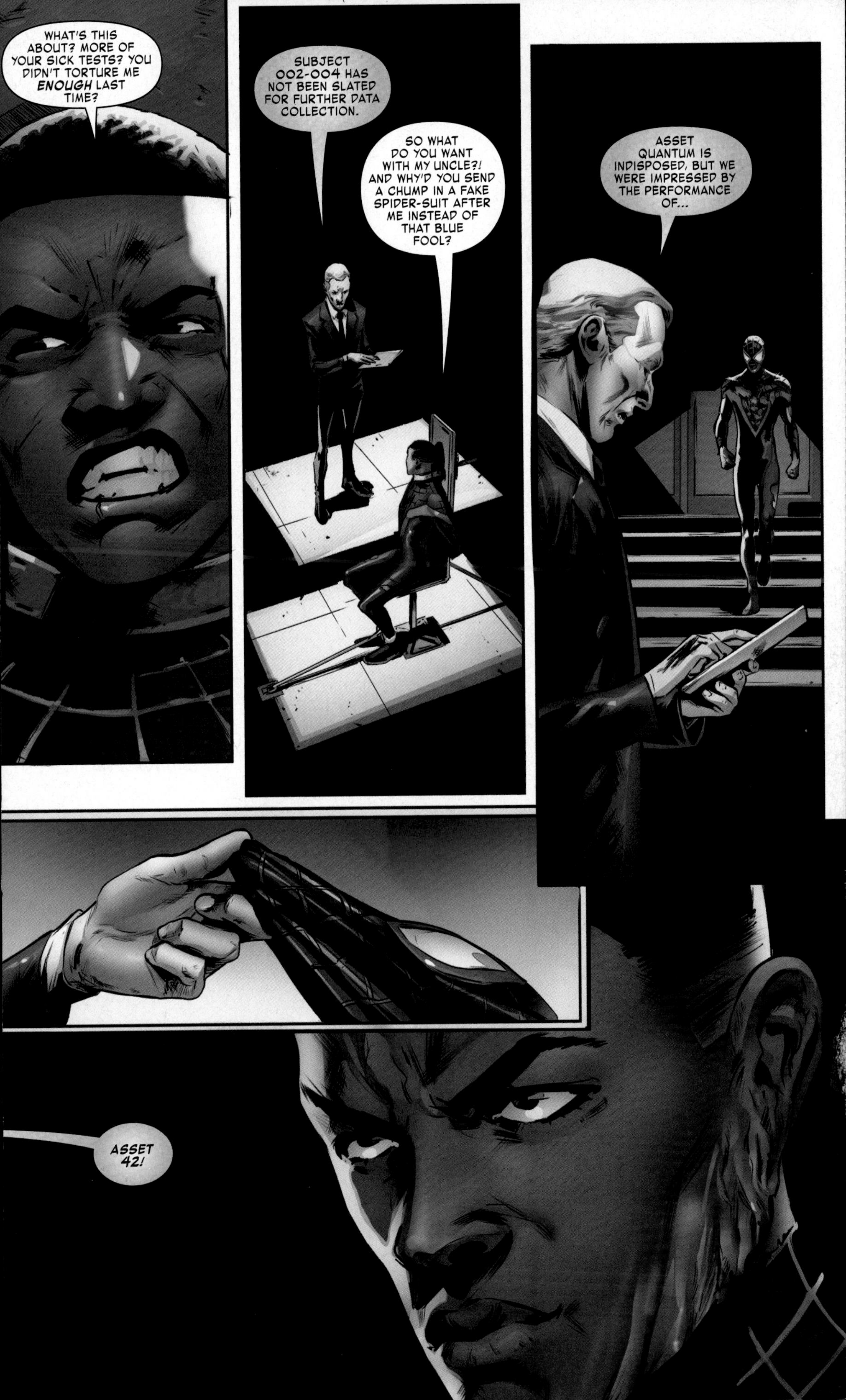
WHAT'S THIS ABOUT? MORE OF YOUR SICK TESTS? YOU DIDN'T TORTURE ME ENOUGH LAST TIME?
SUBJECT 002-004 HAS NOT BEEN SLATED FOR FURTHER DATA COLLECTION.
SO WHAT DO YOU WANT WITH MY UNCLE?! AND WHY'D YOU SEND A CHUMP IN A FAKE SPIDER-SUIT AFTER ME INSTEAD OF THAT BLUE FOOL?
ASSET QUANTUM IS INDISPOSED, BUT WE WERE IMPRESSED BY THE PERFORMANCE OF...
ASSET 42!

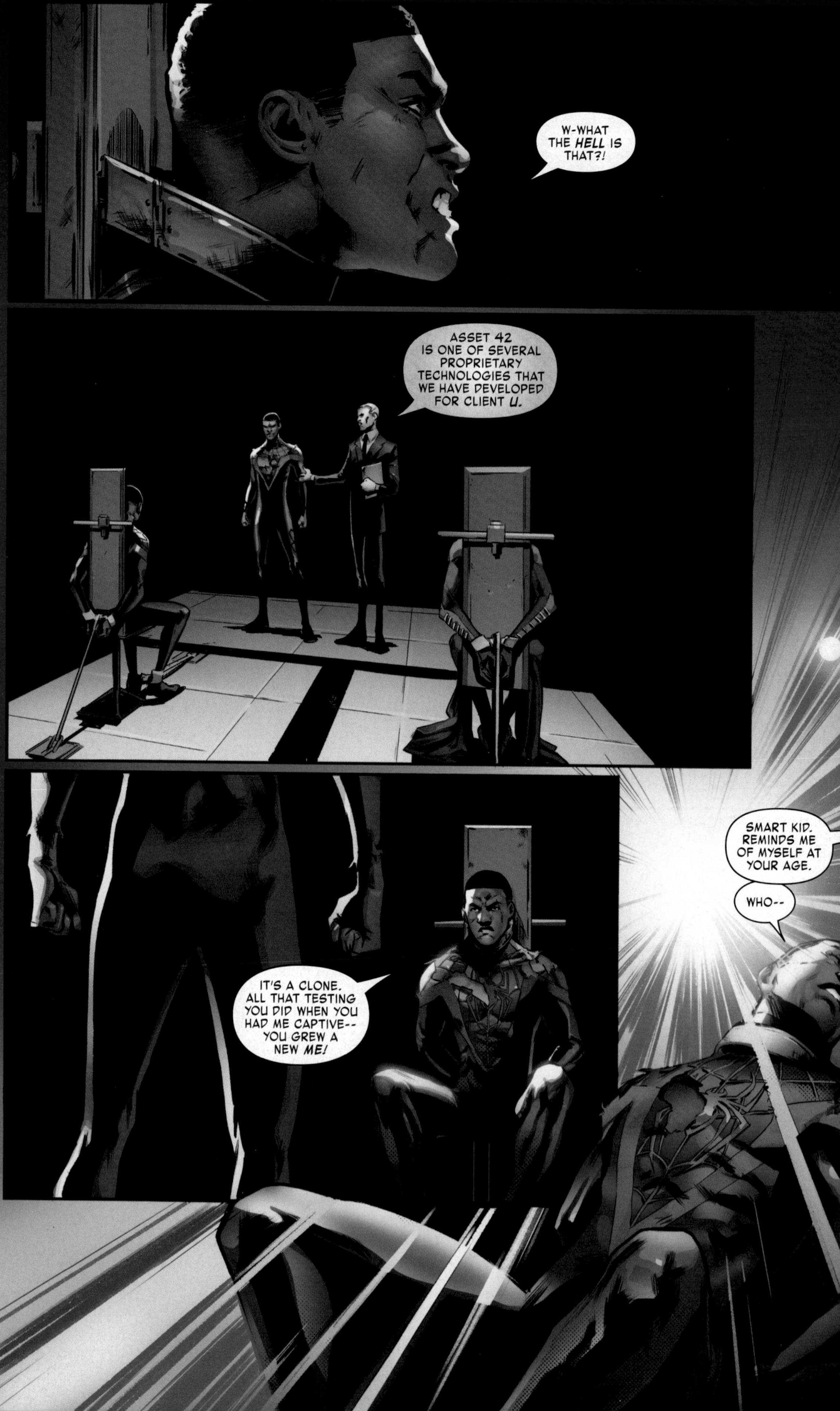
W-WHAT THE HELL IS THAT?!
ASSET 42 IS ONE OF SEVERAL PROPRIETARY TECHNOLOGIES THAT WE HAVE DEVELOPED FOR CLIENT U.
IT'S A CLONE. ALL THAT TESTING YOU DID WHEN YOU HAD ME CAPTIVE-- YOU GREW A NEW ME!
SMART KID. REMINDS ME OF MYSELF AT YOUR AGE.
WHO--

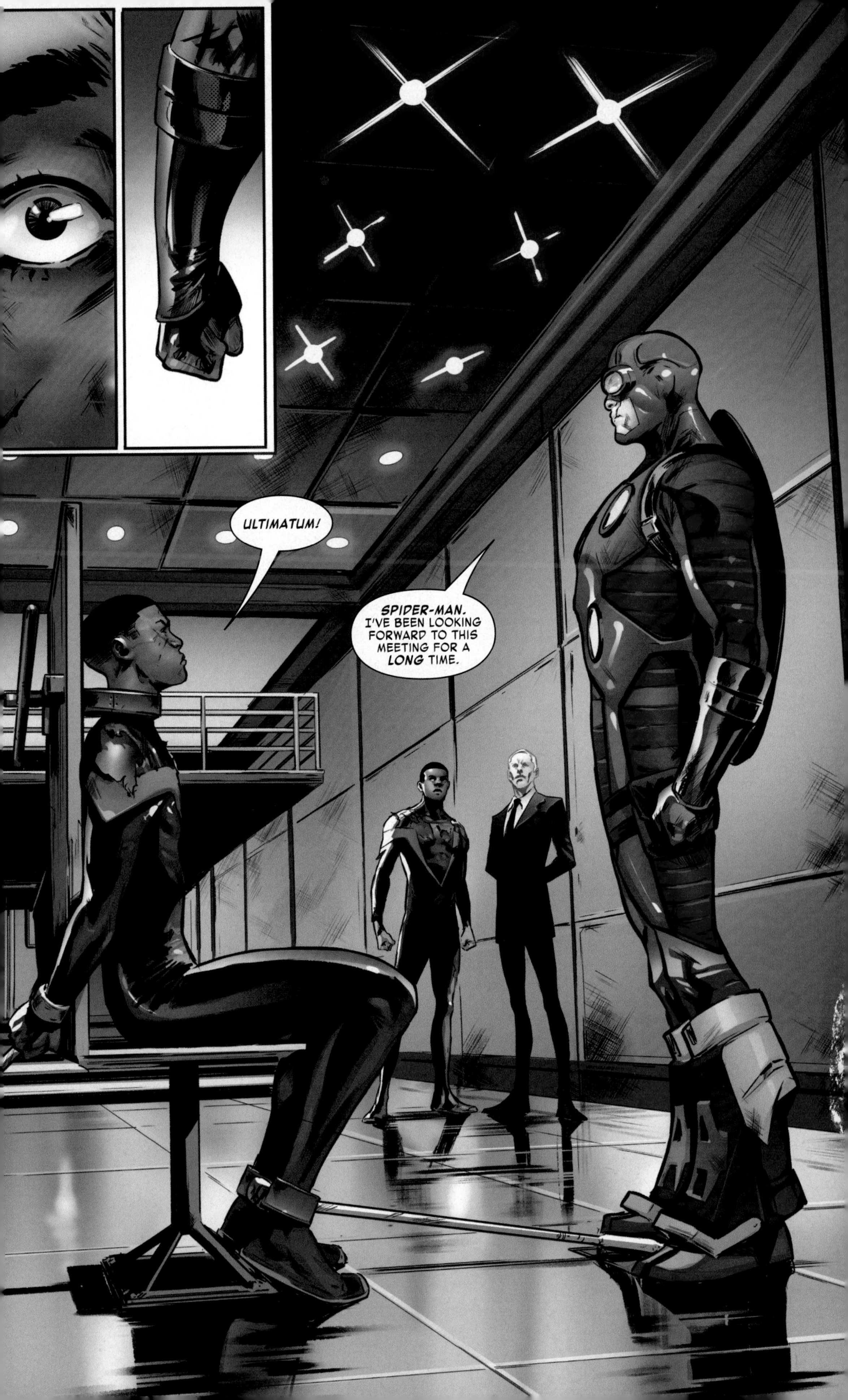
ULTIMATUM!
SPIDER-MAN. I'VE BEEN LOOKING FORWARD TO THIS MEETING FOR A LONG TIME.

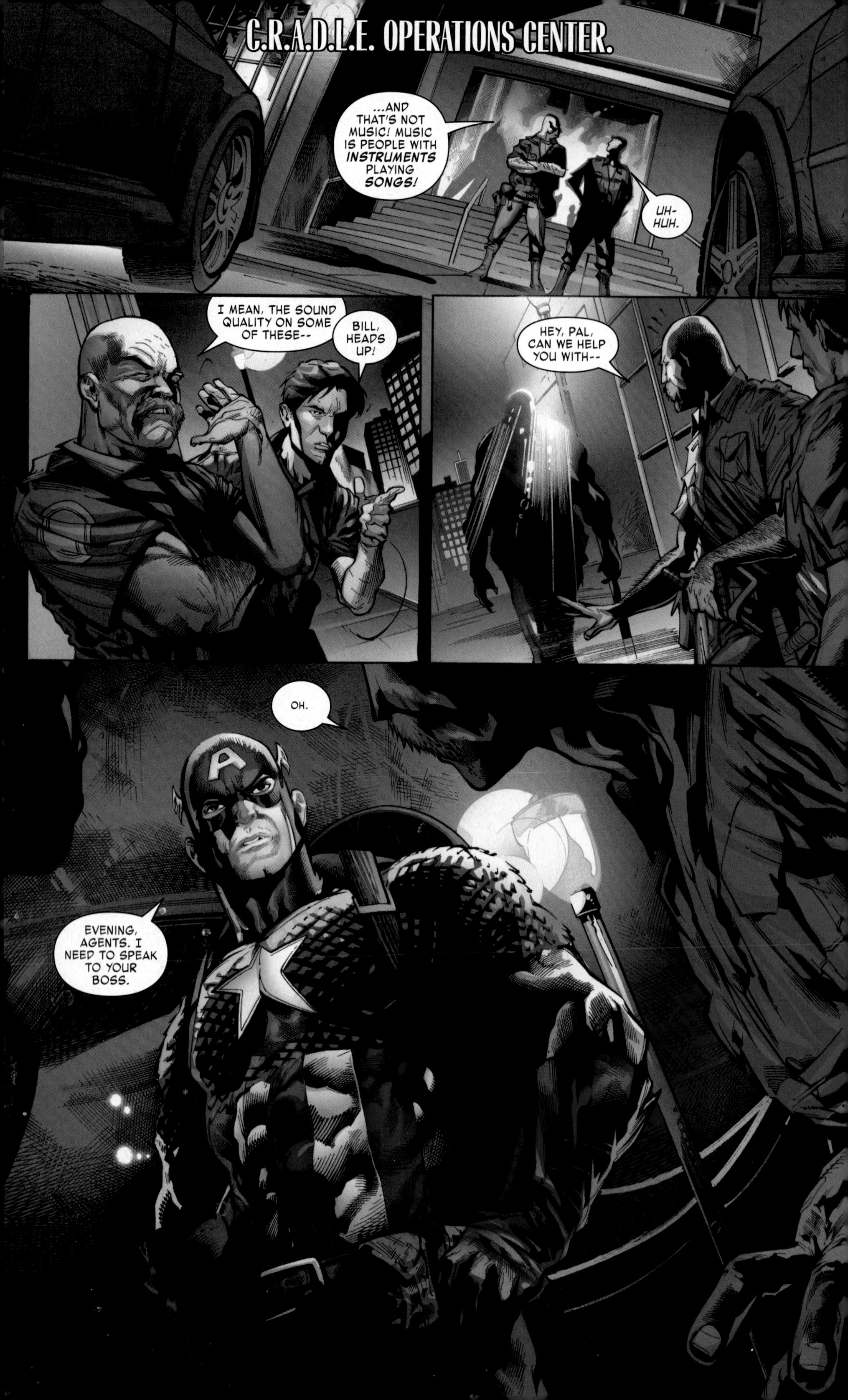
C.R.A.D.L.E. OPERATIONS CENTER.
...AND THAT'S NOT MUSIC! MUSIC IS PEOPLE WITH INSTRUMENTS PLAYING SONGS!
UH-HUH.
I MEAN, THE SOUND QUALITY ON SOME OF THESE--
BILL, HEADS UP!
HEY, PAL, CAN WE HELP YOU WITH--
OH.
EVENING, AGENTS. I NEED TO SPEAK TO YOUR BOSS.

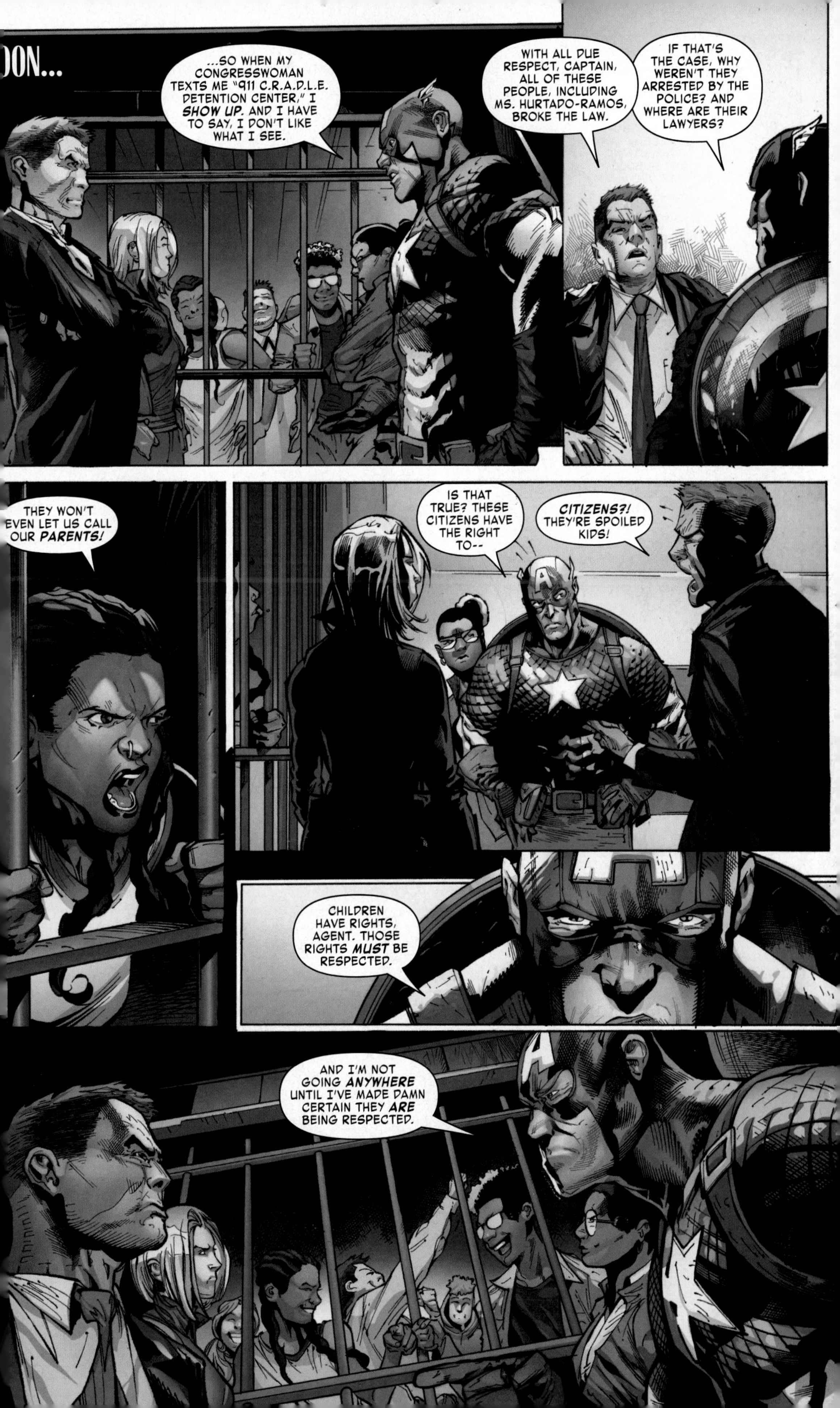

...ON...
...SO WHEN MY CONGRESSWOMAN TEXTS ME "911 C.R.A.D.L.E. DETENTION CENTER," I SHOW UP. AND I HAVE TO SAY, I DON'T LIKE WHAT I SEE.
WITH ALL DUE RESPECT, CAPTAIN, ALL OF THESE PEOPLE, INCLUDING MS. HURTADO-RAMOS, BROKE THE LAW.
IF THAT'S THE CASE, WHY WEREN'T THEY ARRESTED BY THE POLICE? AND WHERE ARE THEIR LAWYERS?
THEY WON'T EVEN LET US CALL OUR PARENTS!
IS THAT TRUE? THESE CITIZENS HAVE THE RIGHT TO--
CITIZENS?! THEY'RE SPOILED KIDS!
CHILDREN HAVE RIGHTS, AGENT. THOSE RIGHTS MUST BE RESPECTED.
AND I'M NOT GOING ANYWHERE UNTIL I'VE MADE DAMN CERTAIN THEY ARE BEING RESPECTED.

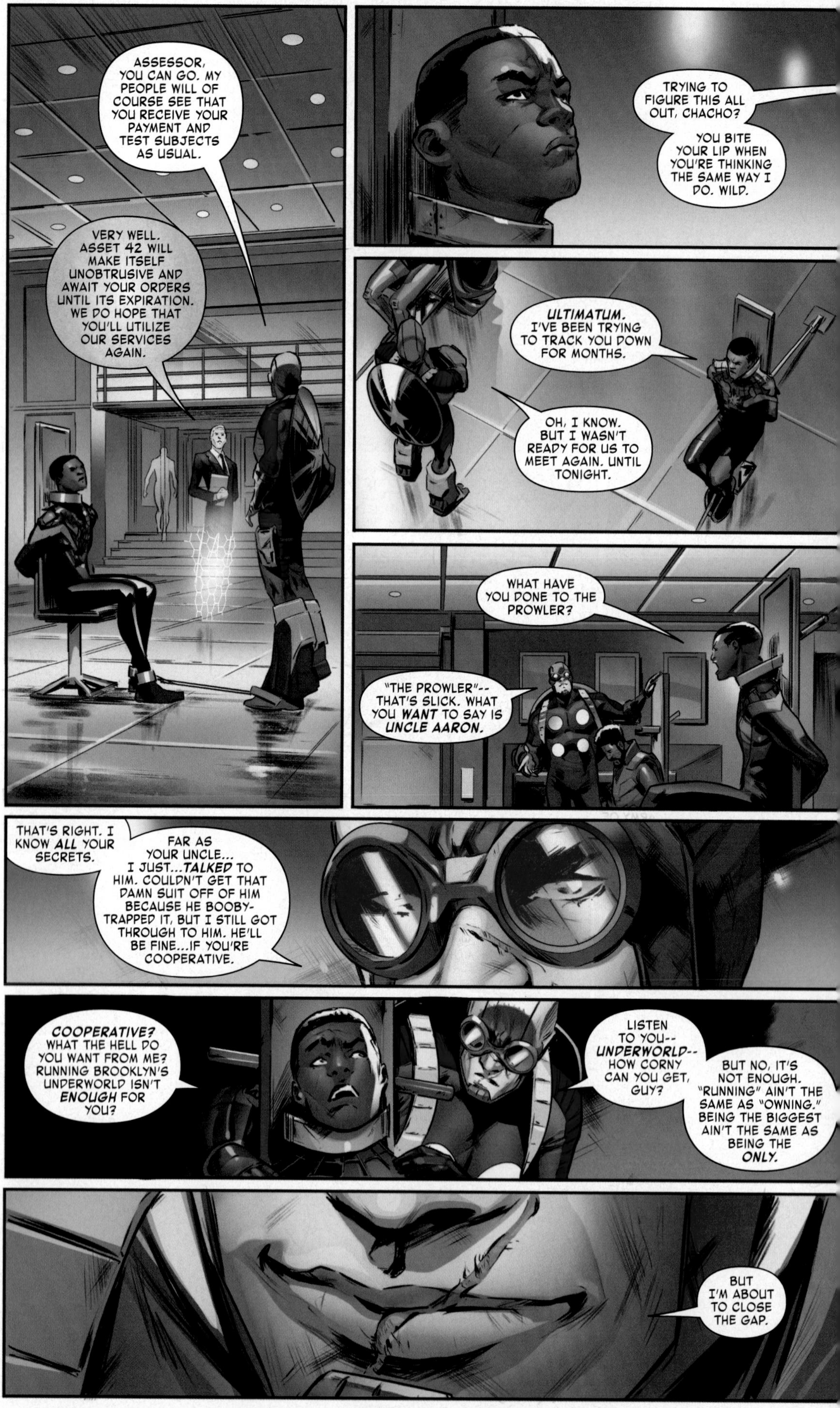
ASSESSOR, YOU CAN GO. MY PEOPLE WILL OF COURSE SEE THAT YOU RECEIVE YOUR PAYMENT AND TEST SUBJECTS AS USUAL.
VERY WELL. ASSET 42 WILL MAKE ITSELF UNOBTRUSIVE AND AWAIT YOUR ORDERS UNTIL ITS EXPIRATION. WE DO HOPE THAT YOU'LL UTILIZE OUR SERVICES AGAIN.
TRYING TO FIGURE THIS ALL OUT, CHACHO?
YOU BITE YOUR LIP WHEN YOU'RE THINKING THE SAME WAY I DO. WILD.
ULTIMATUM. I'VE BEEN TRYING TO TRACK YOU DOWN FOR MONTHS.
OH, I KNOW. BUT I WASN'T READY FOR US TO MEET AGAIN. UNTIL TONIGHT.
WHAT HAVE YOU DONE TO THE PROWLER?
"THE PROWLER"-- THAT'S SLICK. WHAT YOU WANT TO SAY IS UNCLE AARON.
THAT'S RIGHT. I KNOW ALL YOUR SECRETS.
FAR AS YOUR UNCLE... I JUST...TALKED TO HIM. COULDN'T GET THAT DAMN SUIT OFF OF HIM BECAUSE HE BOOBY-TRAPPED IT, BUT I STILL GOT THROUGH TO HIM. HE'LL BE FINE...IF YOU'RE COOPERATIVE.
COOPERATIVE? WHAT THE HELL DO YOU WANT FROM ME? RUNNING BROOKLYN'S UNDERWORLD ISN'T ENOUGH FOR YOU?
LISTEN TO YOU-- UNDERWORLD-- HOW CORNY CAN YOU GET, GUY?
BUT NO, IT'S NOT ENOUGH. "RUNNING" AIN'T THE SAME AS "OWNING." BEING THE BIGGEST AIN'T THE SAME AS BEING THE ONLY.
BUT I'M ABOUT TO CLOSE THE GAP.

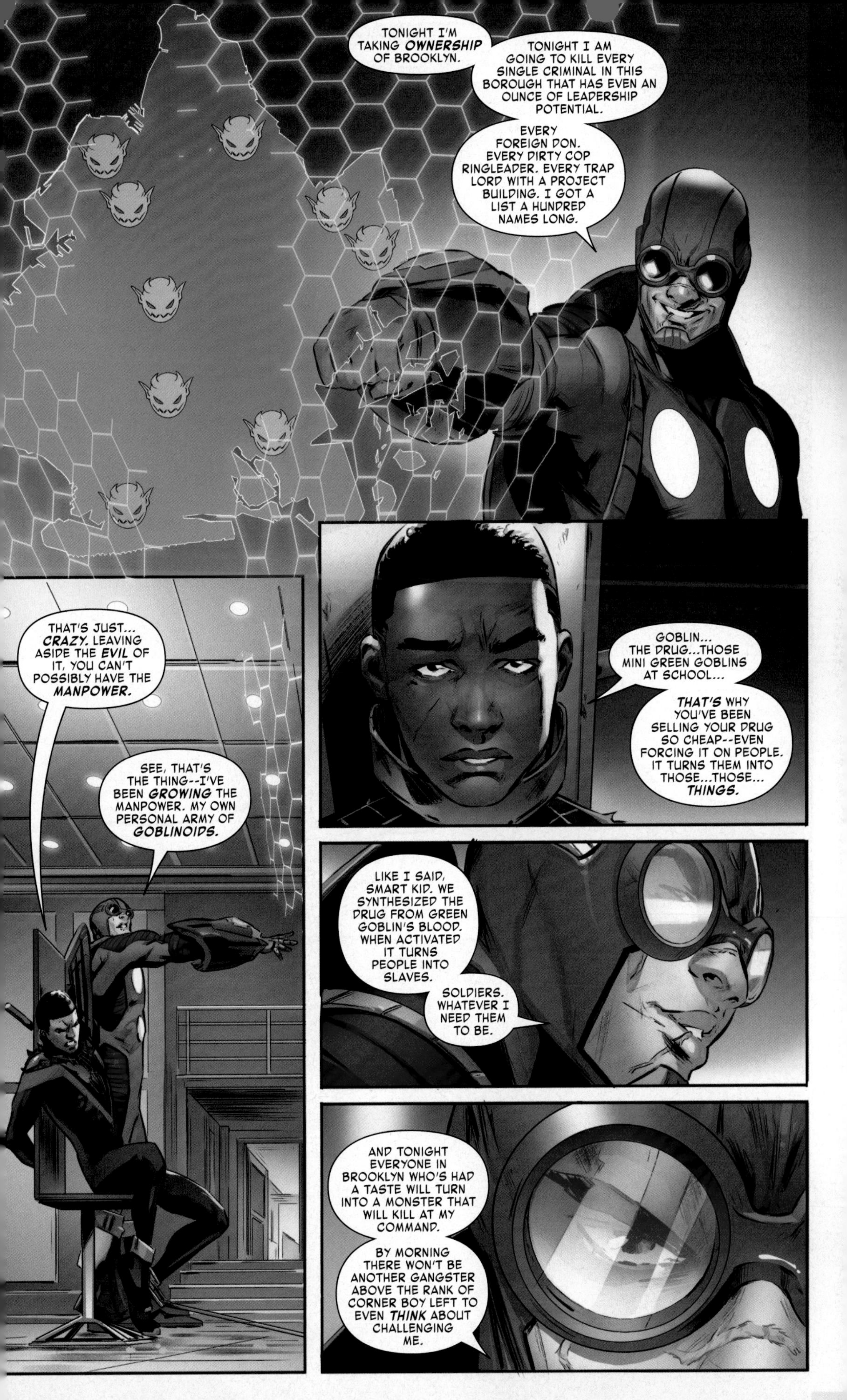
TONIGHT I'M TAKING OWNERSHIP OF BROOKLYN.
TONIGHT I AM GOING TO KILL EVERY SINGLE CRIMINAL IN THIS BOROUGH THAT HAS EVEN AN OUNCE OF LEADERSHIP POTENTIAL.
EVERY FOREIGN DON. EVERY DIRTY COP RINGLEADER. EVERY TRAP LORD WITH A PROJECT BUILDING. I GOT A LIST A HUNDRED NAMES LONG.
THAT'S JUST... CRAZY. LEAVING ASIDE THE EVIL OF IT, YOU CAN'T POSSIBLY HAVE THE MANPOWER.
SEE, THAT'S THE THING--I'VE BEEN GROWING THE MANPOWER. MY OWN PERSONAL ARMY OF GOBLINOIDS.
GOBLIN... THE DRUG...THOSE MINI GREEN GOBLINS AT SCHOOL...
THAT'S WHY YOU'VE BEEN SELLING YOUR DRUG SO CHEAP--EVEN FORCING IT ON PEOPLE. IT TURNS THEM INTO THOSE...THOSE... THINGS.
LIKE I SAID, SMART KID. WE SYNTHESIZED THE DRUG FROM GREEN GOBLIN'S BLOOD. WHEN ACTIVATED IT TURNS PEOPLE INTO SLAVES.
SOLDIERS. WHATEVER I NEED THEM TO BE.
AND TONIGHT EVERYONE IN BROOKLYN WHO'S HAD A TASTE WILL TURN INTO A MONSTER THAT WILL KILL AT MY COMMAND.
BY MORNING THERE WON'T BE ANOTHER GANGSTER ABOVE THE RANK OF CORNER BOY LEFT TO EVEN THINK ABOUT CHALLENGING ME.

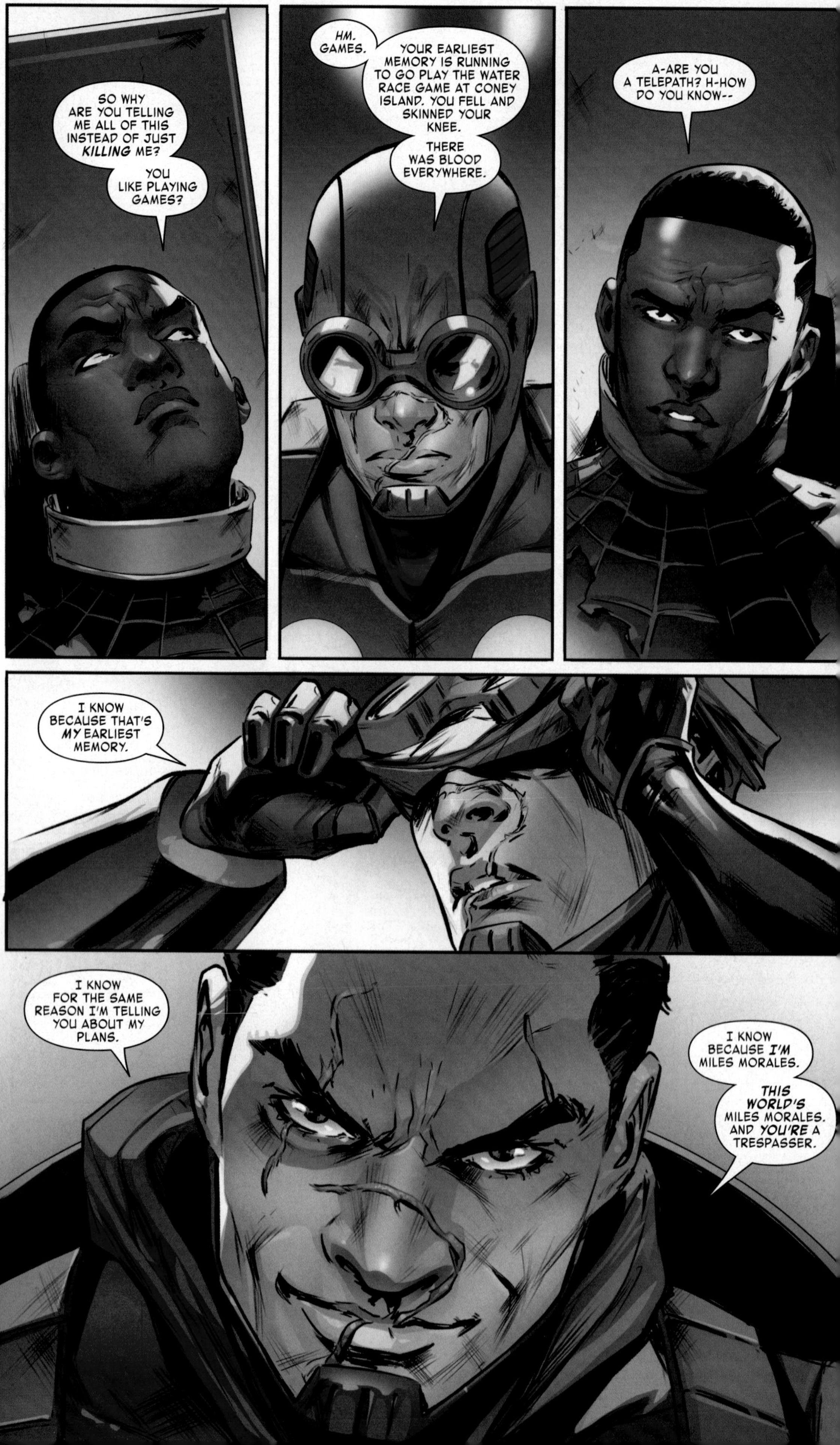
SO WHY ARE YOU TELLING ME ALL OF THIS INSTEAD OF JUST *KILLING* ME?
YOU LIKE PLAYING GAMES?
HM. GAMES.
YOUR EARLIEST MEMORY IS RUNNING TO GO PLAY THE WATER RACE GAME AT CONEY ISLAND. YOU FELL AND SKINNED YOUR KNEE.
THERE WAS BLOOD EVERYWHERE.
A-ARE YOU A TELEPATH? H-HOW DO YOU KNOW--
I KNOW BECAUSE THAT'S *MY* EARLIEST MEMORY.
I KNOW FOR THE SAME REASON I'M TELLING YOU ABOUT MY PLANS.
I KNOW BECAUSE *I'M* MILES MORALES.
THIS WORLD'S MILES MORALES. AND *YOU'RE* A TRESPASSER.

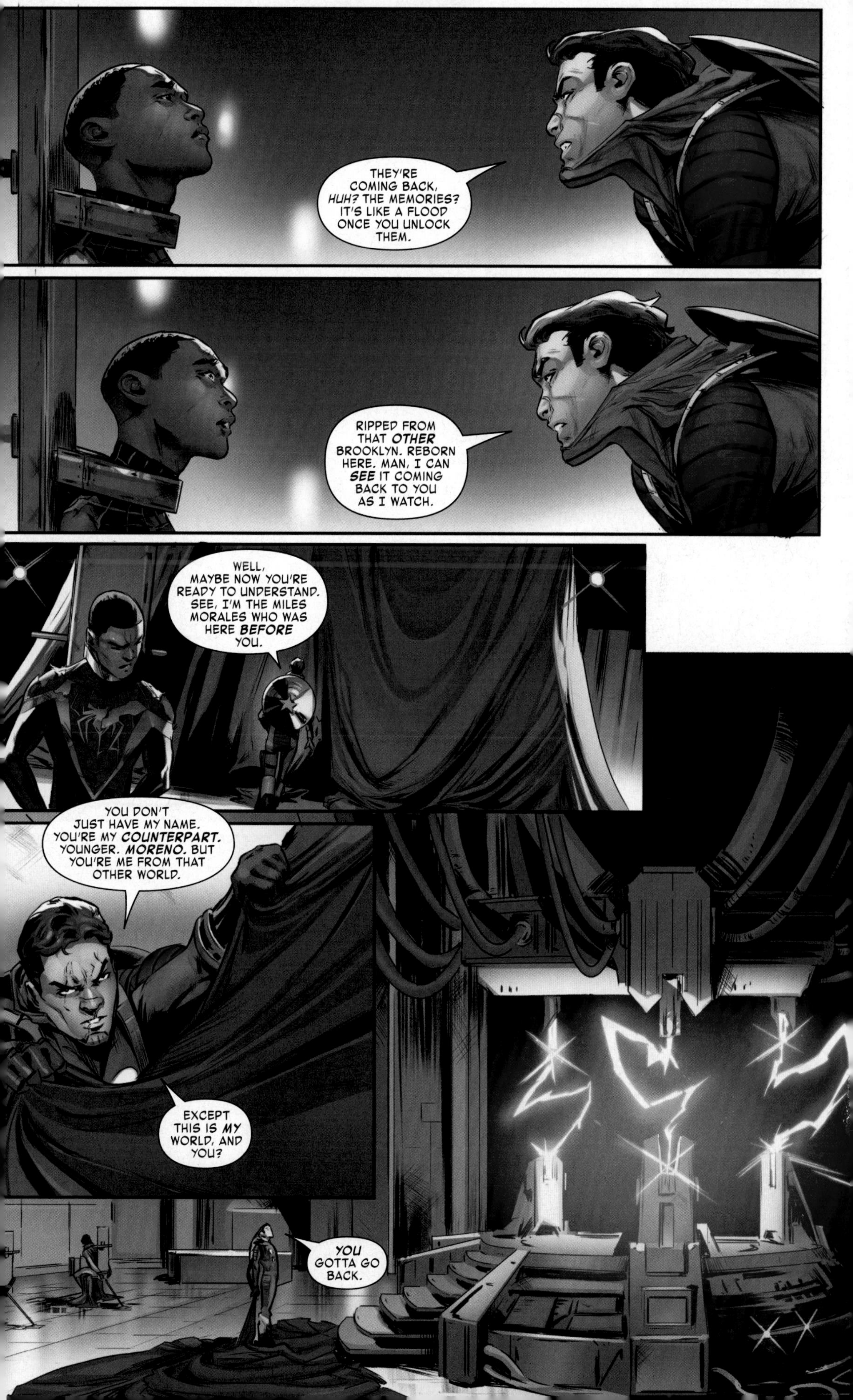
THEY'RE COMING BACK, HUH? THE MEMORIES? IT'S LIKE A FLOOD ONCE YOU UNLOCK THEM.
RIPPED FROM THAT OTHER BROOKLYN. REBORN HERE. MAN, I CAN SEE IT COMING BACK TO YOU AS I WATCH.
WELL, MAYBE NOW YOU'RE READY TO UNDERSTAND. SEE, I'M THE MILES MORALES WHO WAS HERE BEFORE YOU.
YOU DON'T JUST HAVE MY NAME. YOU'RE MY COUNTERPART. YOUNGER. MORENO. BUT YOU'RE ME FROM THAT OTHER WORLD.
EXCEPT THIS IS MY WORLD, AND YOU?
YOU GOTTA GO BACK.

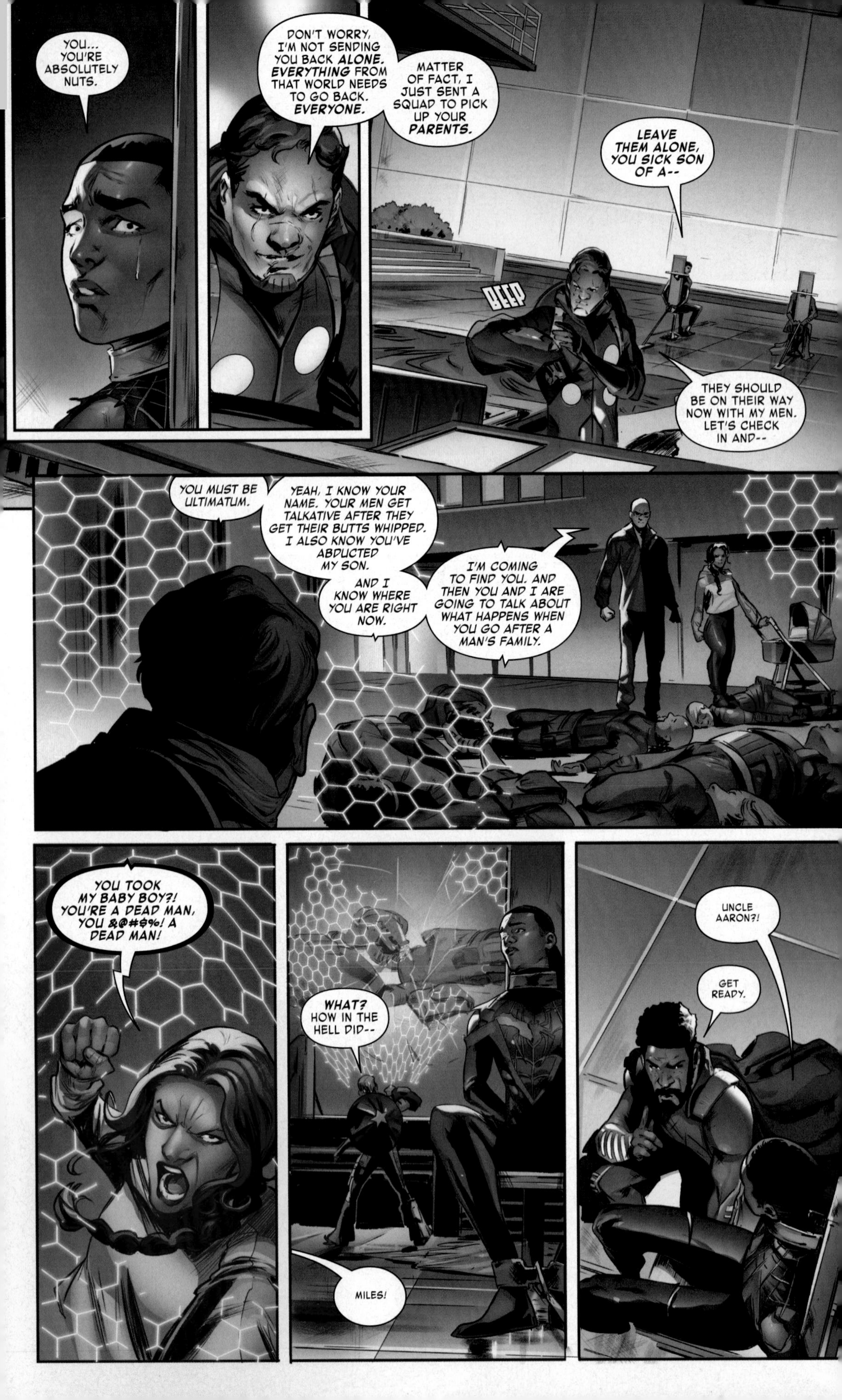

YOU... YOU'RE ABSOLUTELY NUTS.
DON'T WORRY, I'M NOT SENDING YOU BACK ALONE. EVERYTHING FROM THAT WORLD NEEDS TO GO BACK. EVERYONE.
MATTER OF FACT, I JUST SENT A SQUAD TO PICK UP YOUR PARENTS.
LEAVE THEM ALONE, YOU SICK SON OF A--
BEEP
THEY SHOULD BE ON THEIR WAY NOW WITH MY MEN. LET'S CHECK IN AND--
YOU MUST BE ULTIMATUM.
YEAH, I KNOW YOUR NAME. YOUR MEN GET TALKATIVE AFTER THEY GET THEIR BUTTS WHIPPED. I ALSO KNOW YOU'VE ABDUCTED MY SON.
AND I KNOW WHERE YOU ARE RIGHT NOW.
I'M COMING TO FIND YOU. AND THEN YOU AND I ARE GOING TO TALK ABOUT WHAT HAPPENS WHEN YOU GO AFTER A MAN'S FAMILY.
YOU TOOK MY BABY BOY?! YOU'RE A DEAD MAN, YOU &@#$%! A DEAD MAN!
WHAT? HOW IN THE HELL DID--
MILES!
UNCLE AARON?!
GET READY.

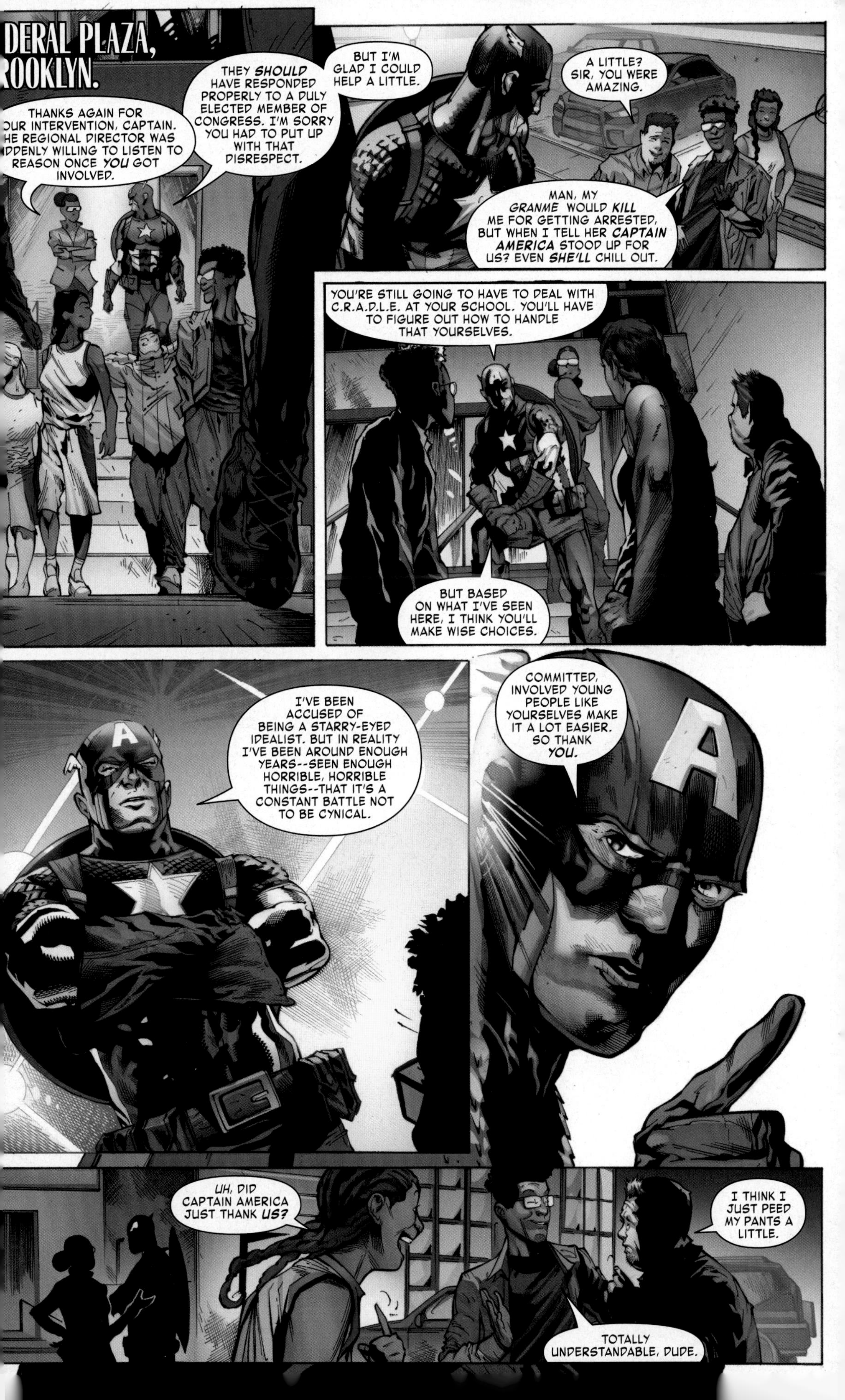

DERAL PLAZA, ROOKLYN.
THANKS AGAIN FOR OUR INTERVENTION, CAPTAIN. HE REGIONAL DIRECTOR WAS DDENLY WILLING TO LISTEN TO REASON ONCE YOU GOT INVOLVED.
THEY SHOULD HAVE RESPONDED PROPERLY TO A DULY ELECTED MEMBER OF CONGRESS. I'M SORRY YOU HAD TO PUT UP WITH THAT DISRESPECT.
BUT I'M GLAD I COULD HELP A LITTLE.
A LITTLE? SIR, YOU WERE AMAZING.
MAN, MY GRANME WOULD KILL ME FOR GETTING ARRESTED, BUT WHEN I TELL HER CAPTAIN AMERICA STOOD UP FOR US? EVEN SHE'LL CHILL OUT.
YOU'RE STILL GOING TO HAVE TO DEAL WITH C.R.A.D.L.E. AT YOUR SCHOOL. YOU'LL HAVE TO FIGURE OUT HOW TO HANDLE THAT YOURSELVES.
BUT BASED ON WHAT I'VE SEEN HERE, I THINK YOU'LL MAKE WISE CHOICES.
I'VE BEEN ACCUSED OF BEING A STARRY-EYED IDEALIST. BUT IN REALITY I'VE BEEN AROUND ENOUGH YEARS--SEEN ENOUGH HORRIBLE, HORRIBLE THINGS--THAT IT'S A CONSTANT BATTLE NOT TO BE CYNICAL.
COMMITTED, INVOLVED YOUNG PEOPLE LIKE YOURSELVES MAKE IT A LOT EASIER. SO THANK YOU.
UH, DID CAPTAIN AMERICA JUST THANK US?
I THINK I JUST PEED MY PANTS A LITTLE.
TOTALLY UNDERSTANDABLE, DUDE.

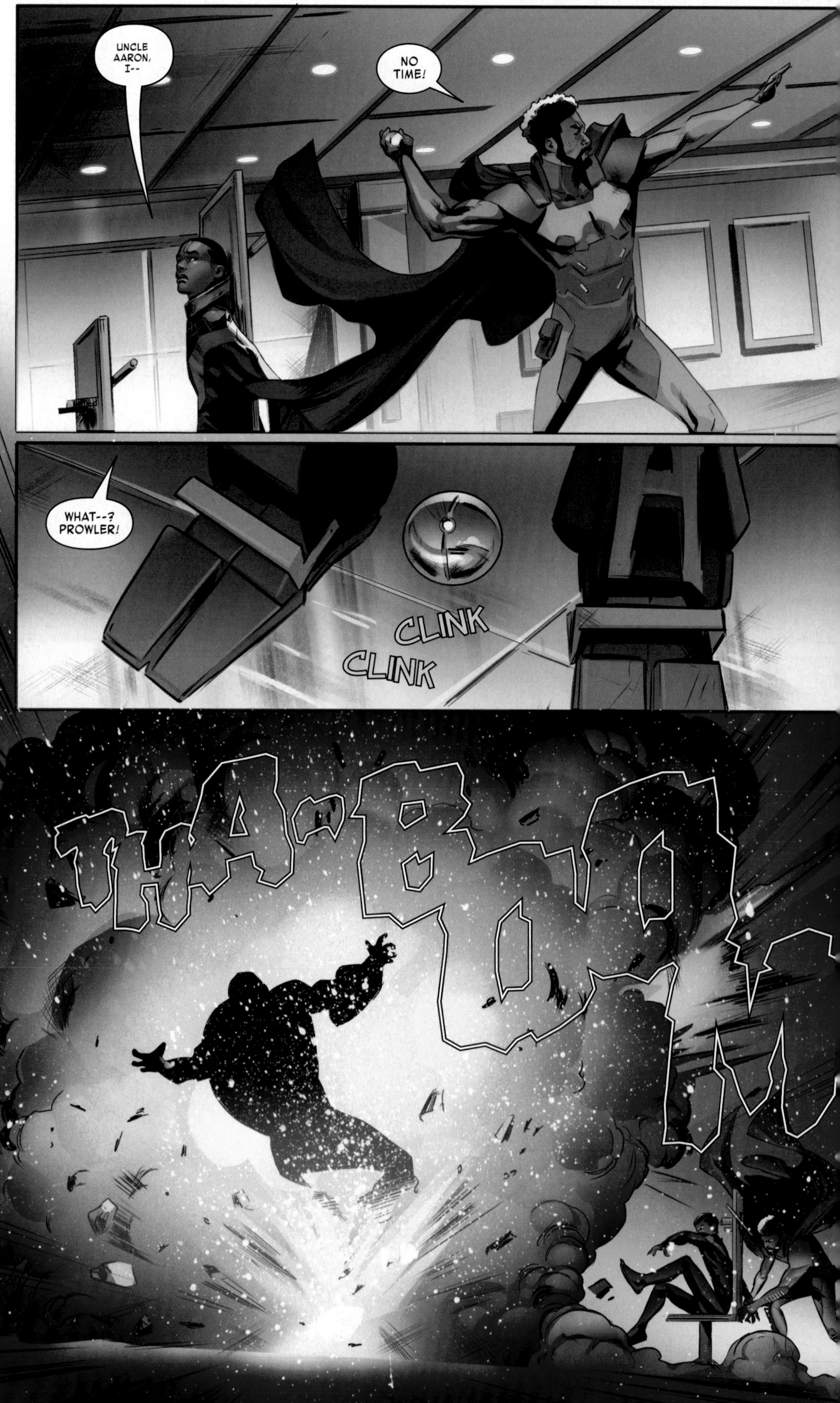
UNCLE AARON, I--
NO TIME!
WHAT--? PROWLER!
CLINK
CLINK
THA-BOOM

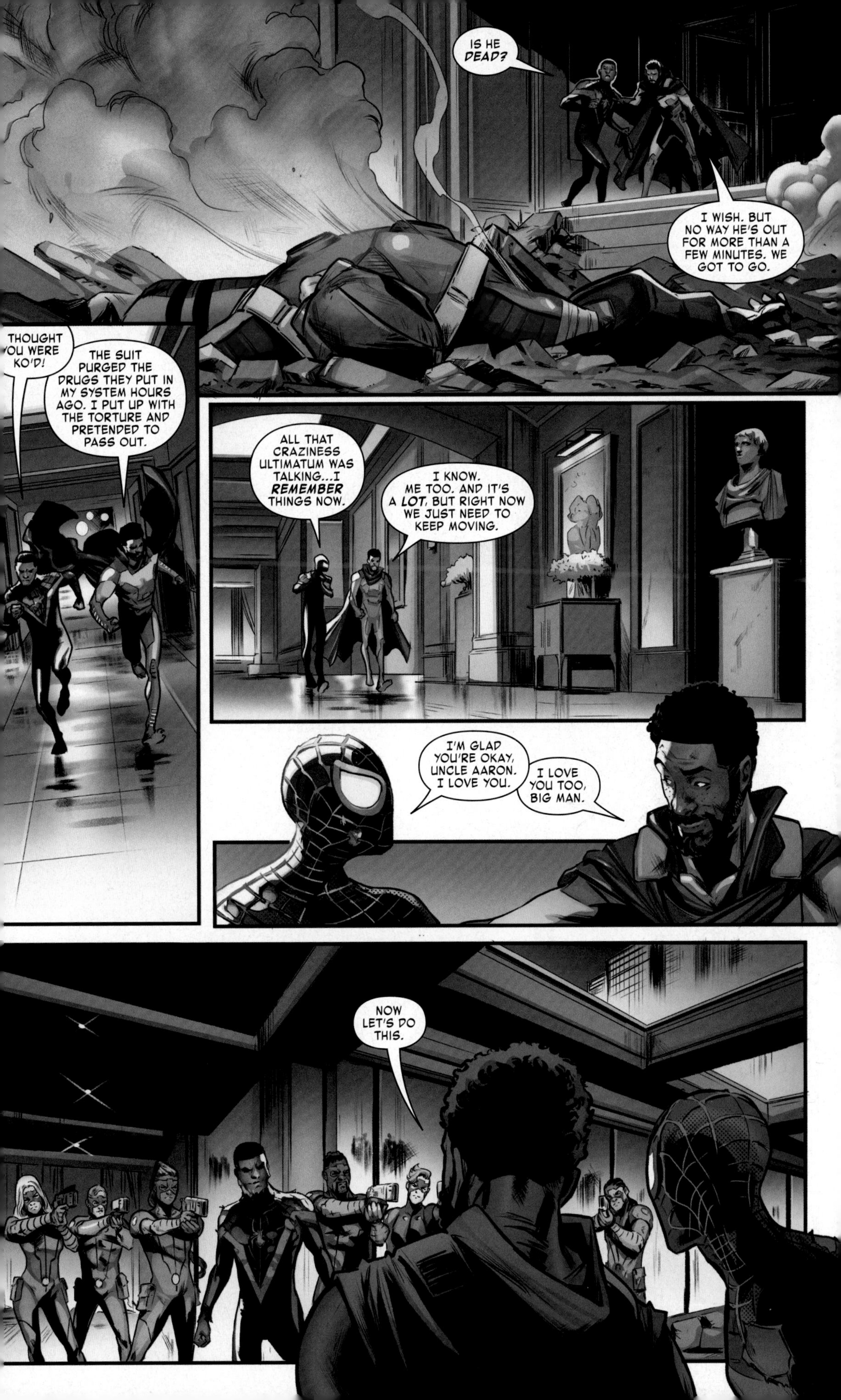
IS HE DEAD?
I WISH. BUT NO WAY HE'S OUT FOR MORE THAN A FEW MINUTES. WE GOT TO GO.
THOUGHT YOU WERE KO'D!
THE SUIT PURGED THE DRUGS THEY PUT IN MY SYSTEM HOURS AGO. I PUT UP WITH THE TORTURE AND PRETENDED TO PASS OUT.
ALL THAT CRAZINESS ULTIMATUM WAS TALKING...I REMEMBER THINGS NOW.
I KNOW. ME TOO. AND IT'S A LOT, BUT RIGHT NOW WE JUST NEED TO KEEP MOVING.
I'M GLAD YOU'RE OKAY, UNCLE AARON. I LOVE YOU.
I LOVE YOU TOO, BIG MAN.
NOW LET'S DO THIS.

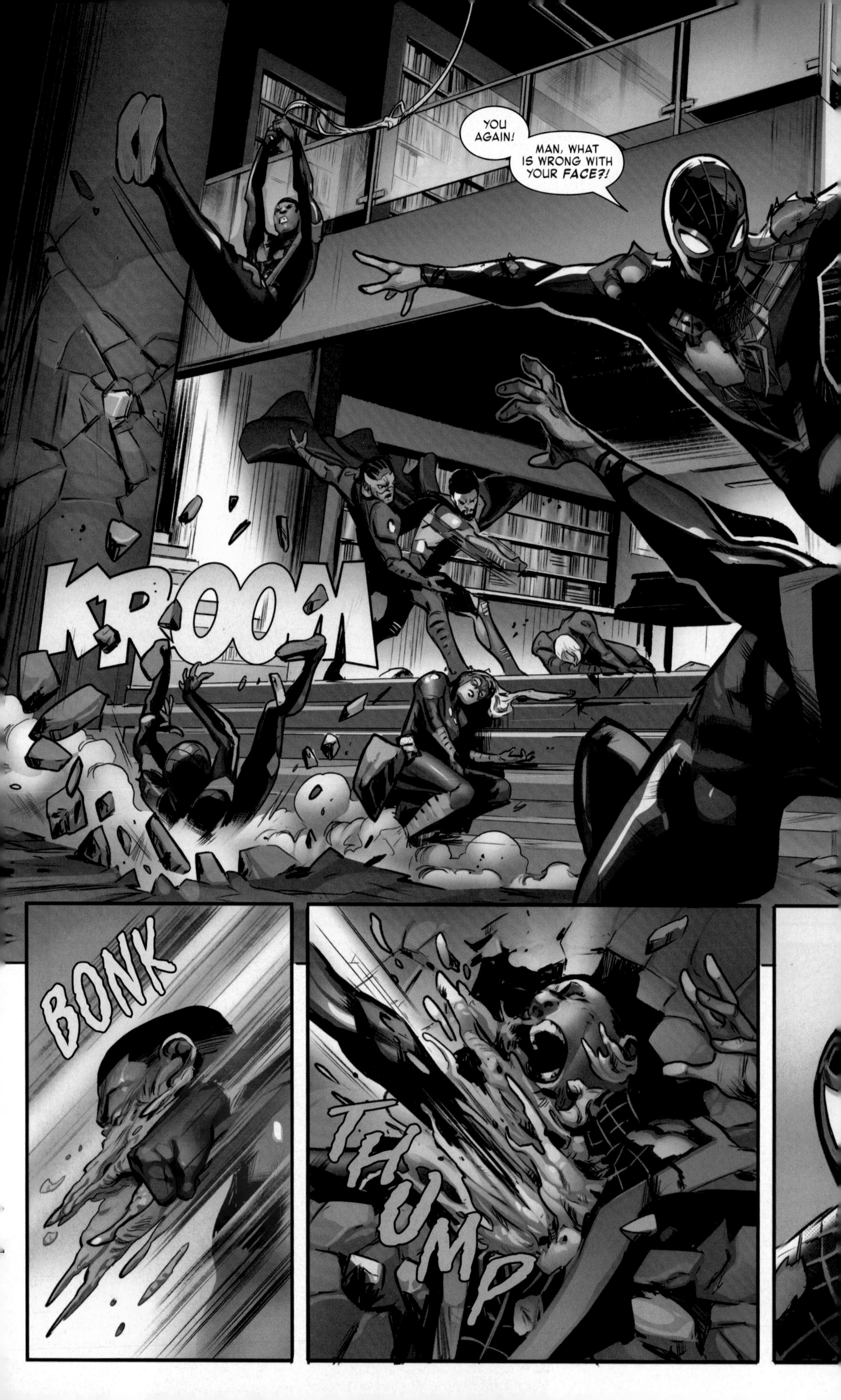
YOU AGAIN!
MAN, WHAT IS WRONG WITH YOUR FACE?!
KROOM
BONK
THUMP

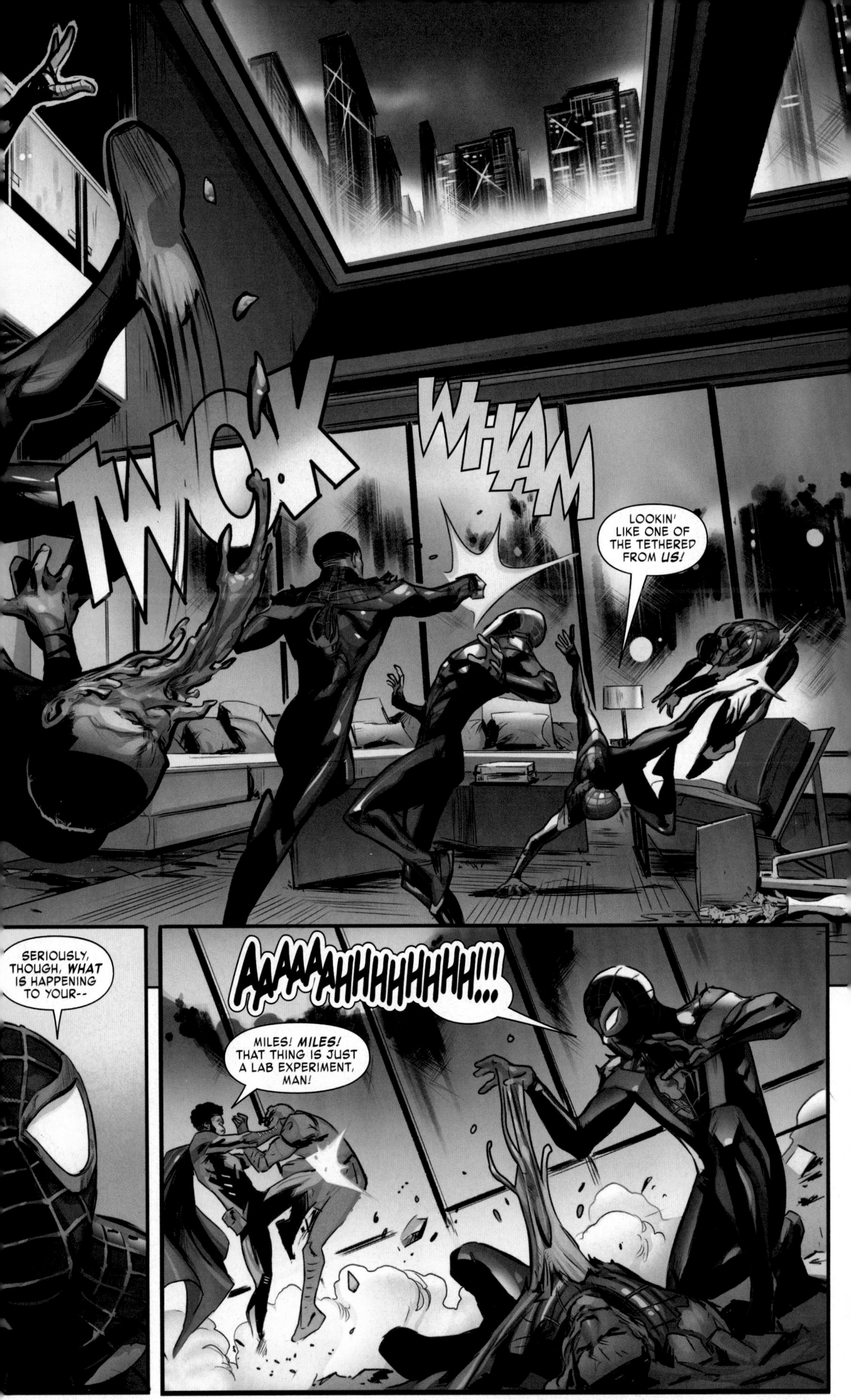
TWOCK
WHAM
LOOKIN' LIKE ONE OF THE TETHERED FROM *US!*
SERIOUSLY, THOUGH, *WHAT* IS HAPPENING TO YOUR--
AAAAAHHHHHHHH!!!...
MILES! *MILES!* THAT THING IS JUST A LAB EXPERIMENT, MAN!

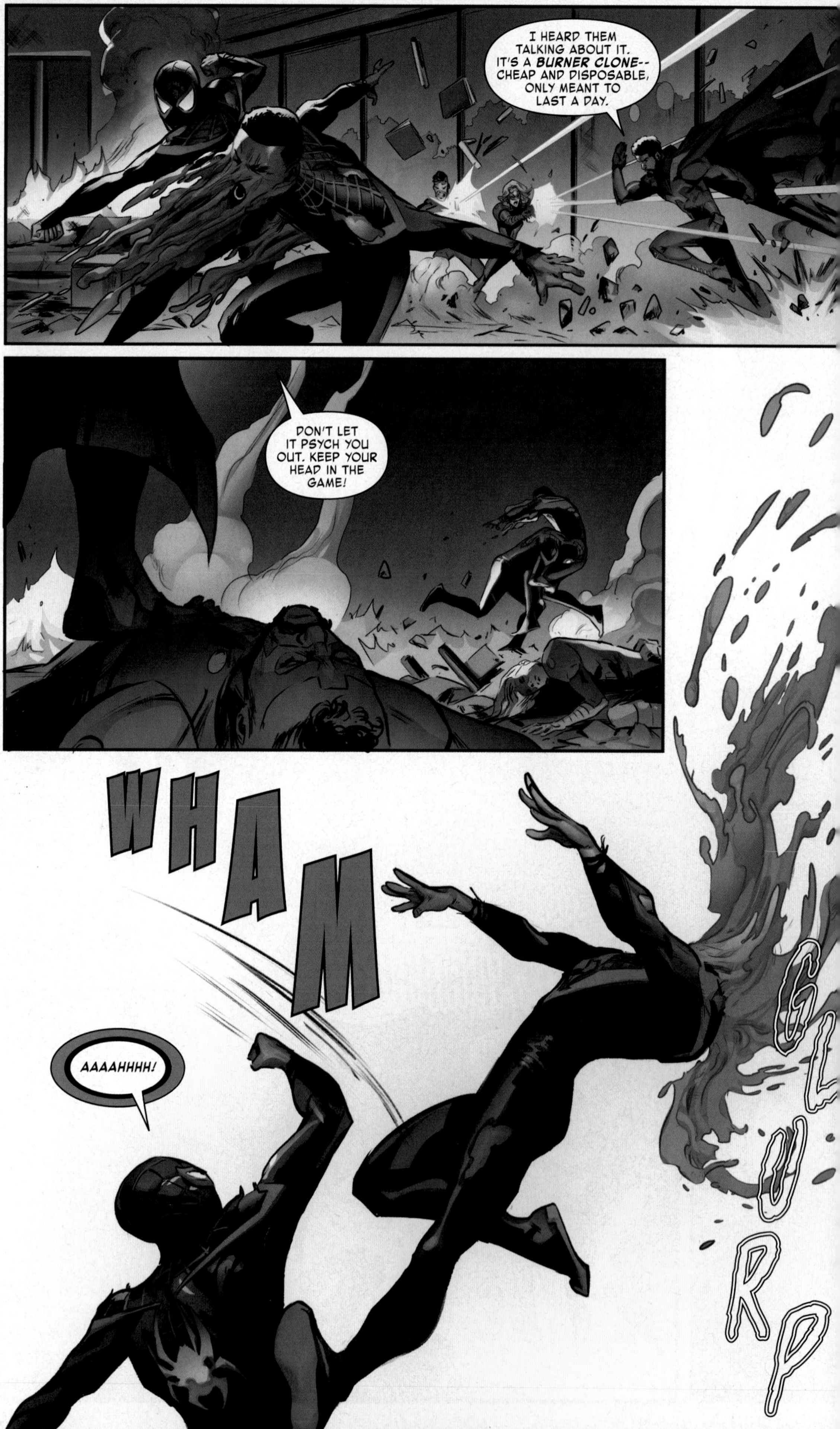
I HEARD THEM TALKING ABOUT IT. IT'S A **BURNER CLONE**-- CHEAP AND DISPOSABLE, ONLY MEANT TO LAST A DAY.
DON'T LET IT PSYCH YOU OUT. KEEP YOUR HEAD IN THE GAME!
WHAM
AAAAHHHH!
GLURP

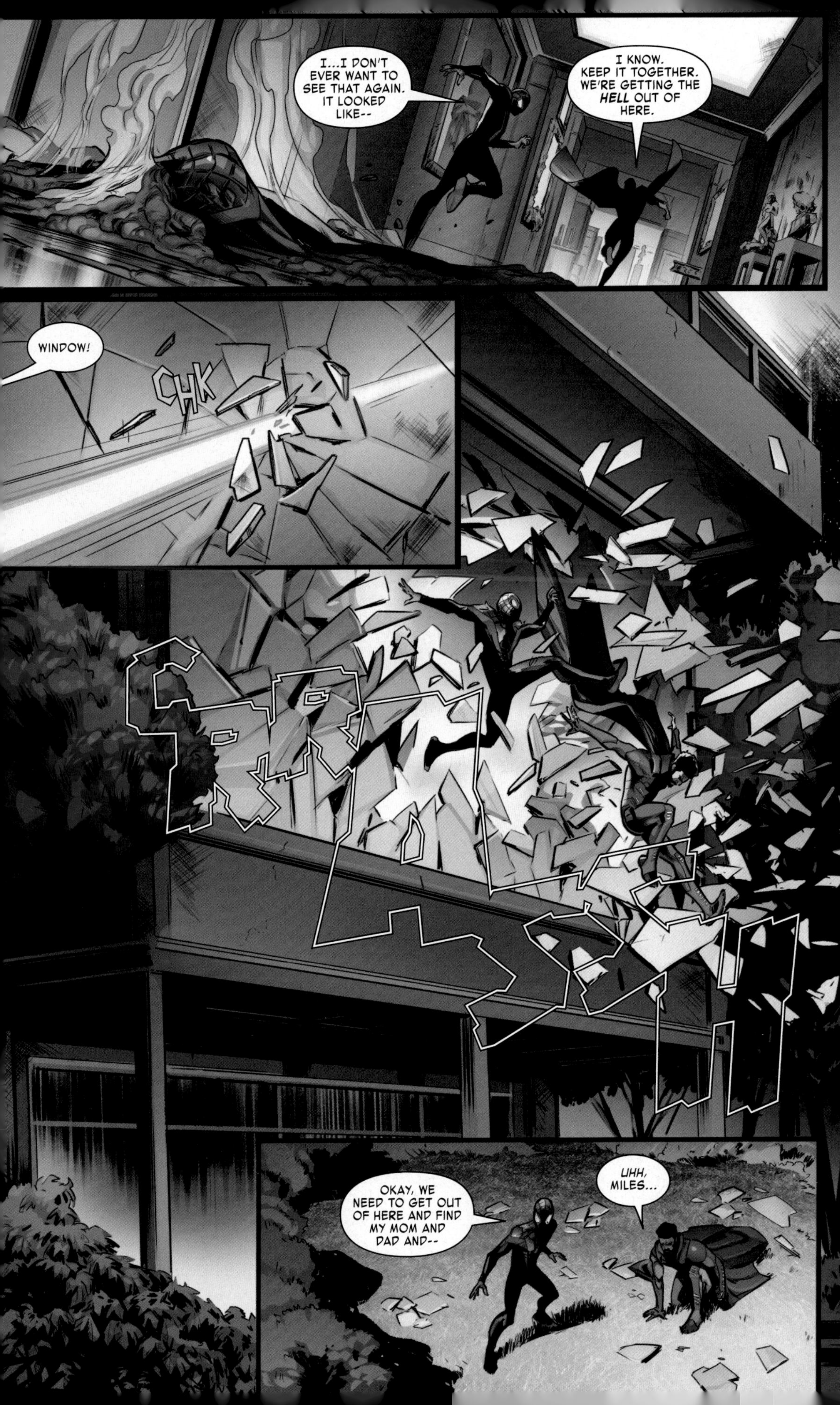
I...I DON'T EVER WANT TO SEE THAT AGAIN. IT LOOKED LIKE--
I KNOW. KEEP IT TOGETHER. WE'RE GETTING THE *HELL* OUT OF HERE.
WINDOW!
CHK
OKAY, WE NEED TO GET OUT OF HERE AND FIND MY MOM AND DAD AND--
UHH, MILES...

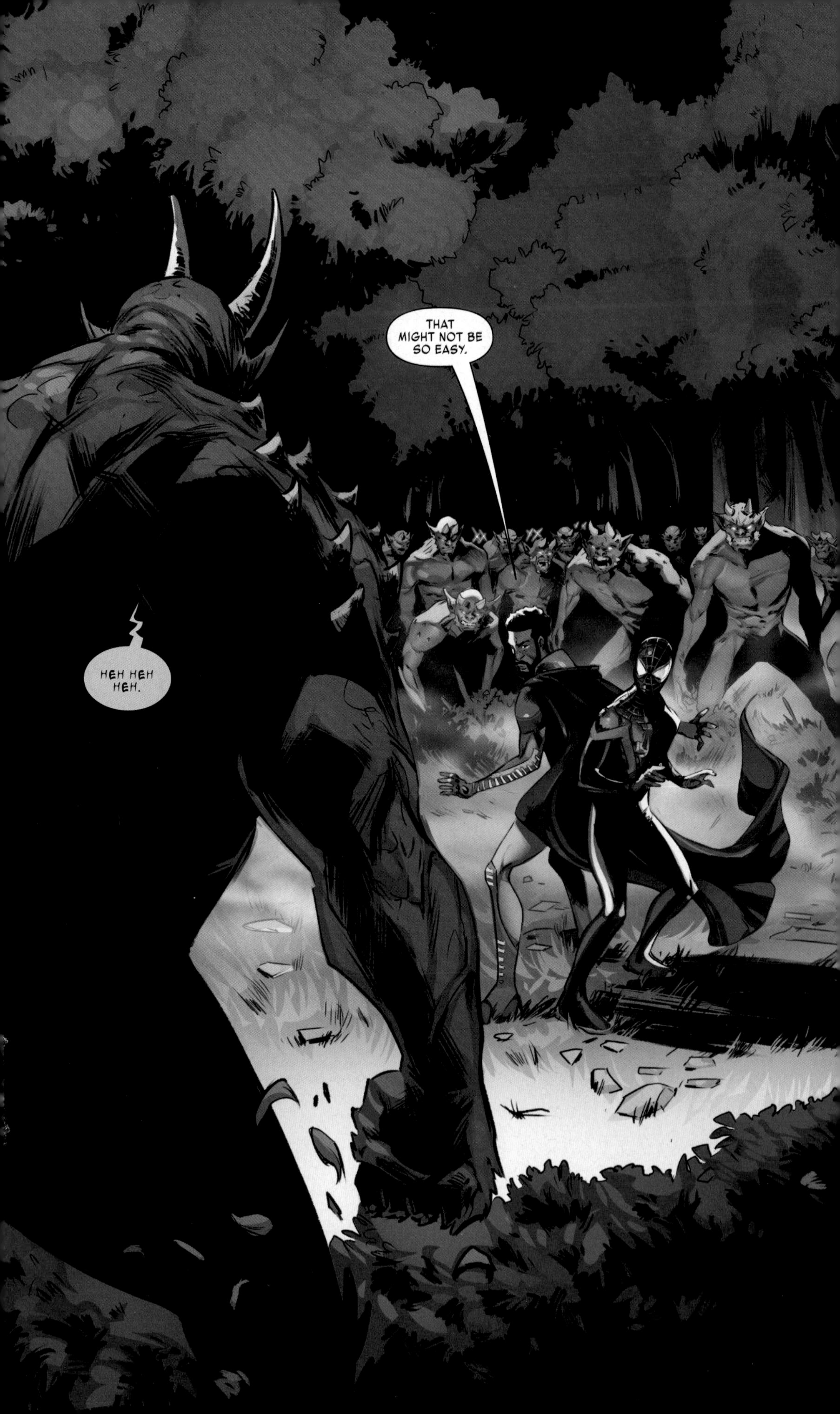
THAT MIGHT NOT BE SO EASY.
HEH HEH HEH.

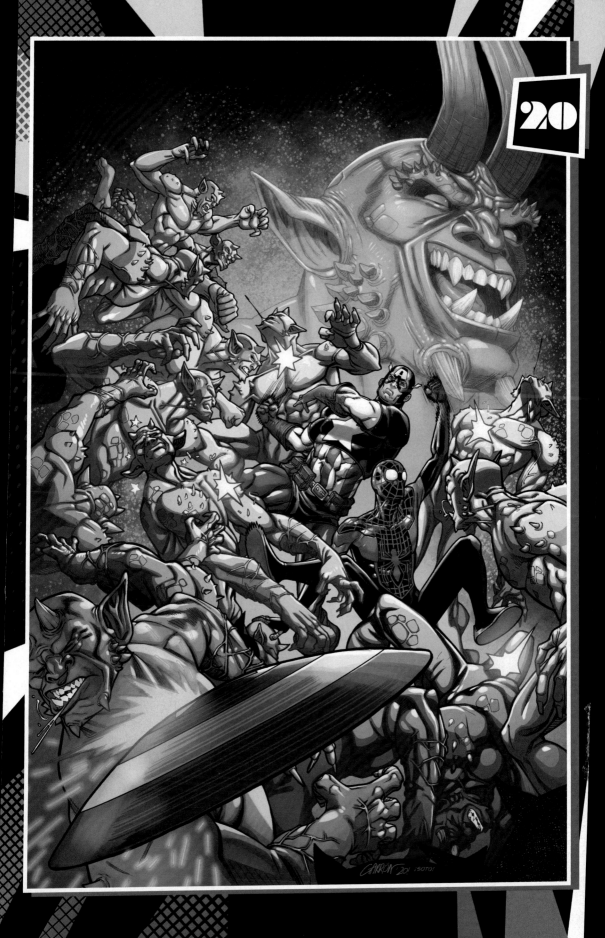

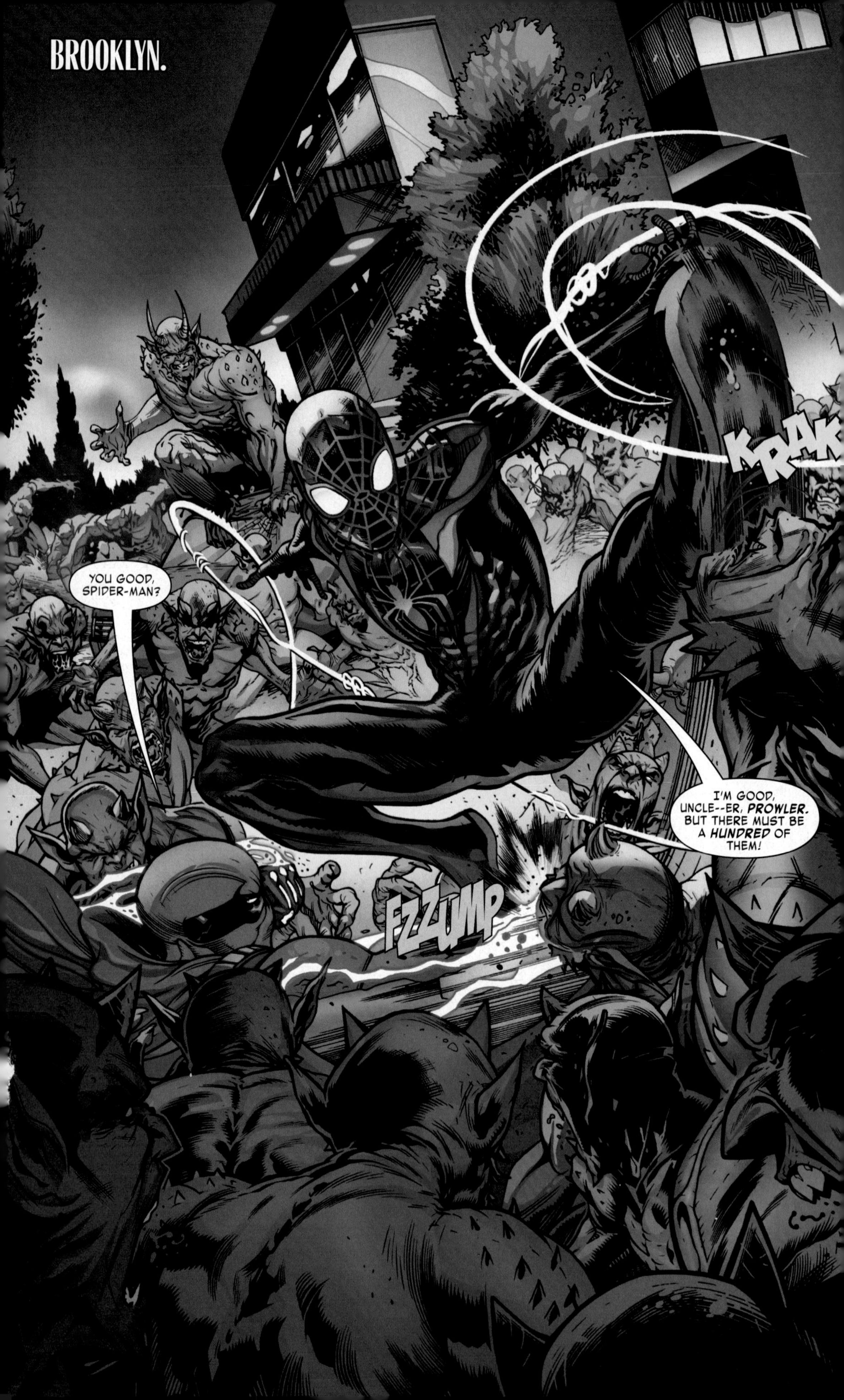
BROOKLYN.
KRAK
YOU GOOD, SPIDER-MAN?
I'M GOOD, UNCLE--ER, PROWLER. BUT THERE MUST BE A HUNDRED OF THEM!
FZZUMP

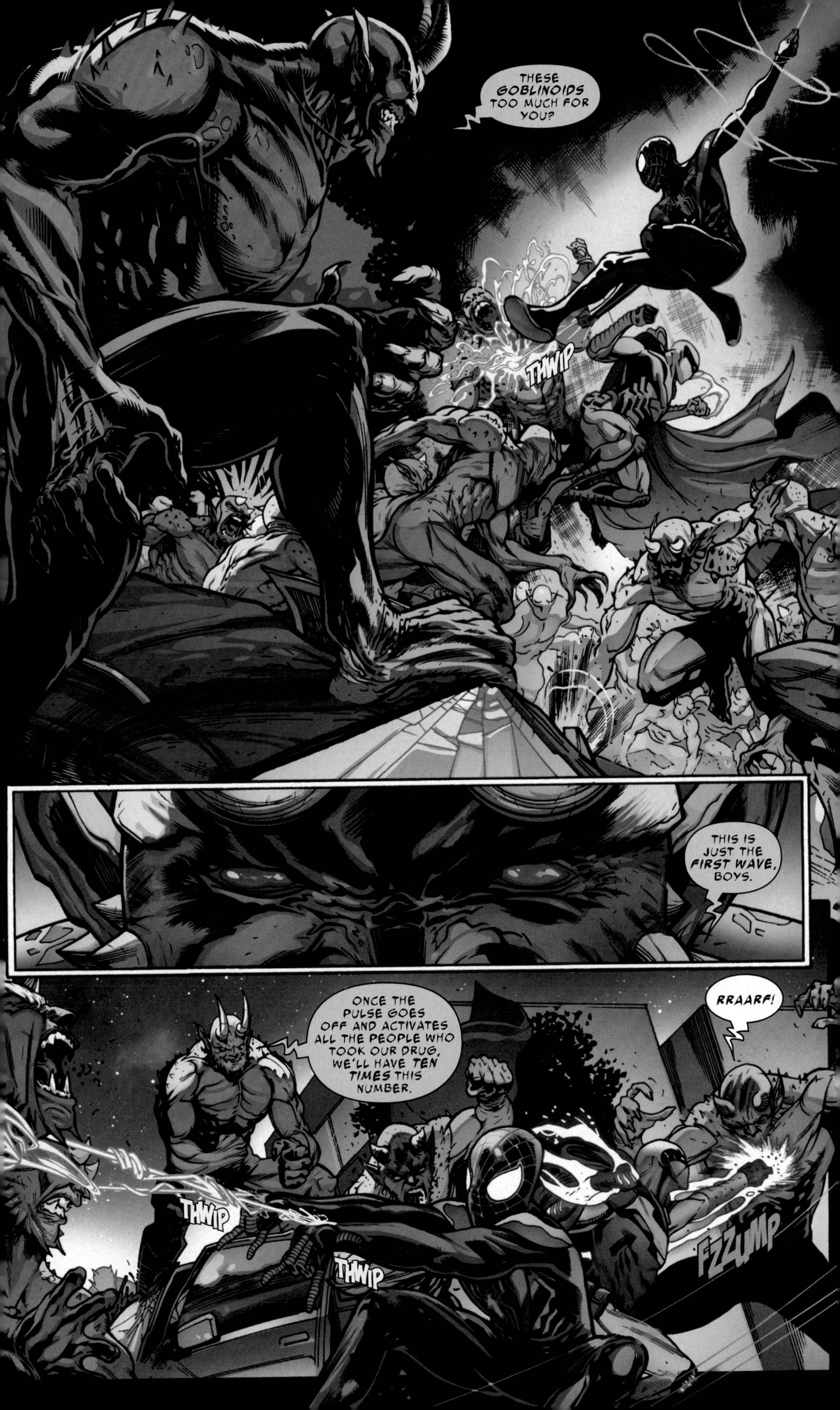
THESE GOBLINOIDS TOO MUCH FOR YOU?
THWIP
THIS IS JUST THE FIRST WAVE, BOYS.
ONCE THE PULSE GOES OFF AND ACTIVATES ALL THE PEOPLE WHO TOOK OUR DRUG, WE'LL HAVE TEN TIMES THIS NUMBER.
RRAARF!
THWIP
THWIP
FZZUMP

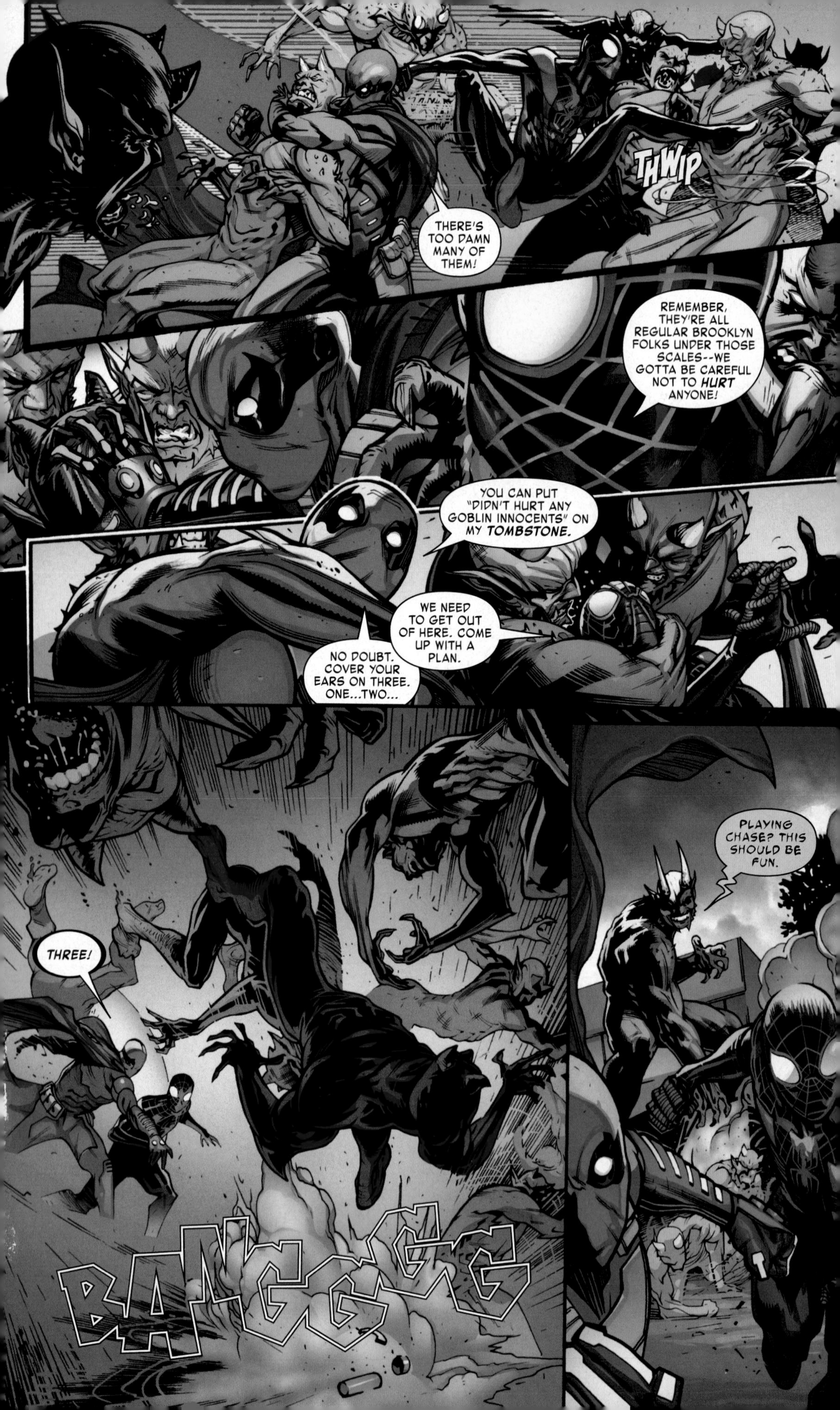
THWIP
THERE'S TOO DAMN MANY OF THEM!
REMEMBER, THEY'RE ALL REGULAR BROOKLYN FOLKS UNDER THOSE SCALES--WE GOTTA BE CAREFUL NOT TO HURT ANYONE!
YOU CAN PUT "DIDN'T HURT ANY GOBLIN INNOCENTS" ON MY TOMBSTONE.
WE NEED TO GET OUT OF HERE. COME UP WITH A PLAN.
NO DOUBT. COVER YOUR EARS ON THREE. ONE...TWO...
THREE!
BANGGGG
PLAYING CHASE? THIS SHOULD BE FUN.

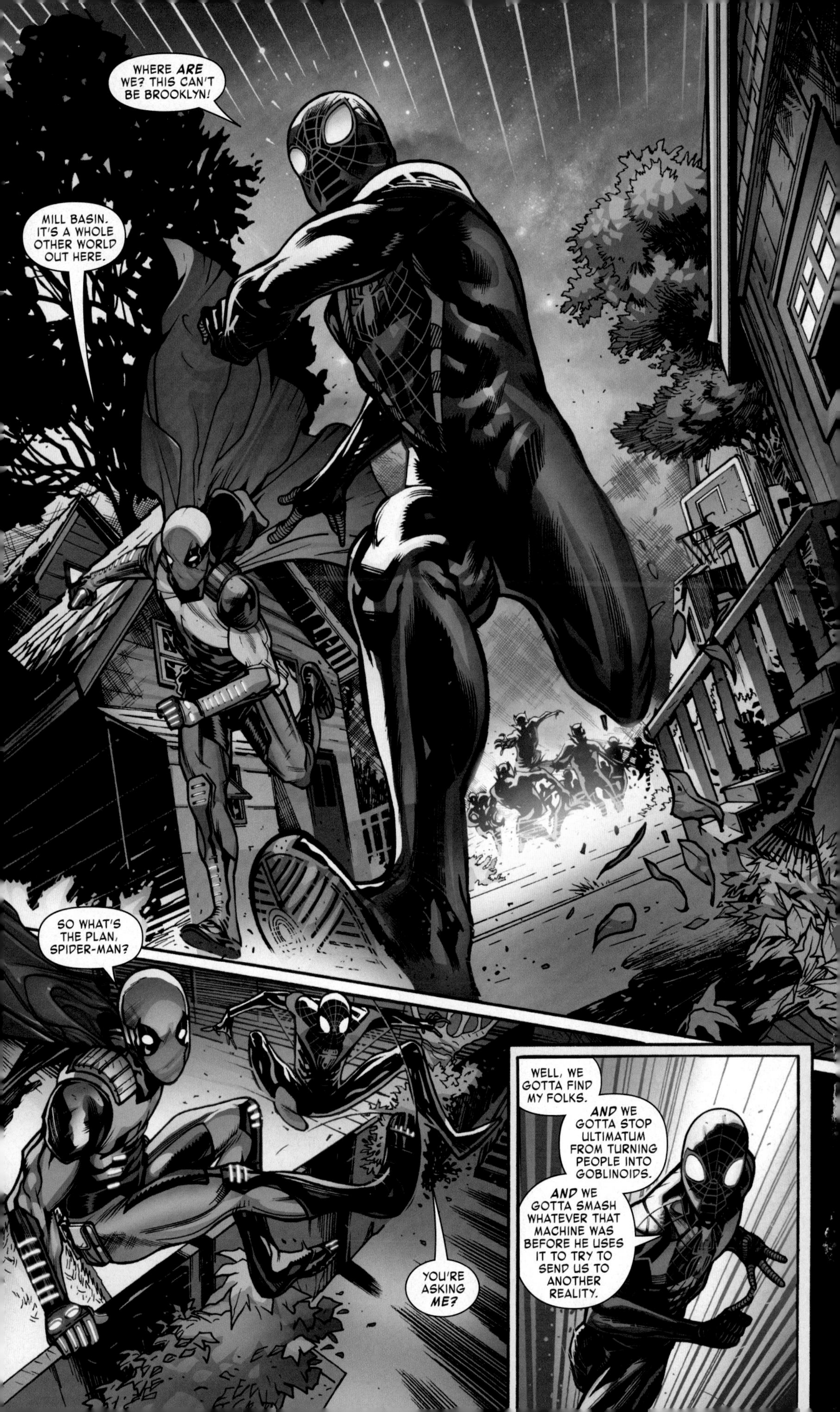
WHERE *ARE* WE? THIS CAN'T BE BROOKLYN!
MILL BASIN. IT'S A WHOLE OTHER WORLD OUT HERE.
SO WHAT'S THE PLAN, SPIDER-MAN?
YOU'RE ASKING *ME?*
WELL, WE GOTTA FIND MY FOLKS.
AND WE GOTTA STOP ULTIMATUM FROM TURNING PEOPLE INTO GOBLINOIDS.
AND WE GOTTA SMASH WHATEVER THAT MACHINE WAS BEFORE HE USES IT TO TRY TO SEND US TO ANOTHER REALITY.

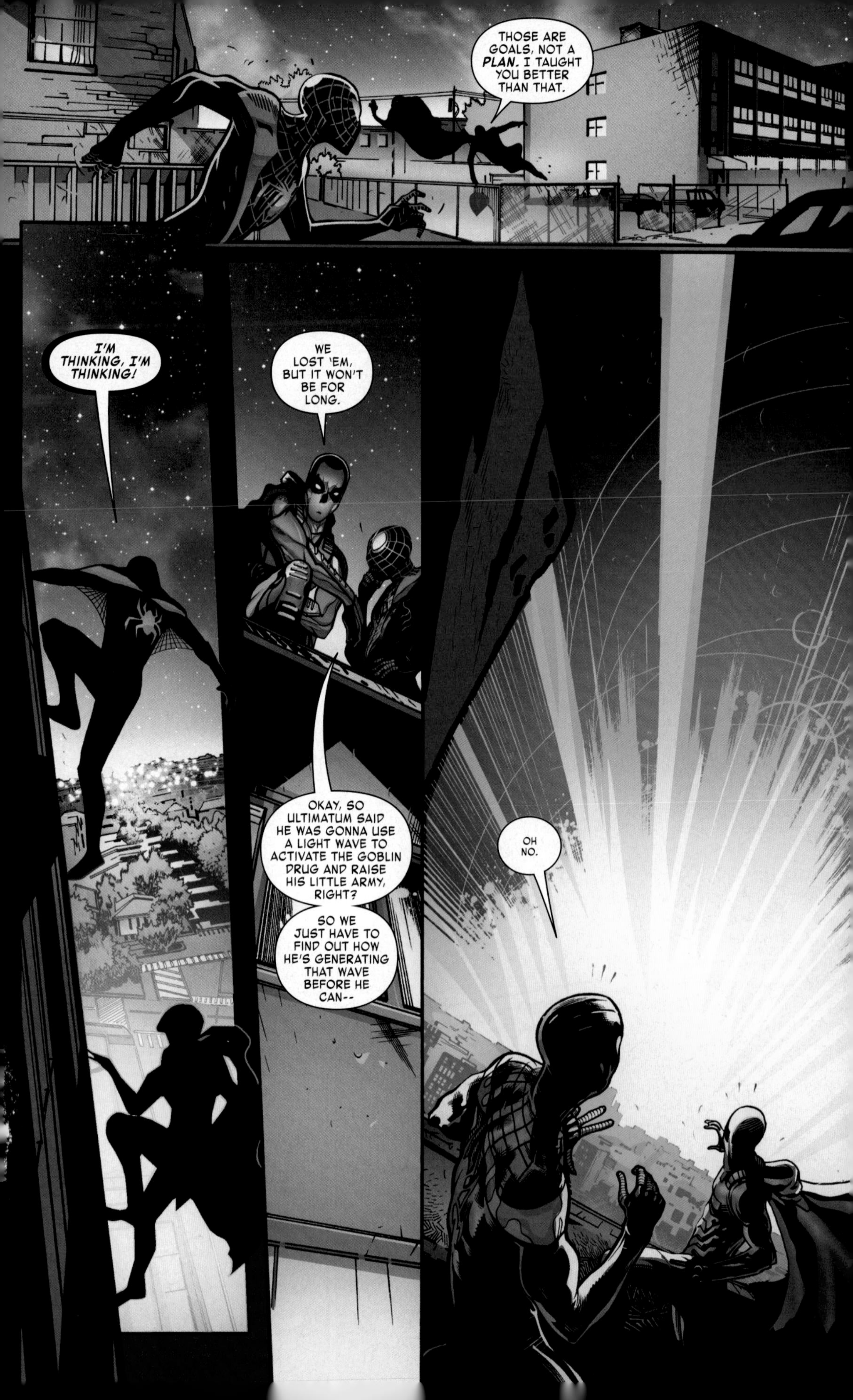
THOSE ARE GOALS, NOT A **PLAN.** I TAUGHT YOU BETTER THAN THAT.
I'M THINKING, I'M THINKING!
WE LOST 'EM, BUT IT WON'T BE FOR LONG.
OKAY, SO ULTIMATUM SAID HE WAS GONNA USE A LIGHT WAVE TO ACTIVATE THE GOBLIN DRUG AND RAISE HIS LITTLE ARMY, RIGHT?
SO WE JUST HAVE TO FIND OUT HOW HE'S GENERATING THAT WAVE BEFORE HE CAN--
OH NO.

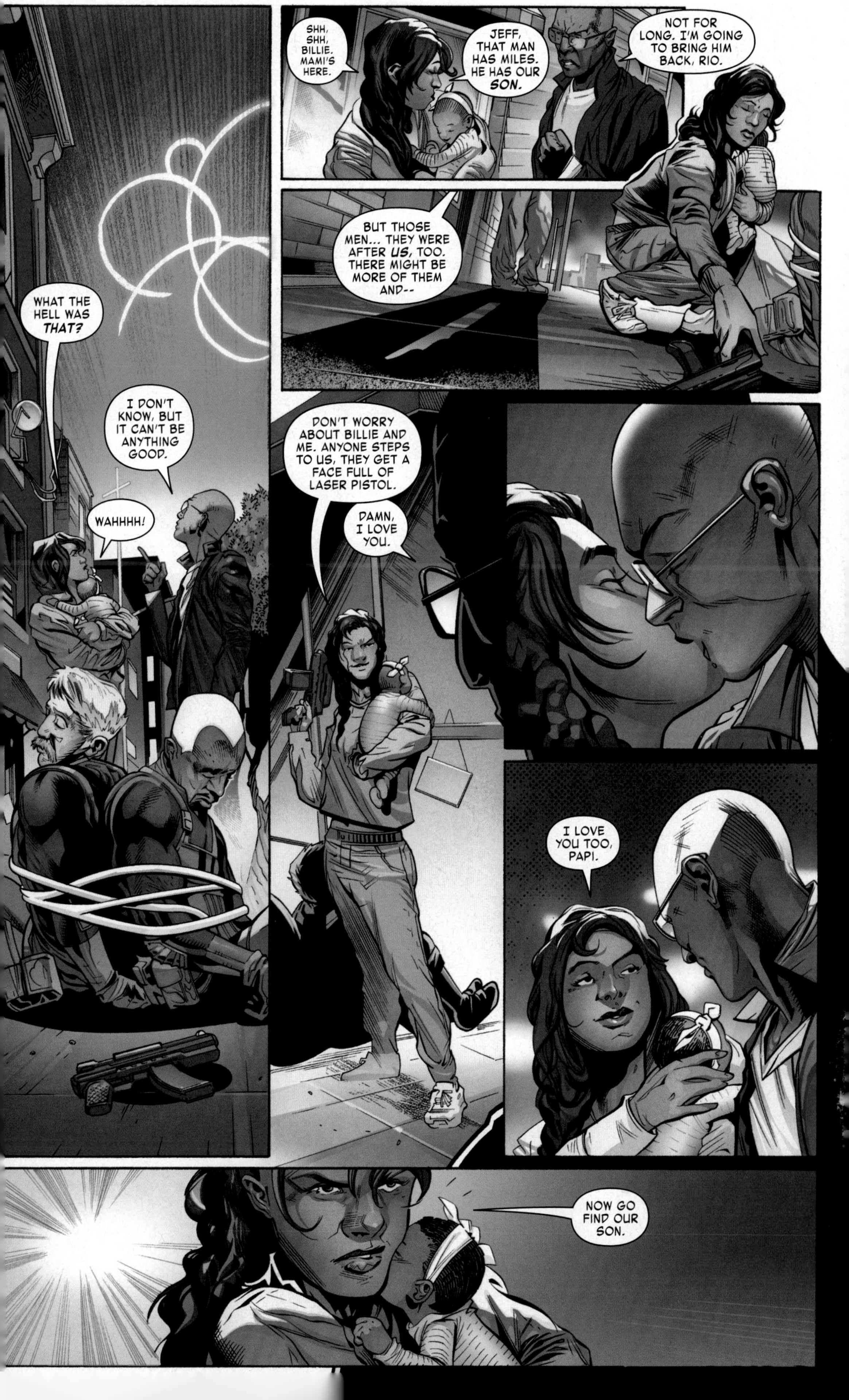

SHH, SHH, BILLIE. MAMI'S HERE.
JEFF, THAT MAN HAS MILES. HE HAS OUR *SON.*
NOT FOR LONG. I'M GOING TO BRING HIM BACK, RIO.
BUT THOSE MEN... THEY WERE AFTER *US,* TOO. THERE MIGHT BE MORE OF THEM AND--
WHAT THE HELL WAS *THAT?*
I DON'T KNOW, BUT IT CAN'T BE ANYTHING GOOD.
WAHHHH!
DON'T WORRY ABOUT BILLIE AND ME. ANYONE STEPS TO US, THEY GET A FACE FULL OF LASER PISTOL.
DAMN, I LOVE YOU.
I LOVE YOU TOO, PAPI.
NOW GO FIND OUR SON.

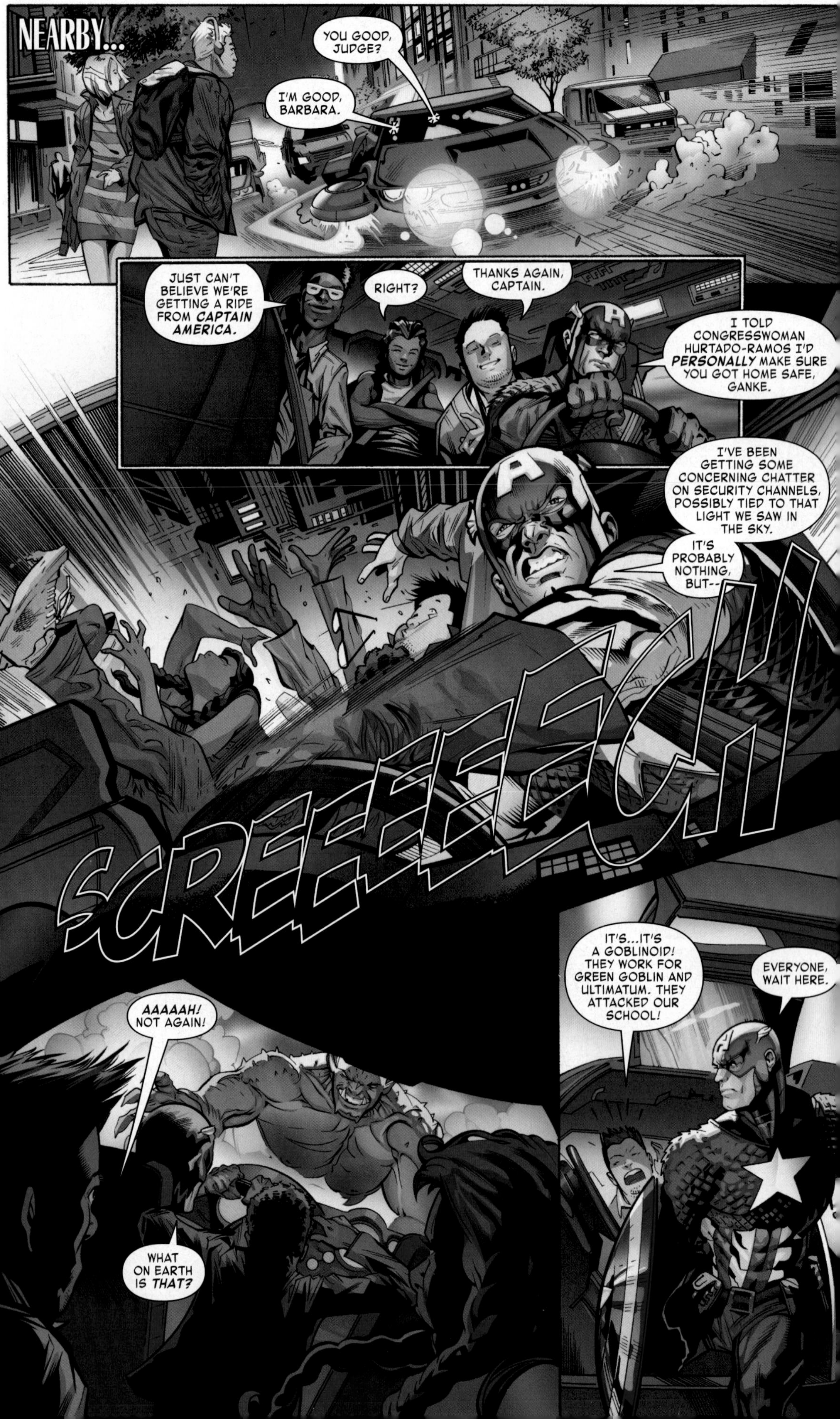
NEARBY...
YOU GOOD, JUDGE?
I'M GOOD, BARBARA.
JUST CAN'T BELIEVE WE'RE GETTING A RIDE FROM CAPTAIN AMERICA.
RIGHT?
THANKS AGAIN, CAPTAIN.
I TOLD CONGRESSWOMAN HURTADO-RAMOS I'D PERSONALLY MAKE SURE YOU GOT HOME SAFE, GANKE.
I'VE BEEN GETTING SOME CONCERNING CHATTER ON SECURITY CHANNELS, POSSIBLY TIED TO THAT LIGHT WE SAW IN THE SKY.
IT'S PROBABLY NOTHING, BUT--
SCREEEEECH
AAAAAH! NOT AGAIN!
WHAT ON EARTH IS THAT?
IT'S...IT'S A GOBLINOID! THEY WORK FOR GREEN GOBLIN AND ULTIMATUM. THEY ATTACKED OUR SCHOOL!
EVERYONE, WAIT HERE.

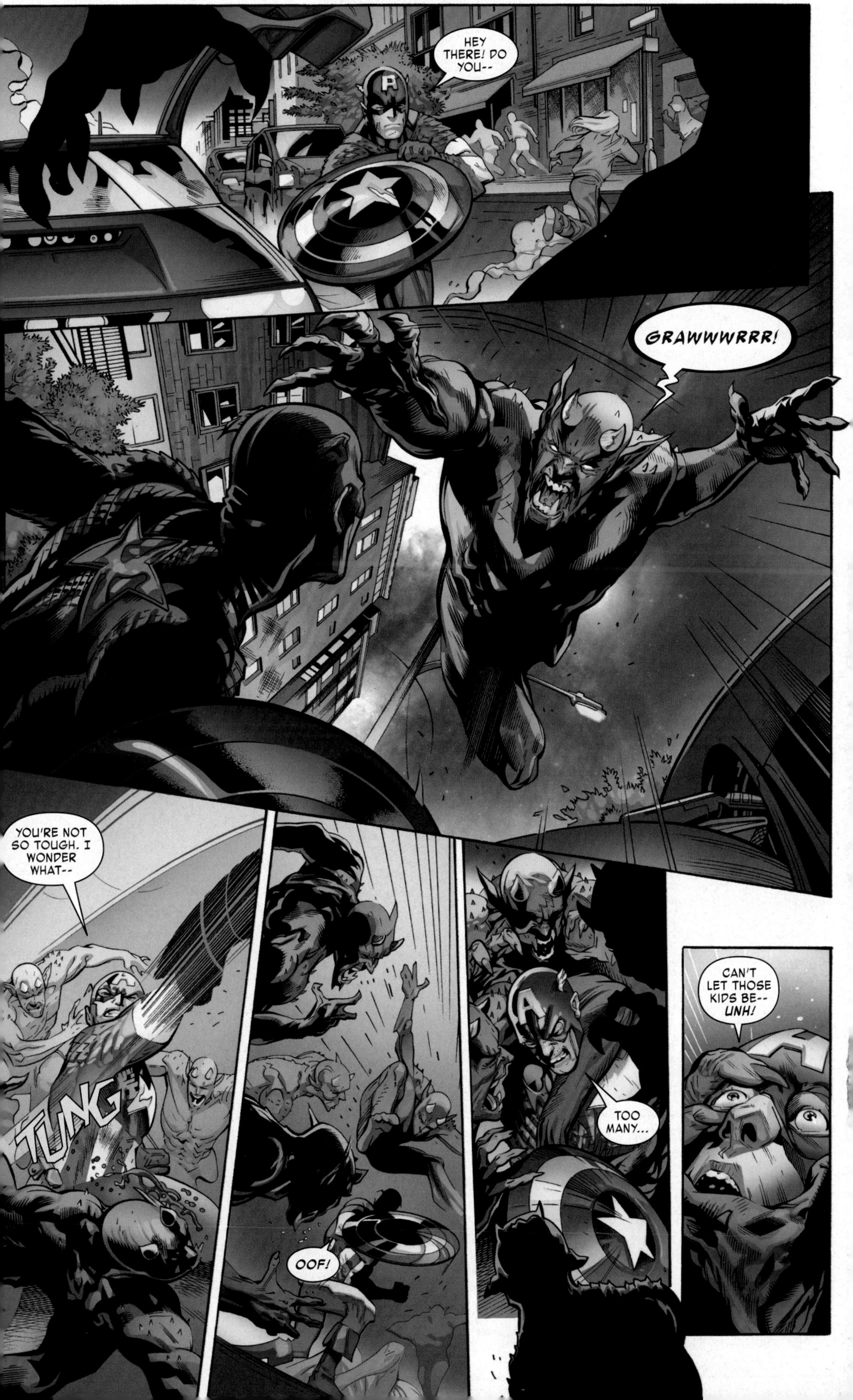
HEY THERE! DO YOU--
GRAWWWRRR!
YOU'RE NOT SO TOUGH. I WONDER WHAT--
TUNG
OOF!
TOO MANY...
CAN'T LET THOSE KIDS BE-- UNH!

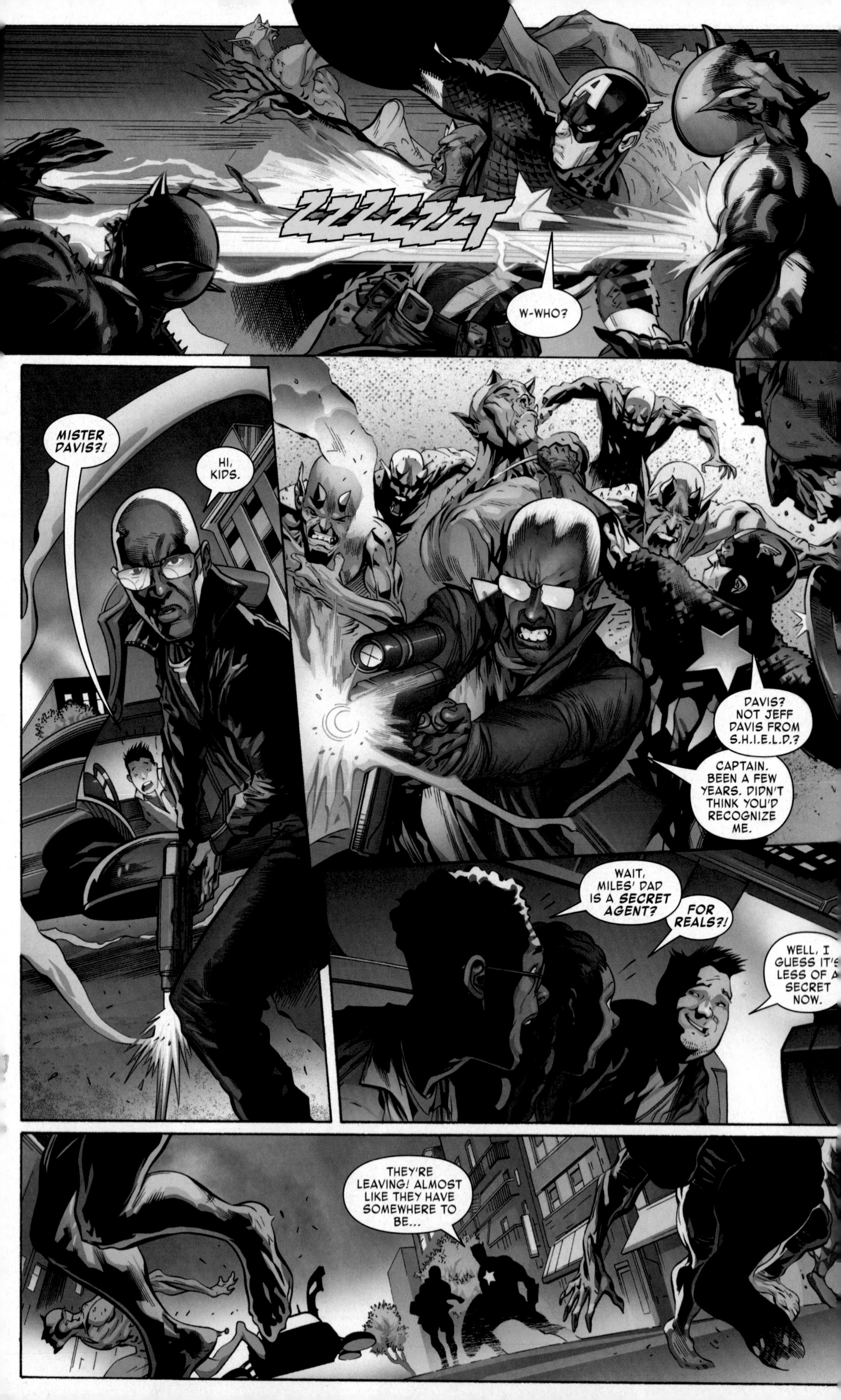
ZZZZZZZT
W-WHO?
MISTER DAVIS?!
HI, KIDS.
DAVIS? NOT JEFF DAVIS FROM S.H.I.E.L.D.?
CAPTAIN. BEEN A FEW YEARS. DIDN'T THINK YOU'D RECOGNIZE ME.
WAIT, MILES' DAD IS A SECRET AGENT?
FOR REALS?!
WELL, I GUESS IT'S LESS OF A SECRET NOW.
THEY'RE LEAVING! ALMOST LIKE THEY HAVE SOMEWHERE TO BE...

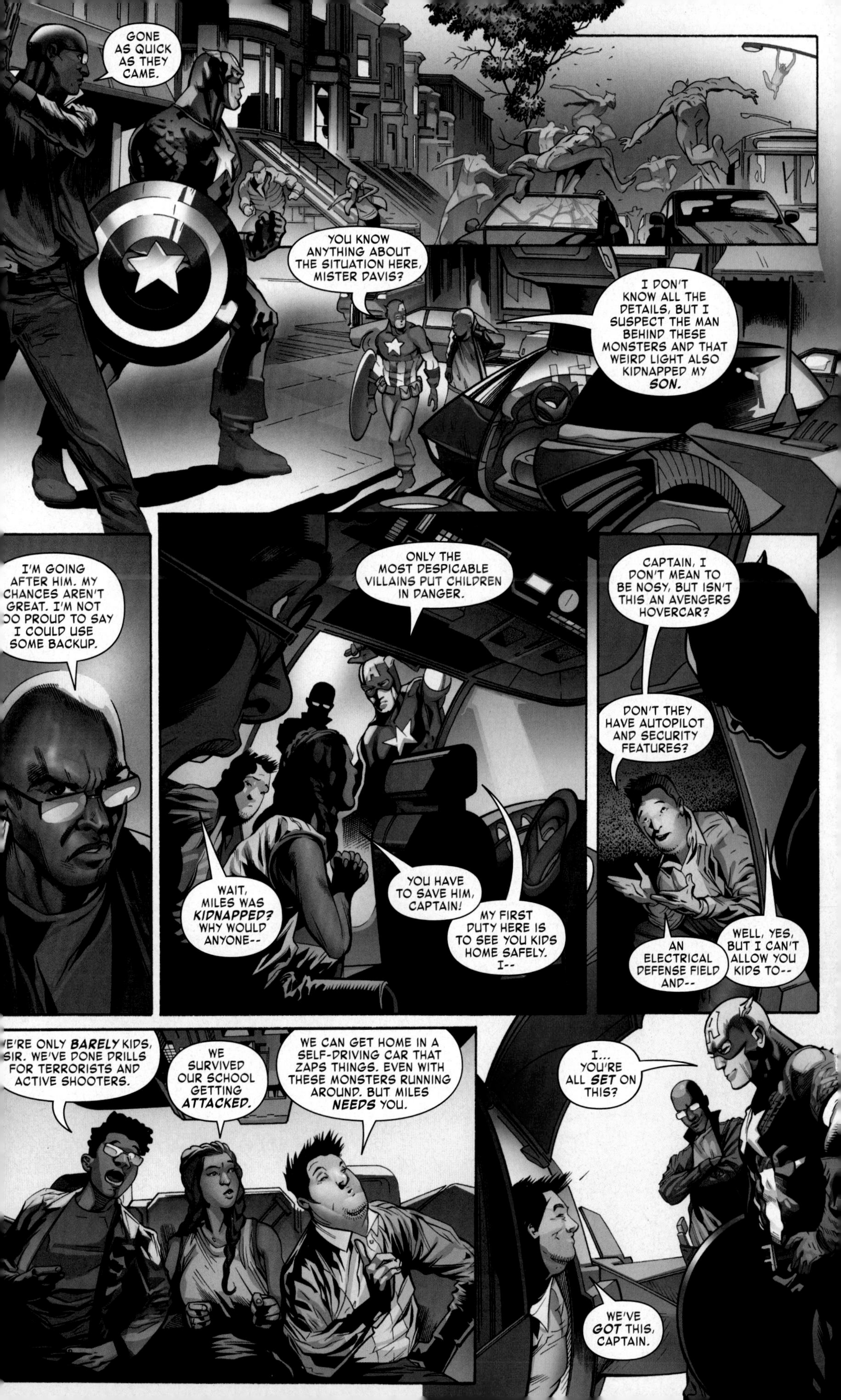
GONE AS QUICK AS THEY CAME.
YOU KNOW ANYTHING ABOUT THE SITUATION HERE, MISTER DAVIS?
I DON'T KNOW ALL THE DETAILS, BUT I SUSPECT THE MAN BEHIND THESE MONSTERS AND THAT WEIRD LIGHT ALSO KIDNAPPED MY SON.
I'M GOING AFTER HIM. MY CHANCES AREN'T GREAT. I'M NOT OO PROUD TO SAY I COULD USE SOME BACKUP.
ONLY THE MOST DESPICABLE VILLAINS PUT CHILDREN IN DANGER.
WAIT, MILES WAS KIDNAPPED? WHY WOULD ANYONE--
YOU HAVE TO SAVE HIM, CAPTAIN!
MY FIRST DUTY HERE IS TO SEE YOU KIDS HOME SAFELY. I--
CAPTAIN, I DON'T MEAN TO BE NOSY, BUT ISN'T THIS AN AVENGERS HOVERCAR?
DON'T THEY HAVE AUTOPILOT AND SECURITY FEATURES?
AN ELECTRICAL DEFENSE FIELD AND--
WELL, YES, BUT I CAN'T ALLOW YOU KIDS TO--
E'RE ONLY BARELY KIDS, SIR. WE'VE DONE DRILLS FOR TERRORISTS AND ACTIVE SHOOTERS.
WE SURVIVED OUR SCHOOL GETTING ATTACKED.
WE CAN GET HOME IN A SELF-DRIVING CAR THAT ZAPS THINGS. EVEN WITH THESE MONSTERS RUNNING AROUND. BUT MILES NEEDS YOU.
I... YOU'RE ALL SET ON THIS?
WE'VE GOT THIS, CAPTAIN.

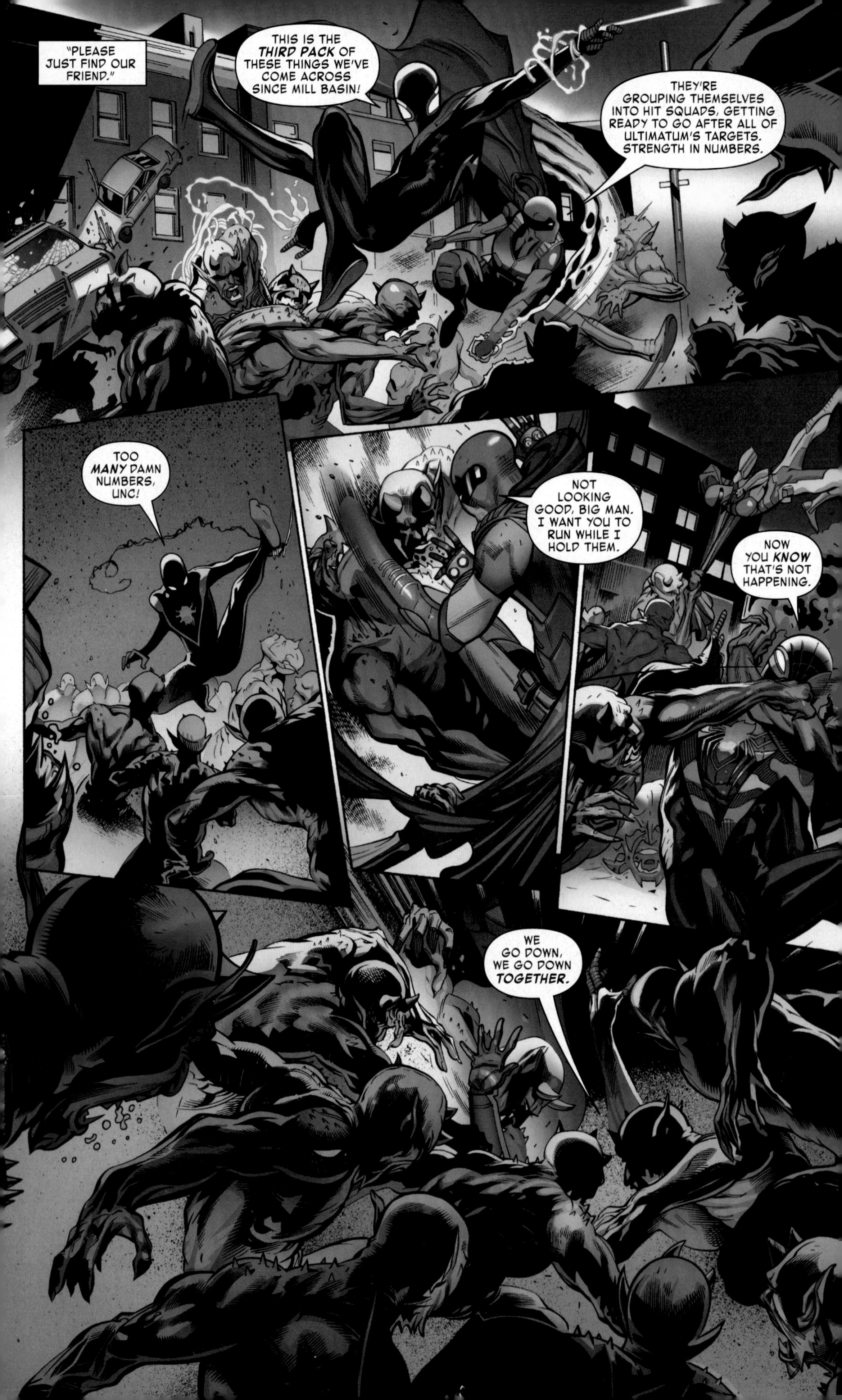
"PLEASE JUST FIND OUR FRIEND."
THIS IS THE *THIRD PACK* OF THESE THINGS WE'VE COME ACROSS SINCE MILL BASIN!
THEY'RE GROUPING THEMSELVES INTO HIT SQUADS, GETTING READY TO GO AFTER ALL OF ULTIMATUM'S TARGETS. STRENGTH IN NUMBERS.
TOO *MANY* DAMN NUMBERS, UNC!
NOT LOOKING GOOD, BIG MAN. I WANT YOU TO RUN WHILE I HOLD THEM.
NOW YOU *KNOW* THAT'S NOT HAPPENING.
WE GO DOWN, WE GO DOWN *TOGETHER.*

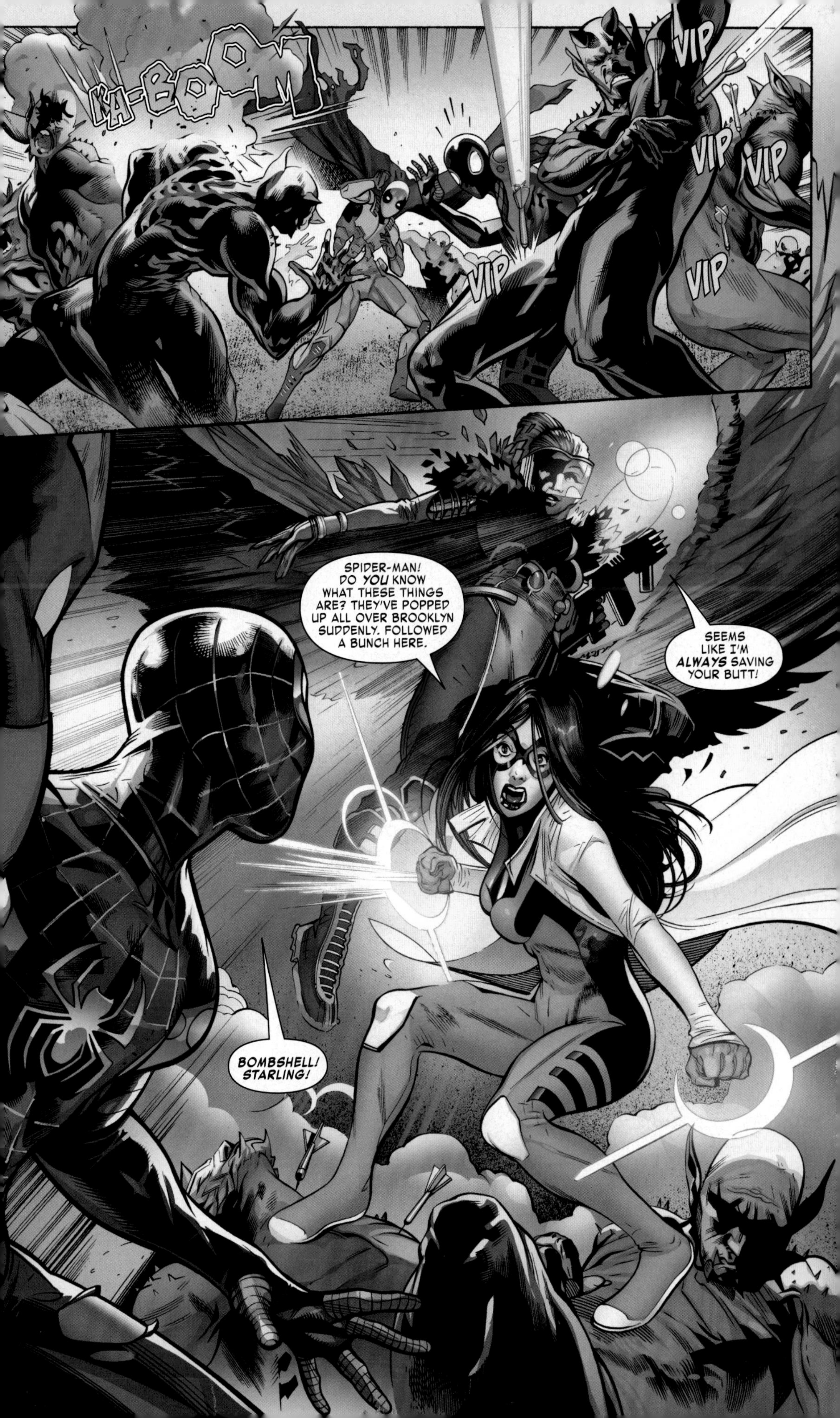

KA-BOOM
VIP
VIP
VIP
VIP
VIP
SPIDER-MAN! DO YOU KNOW WHAT THESE THINGS ARE? THEY'VE POPPED UP ALL OVER BROOKLYN SUDDENLY. FOLLOWED A BUNCH HERE.
SEEMS LIKE I'M ALWAYS SAVING YOUR BUTT!
BOMBSHELL! STARLING!

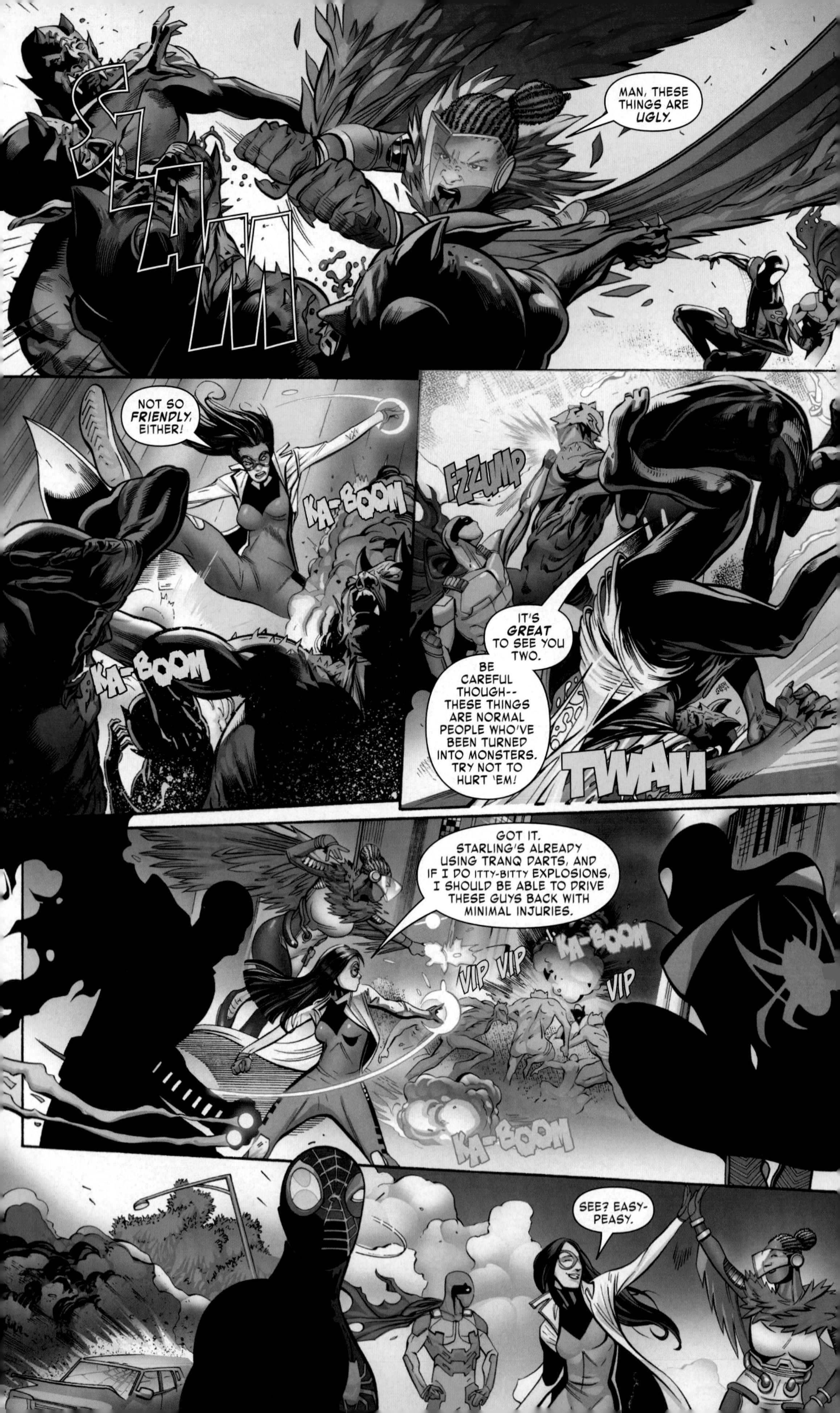
SLAM
MAN, THESE THINGS ARE UGLY.
NOT SO FRIENDLY, EITHER!
KA-BOOM
KA-BOOM
FZZUMP
IT'S GREAT TO SEE YOU TWO.
BE CAREFUL THOUGH-- THESE THINGS ARE NORMAL PEOPLE WHO'VE BEEN TURNED INTO MONSTERS. TRY NOT TO HURT 'EM!
TWAM
GOT IT. STARLING'S ALREADY USING TRANQ DARTS, AND IF I DO ITTY-BITTY EXPLOSIONS, I SHOULD BE ABLE TO DRIVE THESE GUYS BACK WITH MINIMAL INJURIES.
VIP VIP
KA-BOOM
VIP
KA-BOOM
SEE? EASY-PEASY.

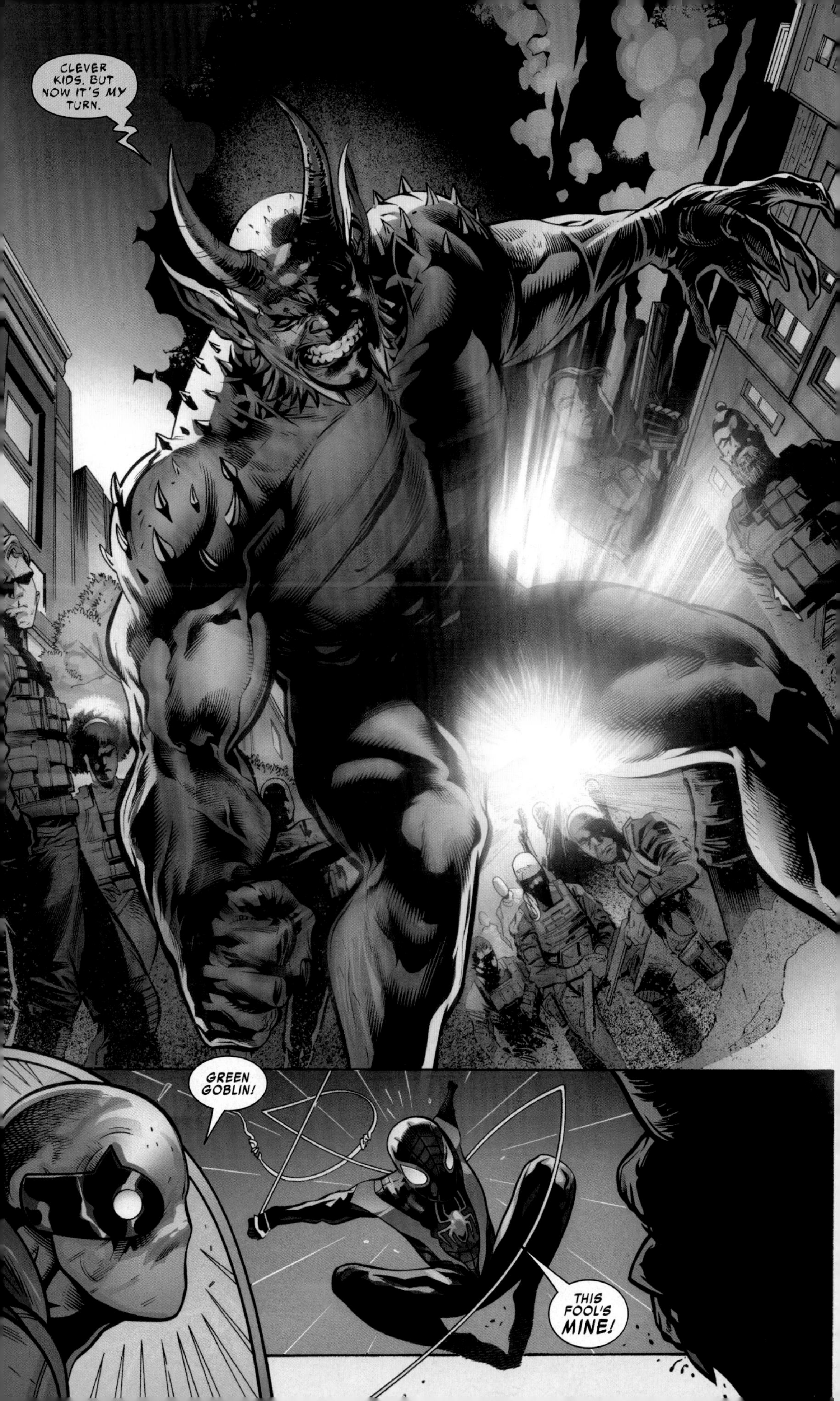
CLEVER KIDS. BUT NOW IT'S MY TURN.
GREEN GOBLIN!
THIS FOOL'S MINE!

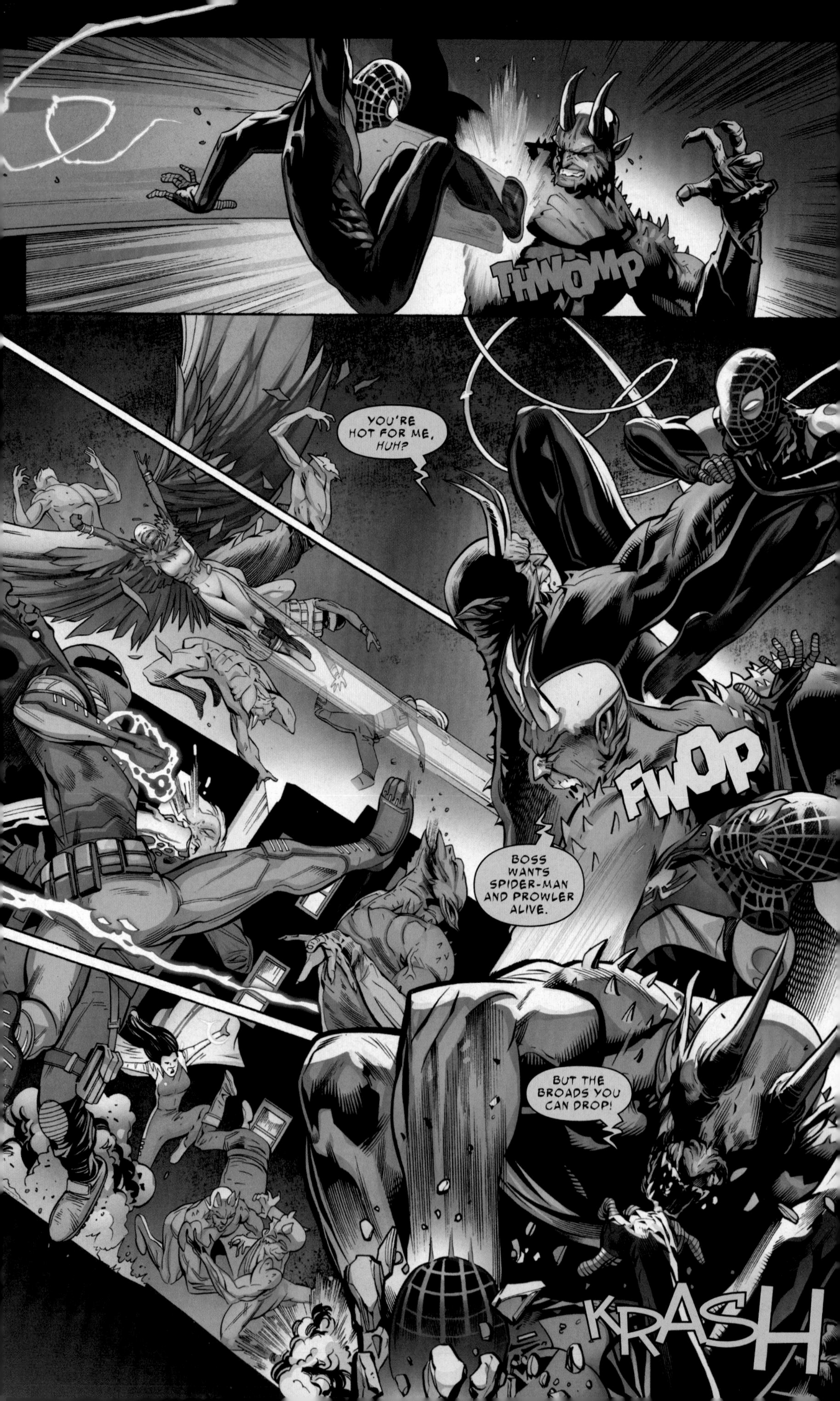
THWOMP
YOU'RE HOT FOR ME, HUH?
FWOP
BOSS WANTS SPIDER-MAN AND PROWLER ALIVE.
BUT THE BROADS YOU CAN DROP!
KRASH

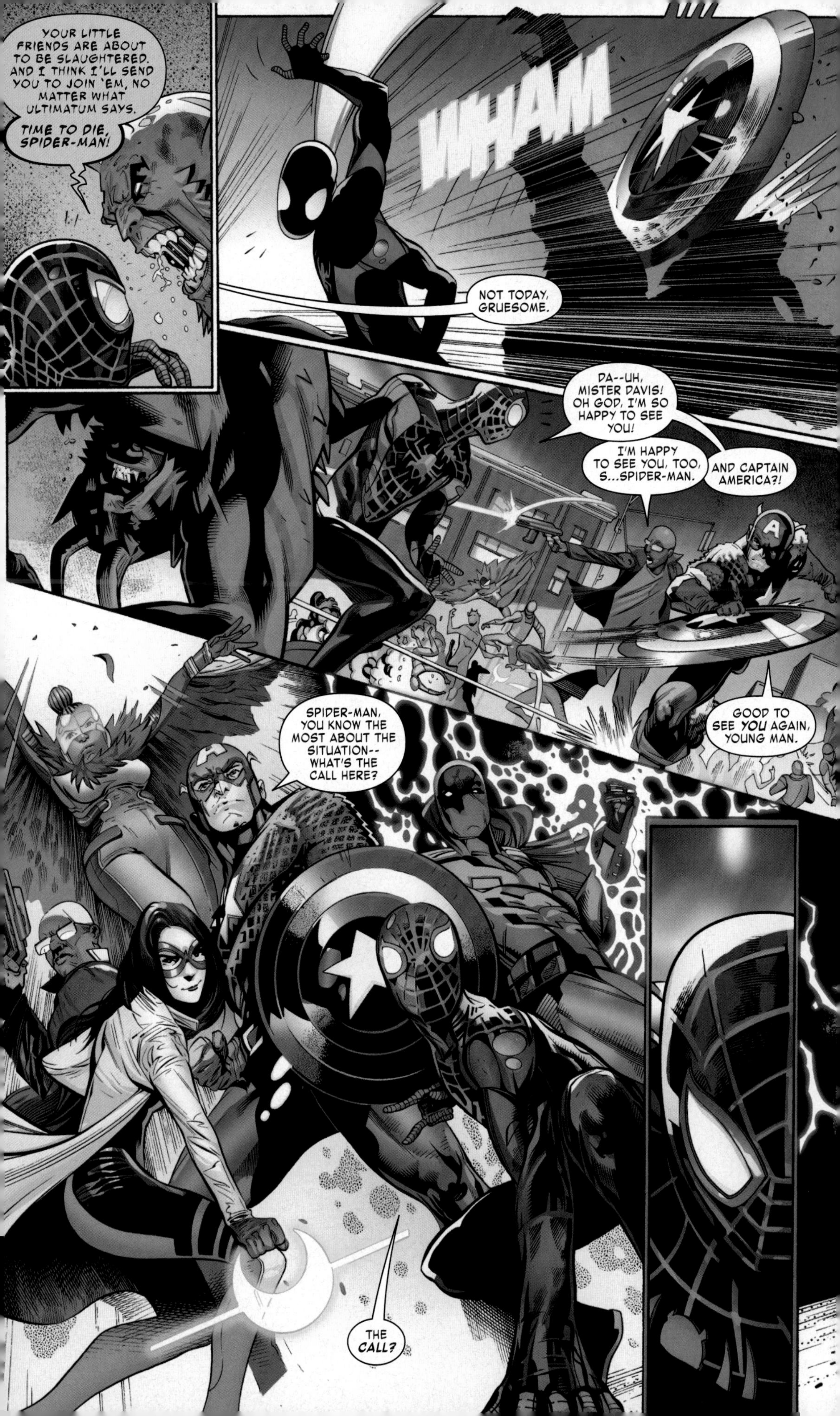

YOUR LITTLE FRIENDS ARE ABOUT TO BE SLAUGHTERED. AND I THINK I'LL SEND YOU TO JOIN 'EM, NO MATTER WHAT ULTIMATUM SAYS.
TIME TO DIE, SPIDER-MAN!
WHAM
NOT TODAY, GRUESOME.
DA--UH, MISTER DAVIS! OH GOD, I'M SO HAPPY TO SEE YOU!
I'M HAPPY TO SEE YOU, TOO, S...SPIDER-MAN.
AND CAPTAIN AMERICA?!
GOOD TO SEE YOU AGAIN, YOUNG MAN.
SPIDER-MAN, YOU KNOW THE MOST ABOUT THE SITUATION--WHAT'S THE CALL HERE?
THE CALL?

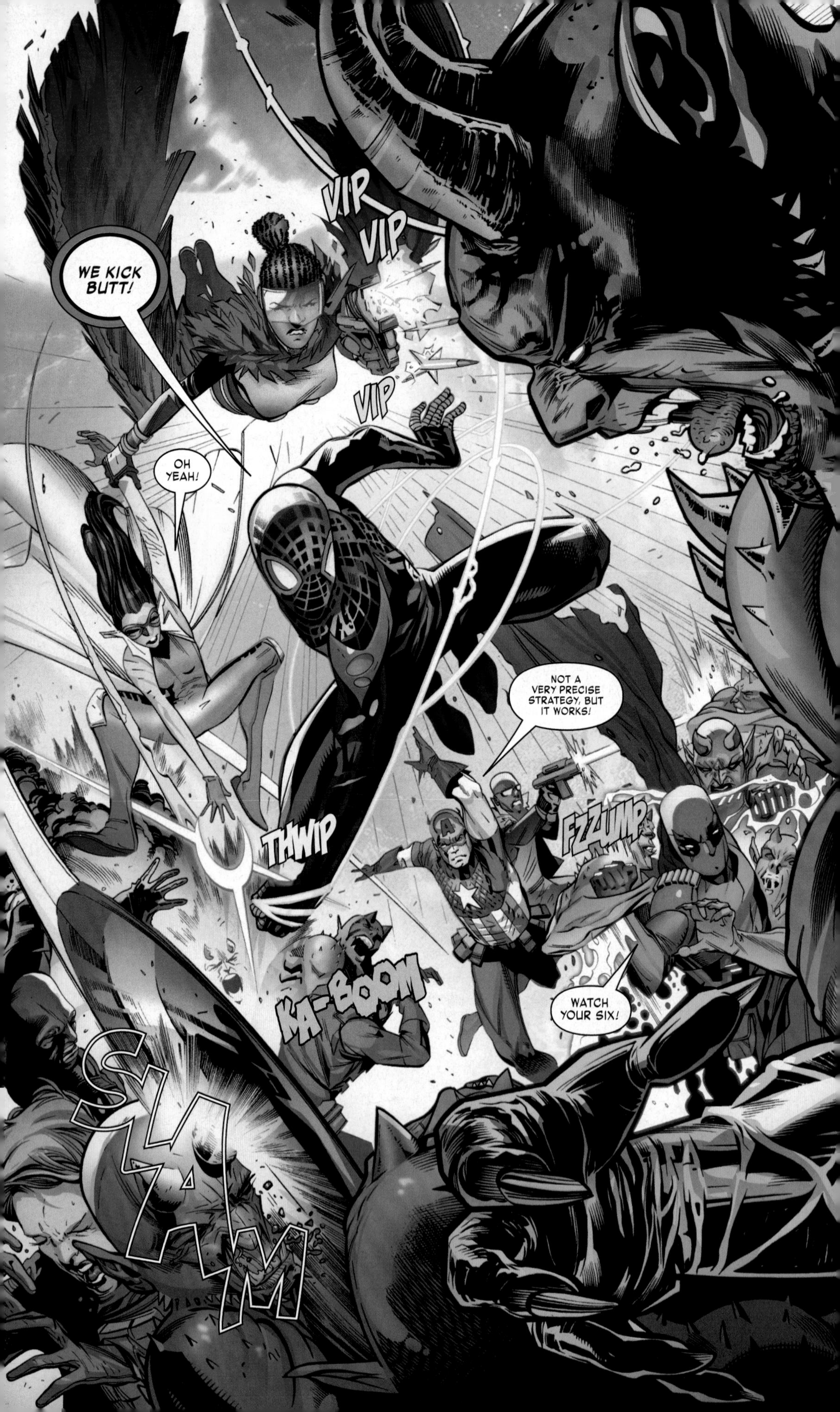
VIP
VIP
WE KICK BUTT!
VIP
OH YEAH!
NOT A VERY PRECISE STRATEGY, BUT IT WORKS!
THWIP
FZZUMP
KA-BOOM
WATCH YOUR SIX!
SLAM

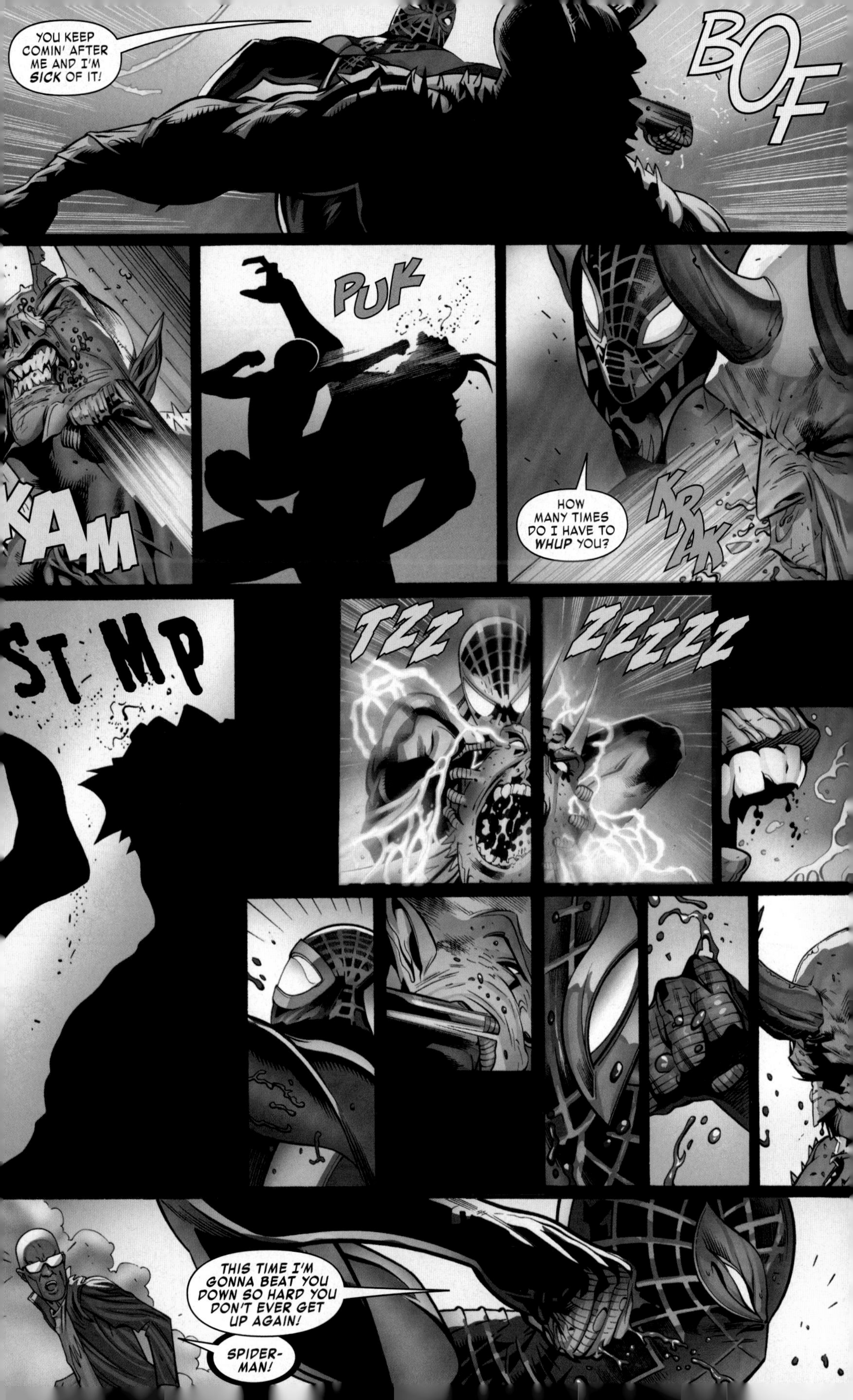

YOU KEEP COMIN' AFTER ME AND I'M SICK OF IT!
BOF
KAM
PUK
HOW MANY TIMES DO I HAVE TO WHUP YOU?
KRAK
ST MP
TZZ
ZZZZZ
THIS TIME I'M GONNA BEAT YOU DOWN SO HARD YOU DON'T EVER GET UP AGAIN!
SPIDER-MAN!

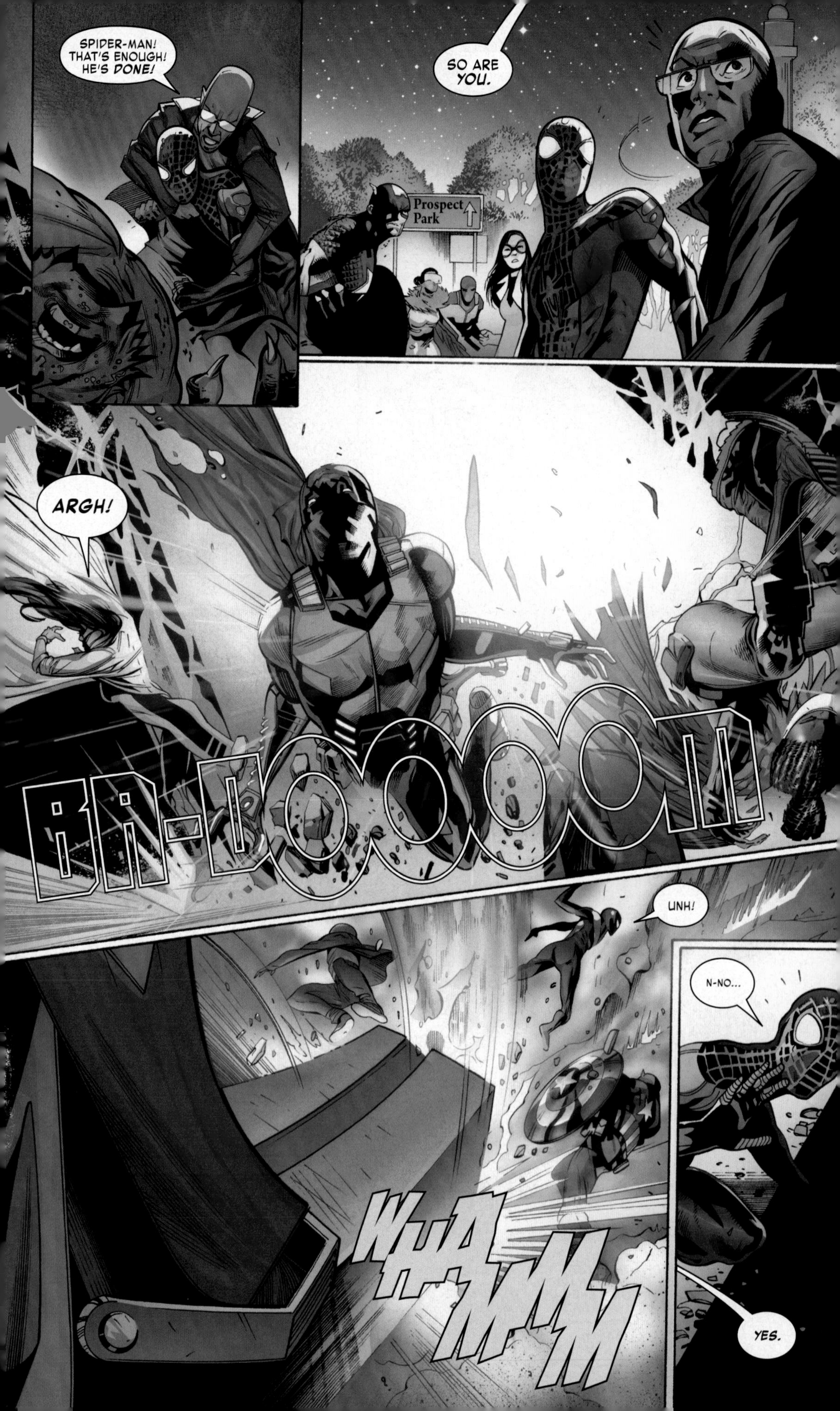
SPIDER-MAN! THAT'S ENOUGH! HE'S DONE!
SO ARE YOU.
Prospect Park
ARGH!
BR-DOOOOM
UNH!
N-NO...
WHAM
YES.

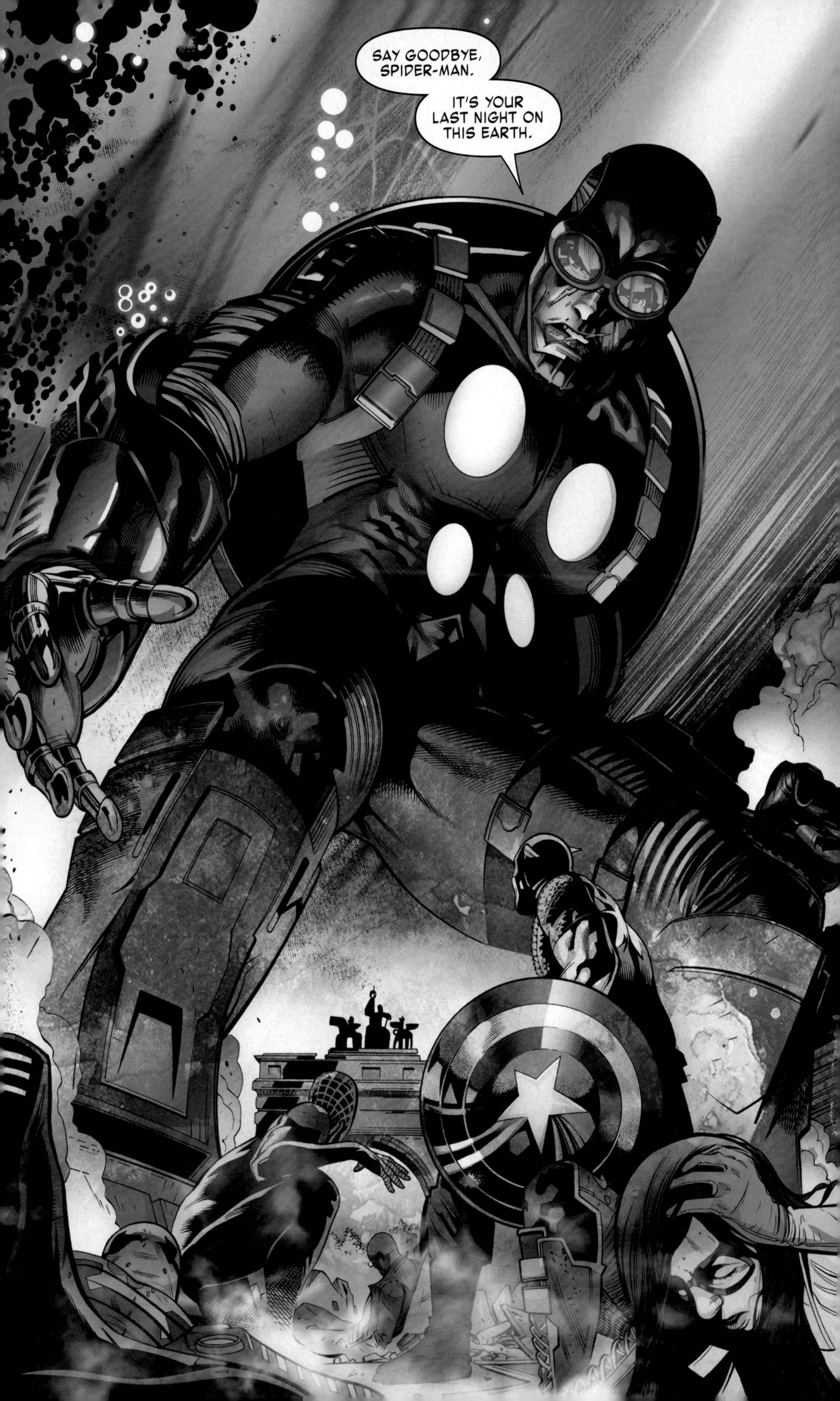
SAY GOODBYE, SPIDER-MAN.
IT'S YOUR LAST NIGHT ON THIS EARTH.

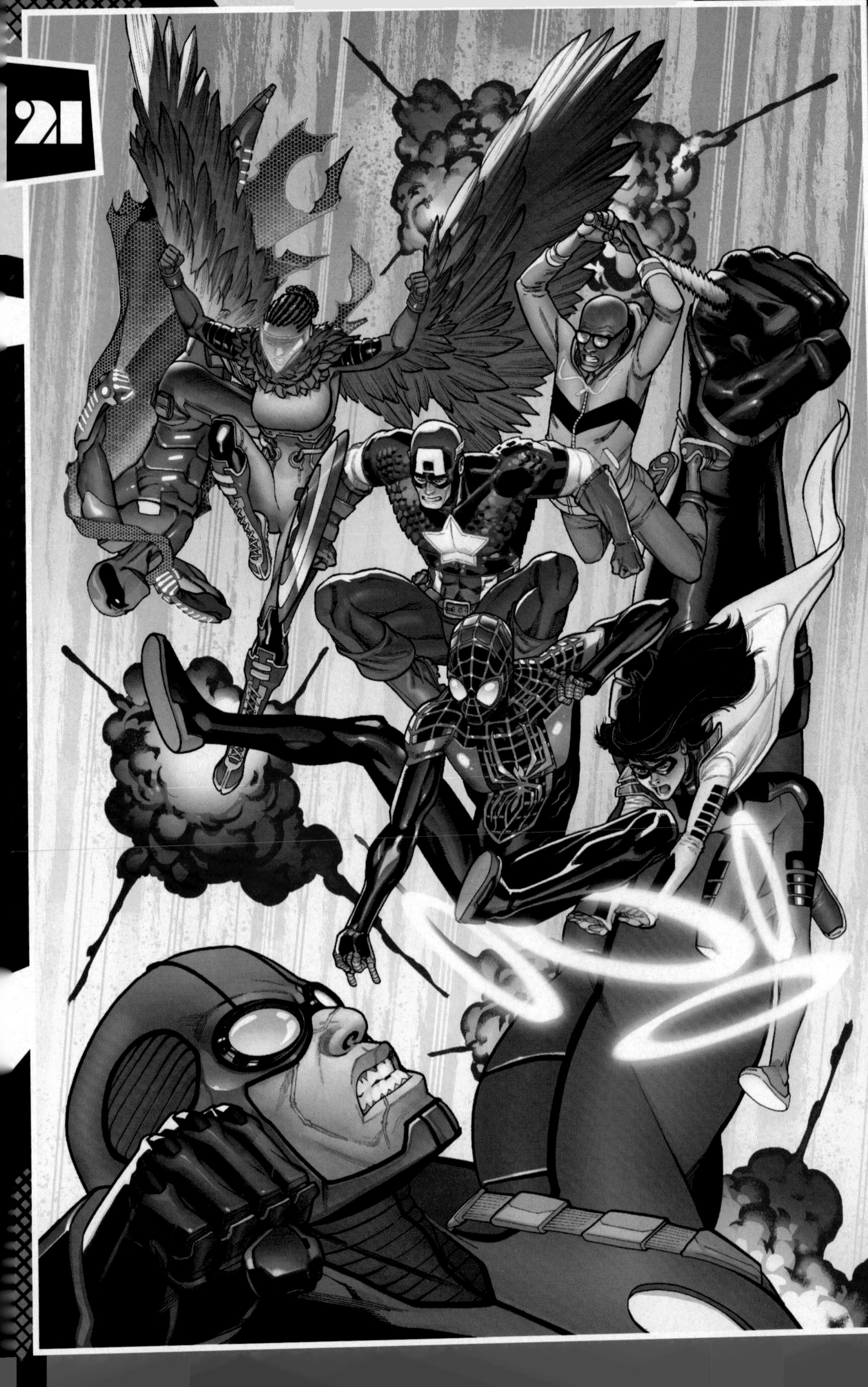
21

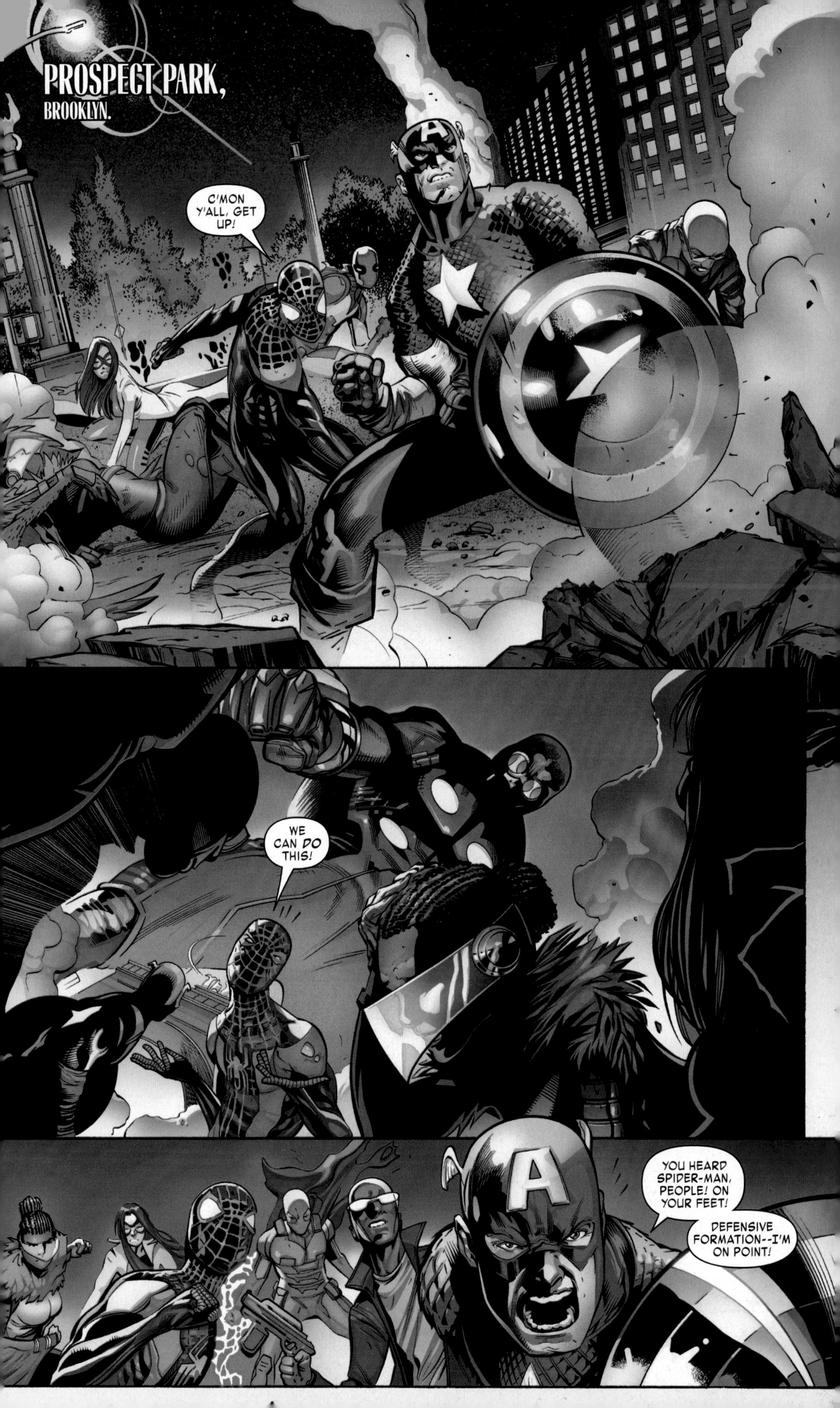
PROSPECT PARK,
BROOKLYN.
C'MON Y'ALL, GET UP!
WE CAN DO THIS!
YOU HEARD SPIDER-MAN, PEOPLE! ON YOUR FEET!
DEFENSIVE FORMATION--I'M ON POINT!

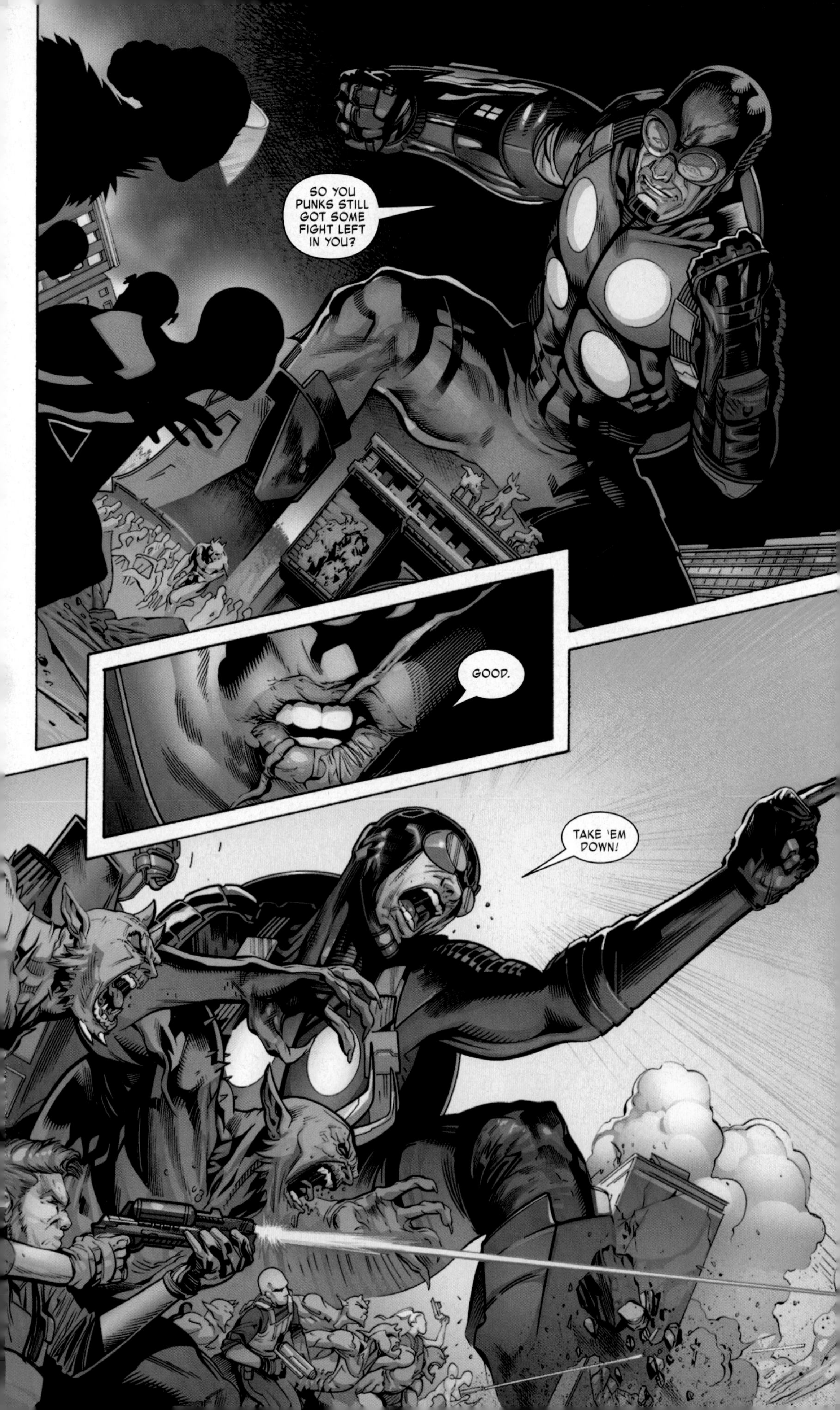
SO YOU PUNKS STILL GOT SOME FIGHT LEFT IN YOU?
GOOD.
TAKE 'EM DOWN!

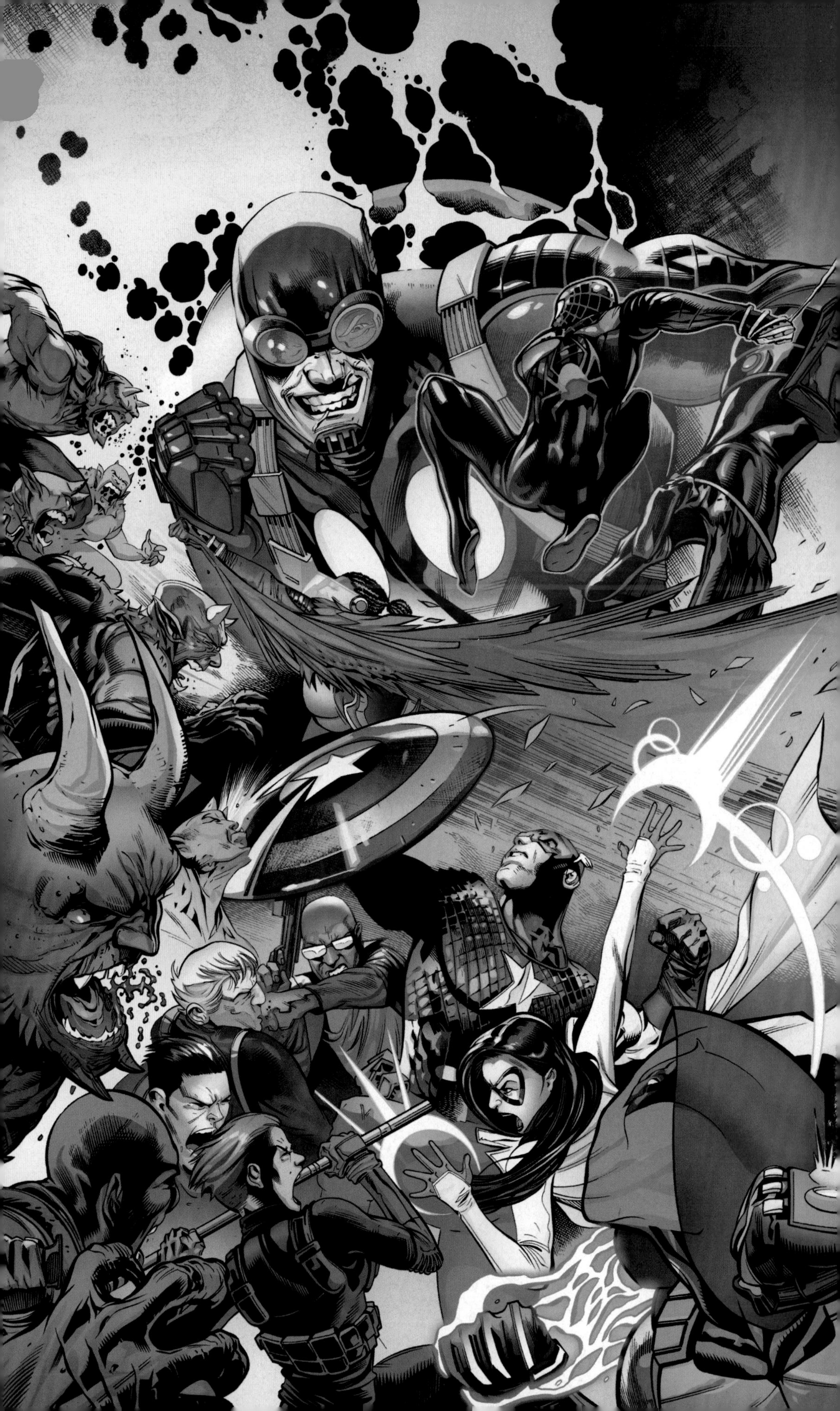

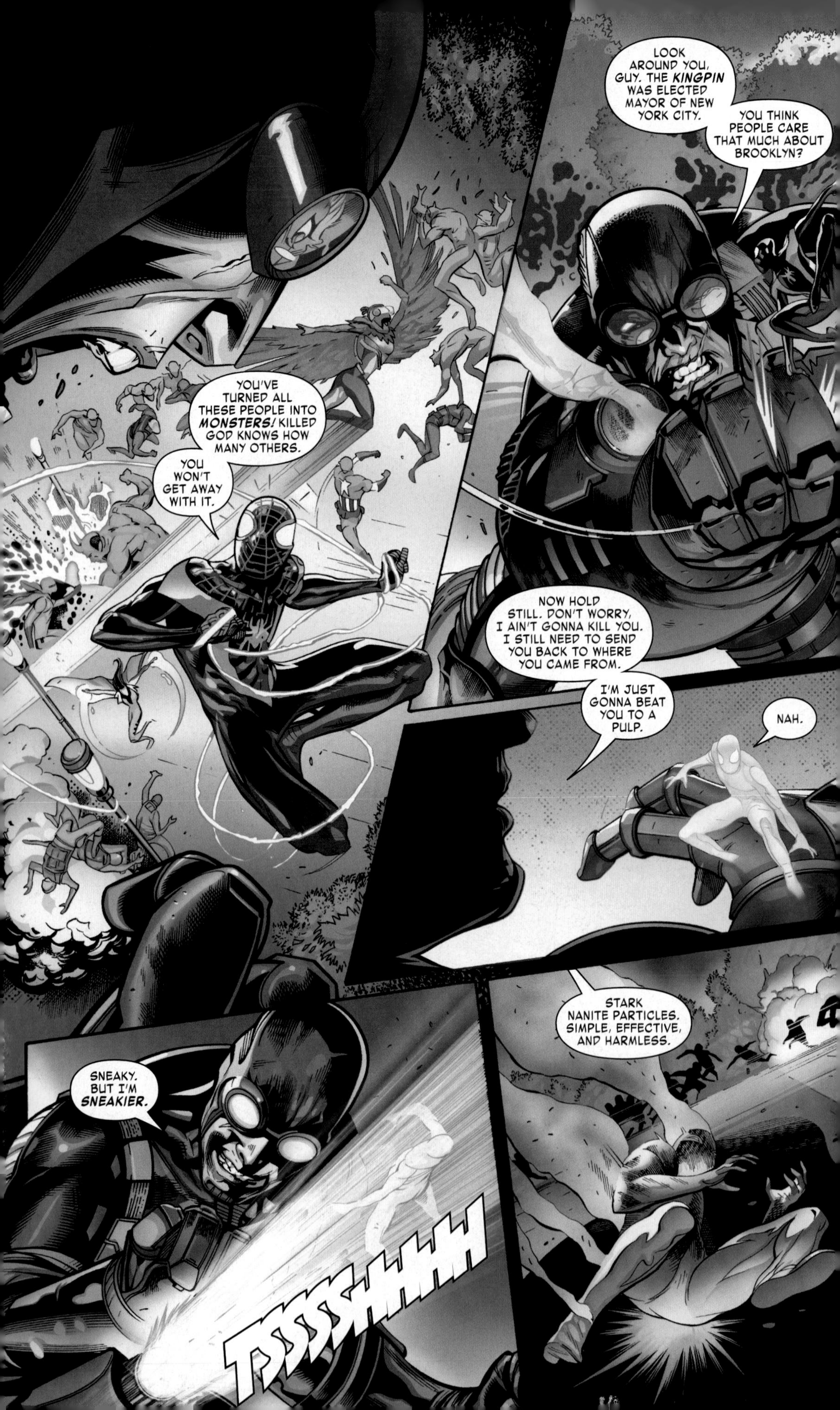

YOU'VE TURNED ALL THESE PEOPLE INTO MONSTERS! KILLED GOD KNOWS HOW MANY OTHERS.
YOU WON'T GET AWAY WITH IT.
LOOK AROUND YOU, GUY. THE KINGPIN WAS ELECTED MAYOR OF NEW YORK CITY.
YOU THINK PEOPLE CARE THAT MUCH ABOUT BROOKLYN?
NOW HOLD STILL. DON'T WORRY, I AIN'T GONNA KILL YOU. I STILL NEED TO SEND YOU BACK TO WHERE YOU CAME FROM.
I'M JUST GONNA BEAT YOU TO A PULP.
NAH.
SNEAKY. BUT I'M SNEAKIER.
TSSSSHHHHH
STARK NANITE PARTICLES. SIMPLE, EFFECTIVE, AND HARMLESS.

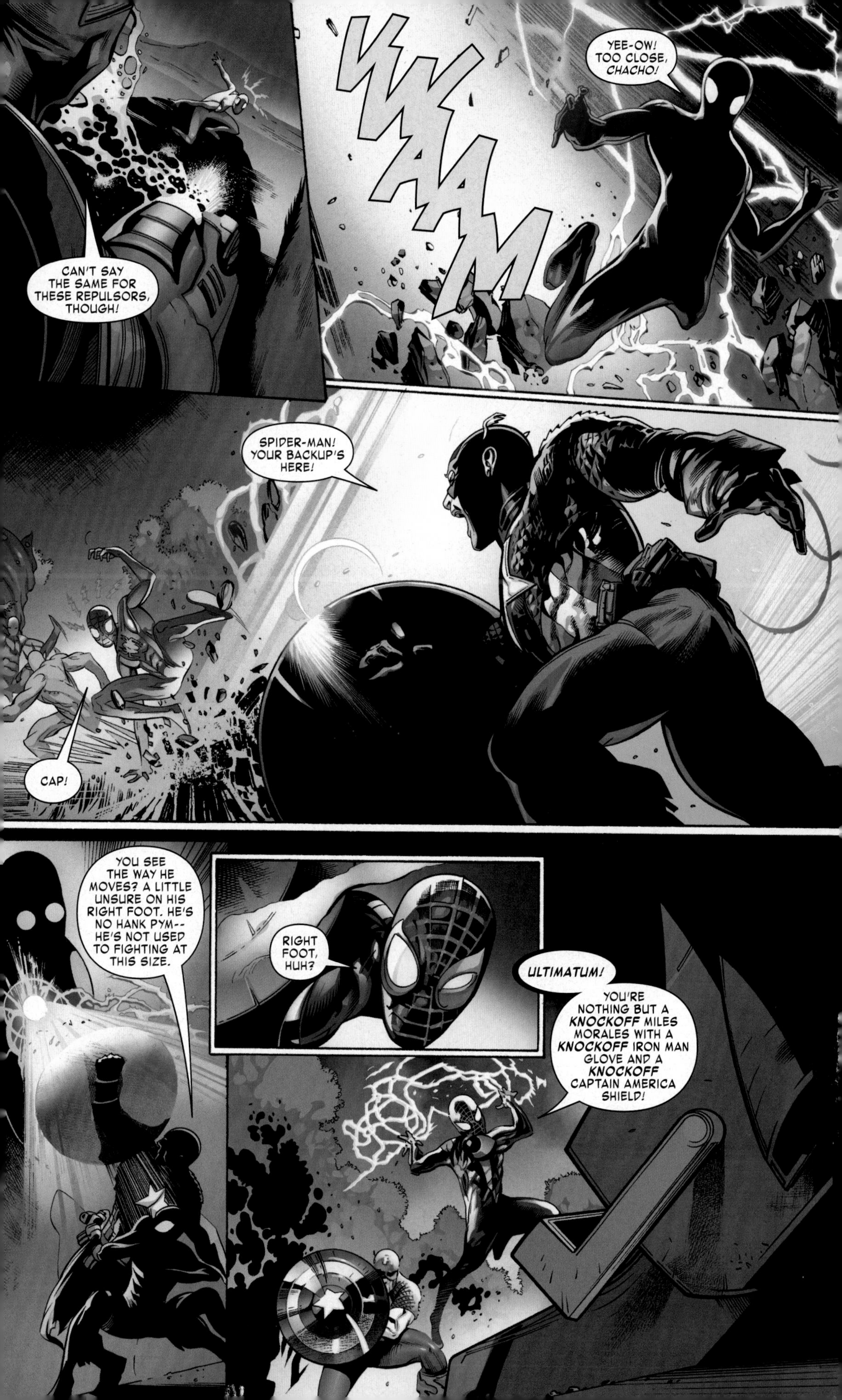
CAN'T SAY THE SAME FOR THESE REPULSORS, THOUGH!
VVVVAAAM
YEE-OW! TOO CLOSE, CHACHO!
SPIDER-MAN! YOUR BACKUP'S HERE!
CAP!
YOU SEE THE WAY HE MOVES? A LITTLE UNSURE ON HIS RIGHT FOOT. HE'S NO HANK PYM-- HE'S NOT USED TO FIGHTING AT THIS SIZE.
RIGHT FOOT, HUH?
ULTIMATUM!
YOU'RE NOTHING BUT A KNOCKOFF MILES MORALES WITH A KNOCKOFF IRON MAN GLOVE AND A KNOCKOFF CAPTAIN AMERICA SHIELD!

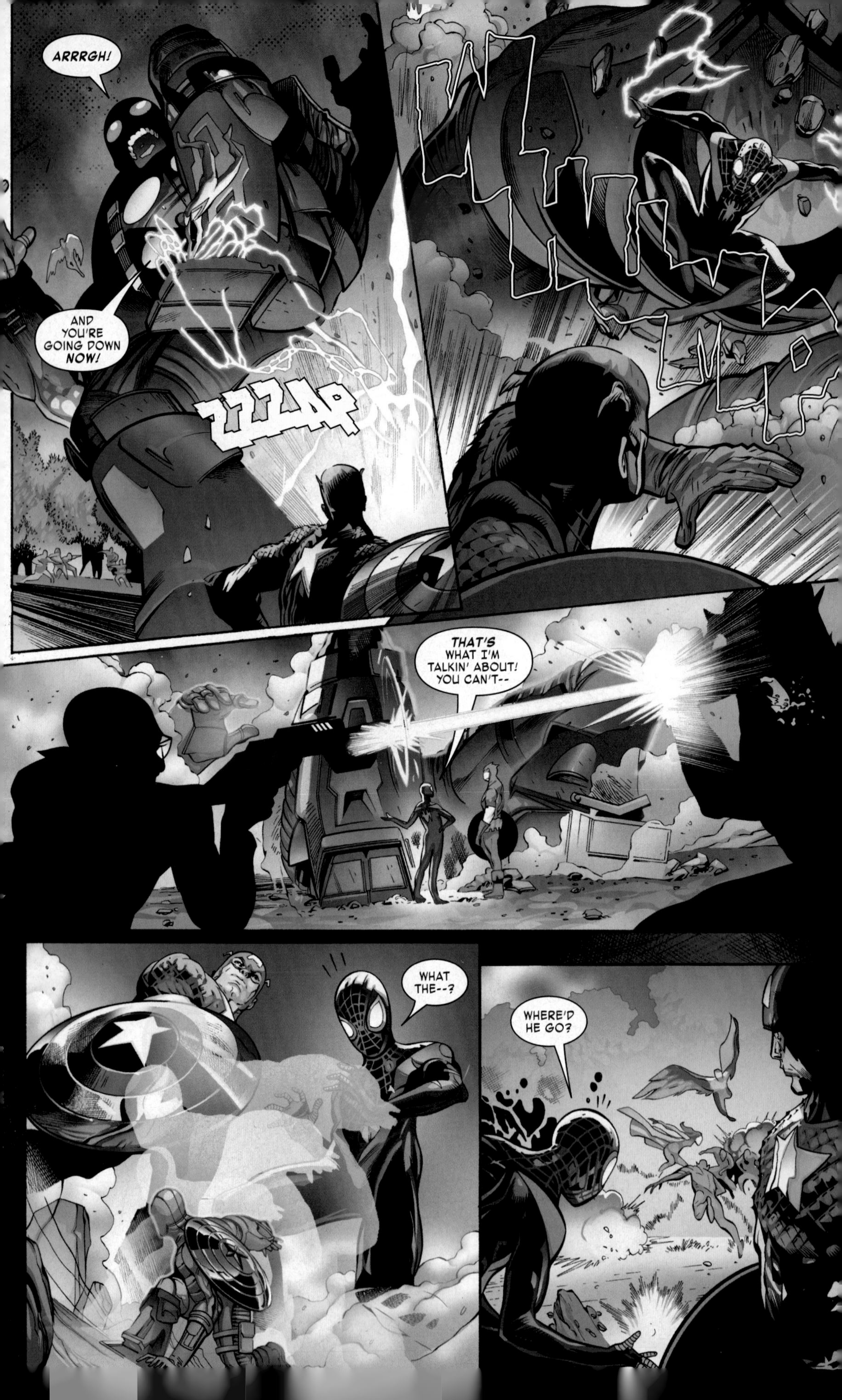
ARRRGH!
AND YOU'RE GOING DOWN NOW!
ZZZZAP
THAT'S WHAT I'M TALKIN' ABOUT! YOU CAN'T--
WHAT THE--?
WHERE'D HE GO?

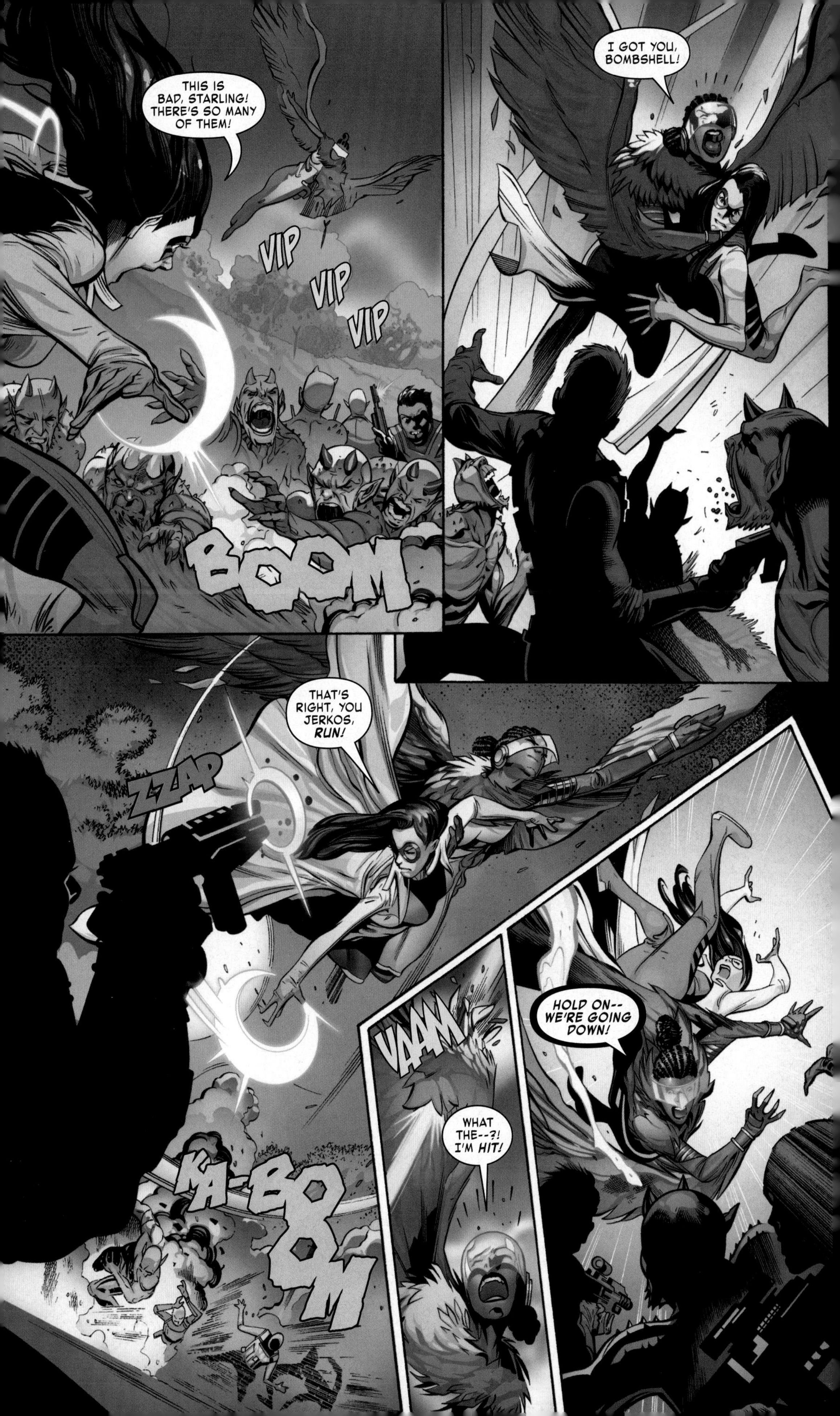
THIS IS BAD, STARLING! THERE'S SO MANY OF THEM!
VIP
VIP
VIP
BOOM
I GOT YOU, BOMBSHELL!
THAT'S RIGHT, YOU JERKOS, RUN!
ZZZAP
KA-BOOOM
VAAM
WHAT THE--?! I'M HIT!
HOLD ON--WE'RE GOING DOWN!

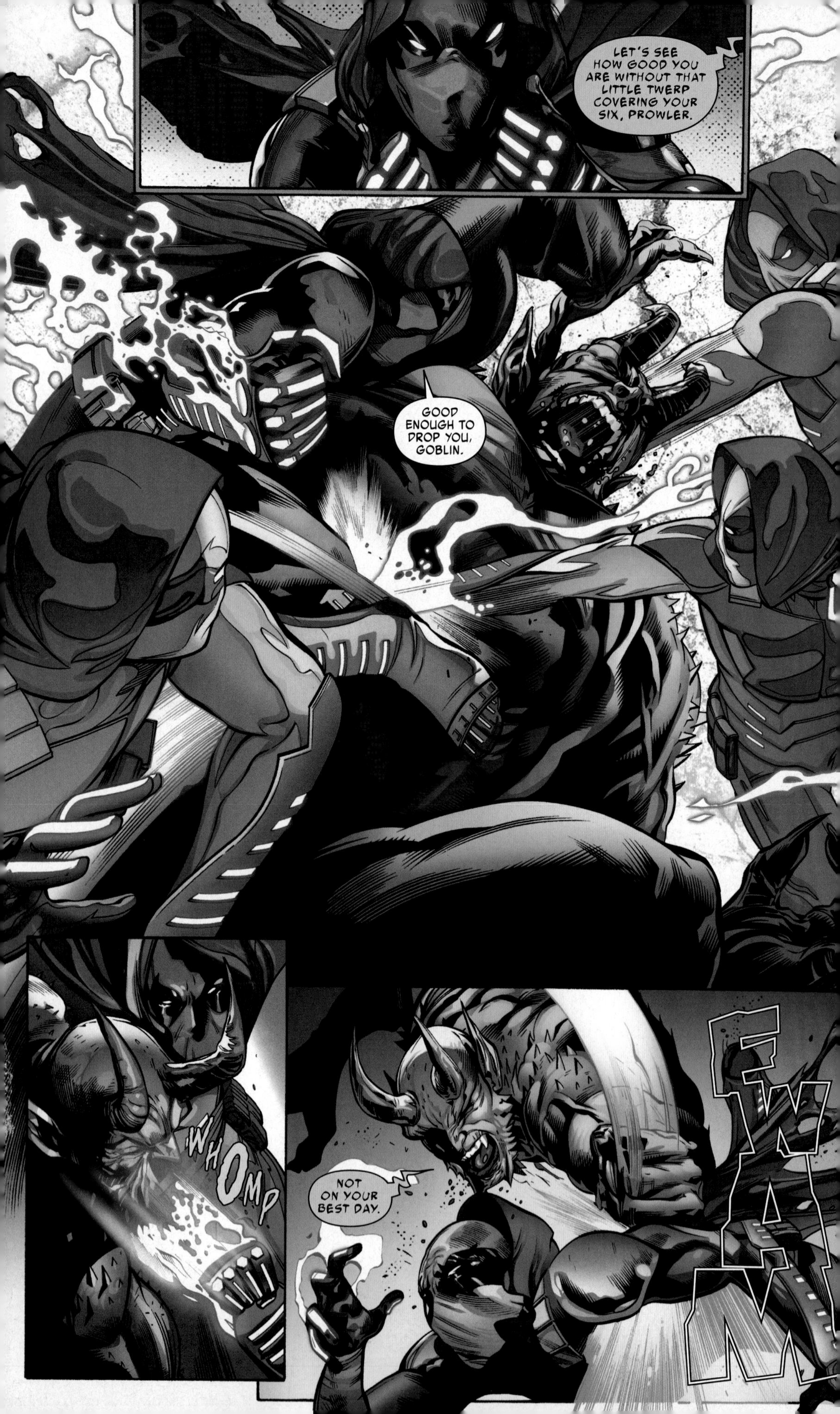
LET'S SEE HOW GOOD YOU ARE WITHOUT THAT LITTLE TWERP COVERING YOUR SIX, PROWLER.
GOOD ENOUGH TO DROP YOU, GOBLIN.
WHOMP
NOT ON YOUR BEST DAY.
FWAM

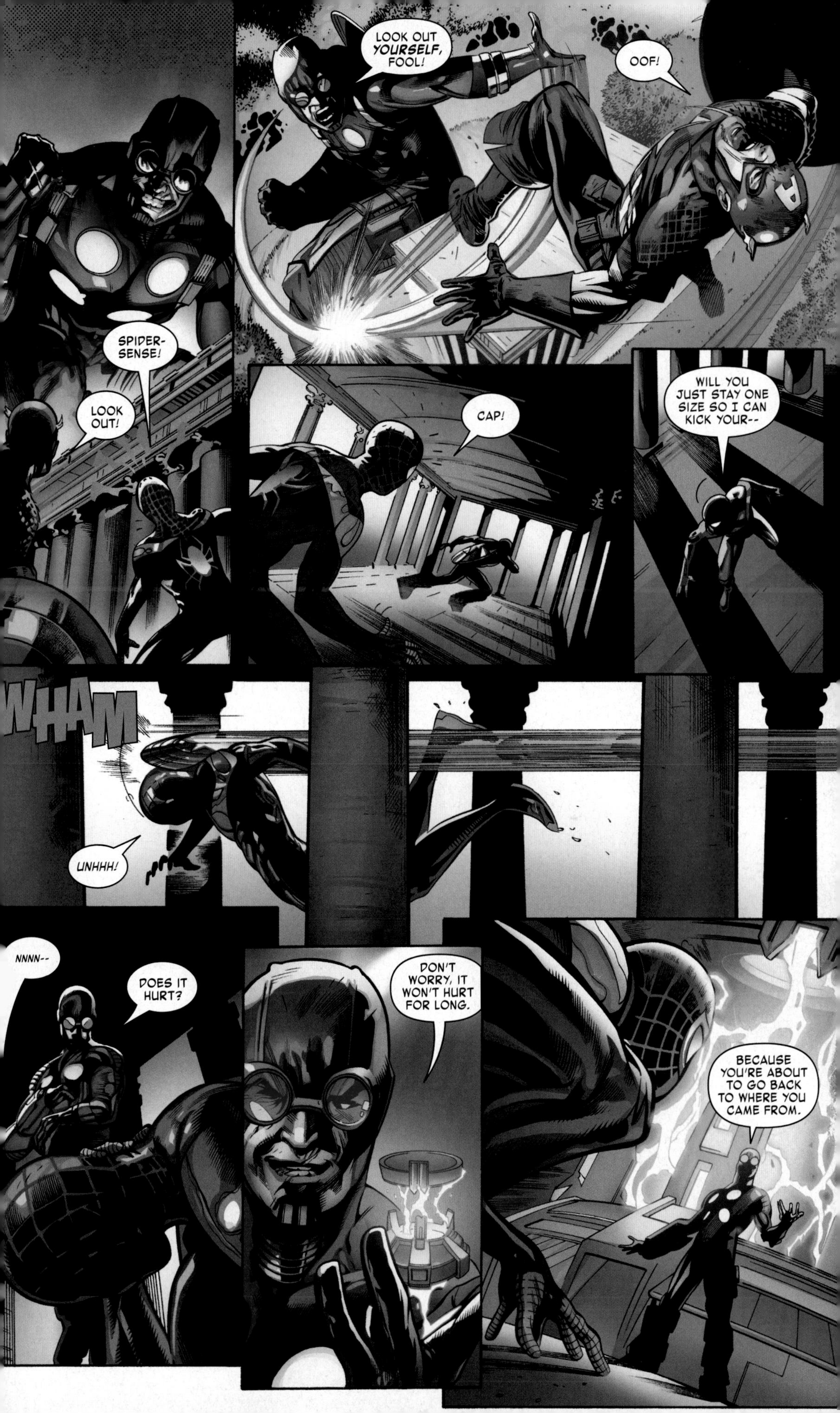

LOOK OUT YOURSELF, FOOL!
OOF!
SPIDER-SENSE!
LOOK OUT!
CAP!
WILL YOU JUST STAY ONE SIZE SO I CAN KICK YOUR--
WHAM
UNHHH!
NNNN--
DOES IT HURT?
DON'T WORRY, IT WON'T HURT FOR LONG.
BECAUSE YOU'RE ABOUT TO GO BACK TO WHERE YOU CAME FROM.

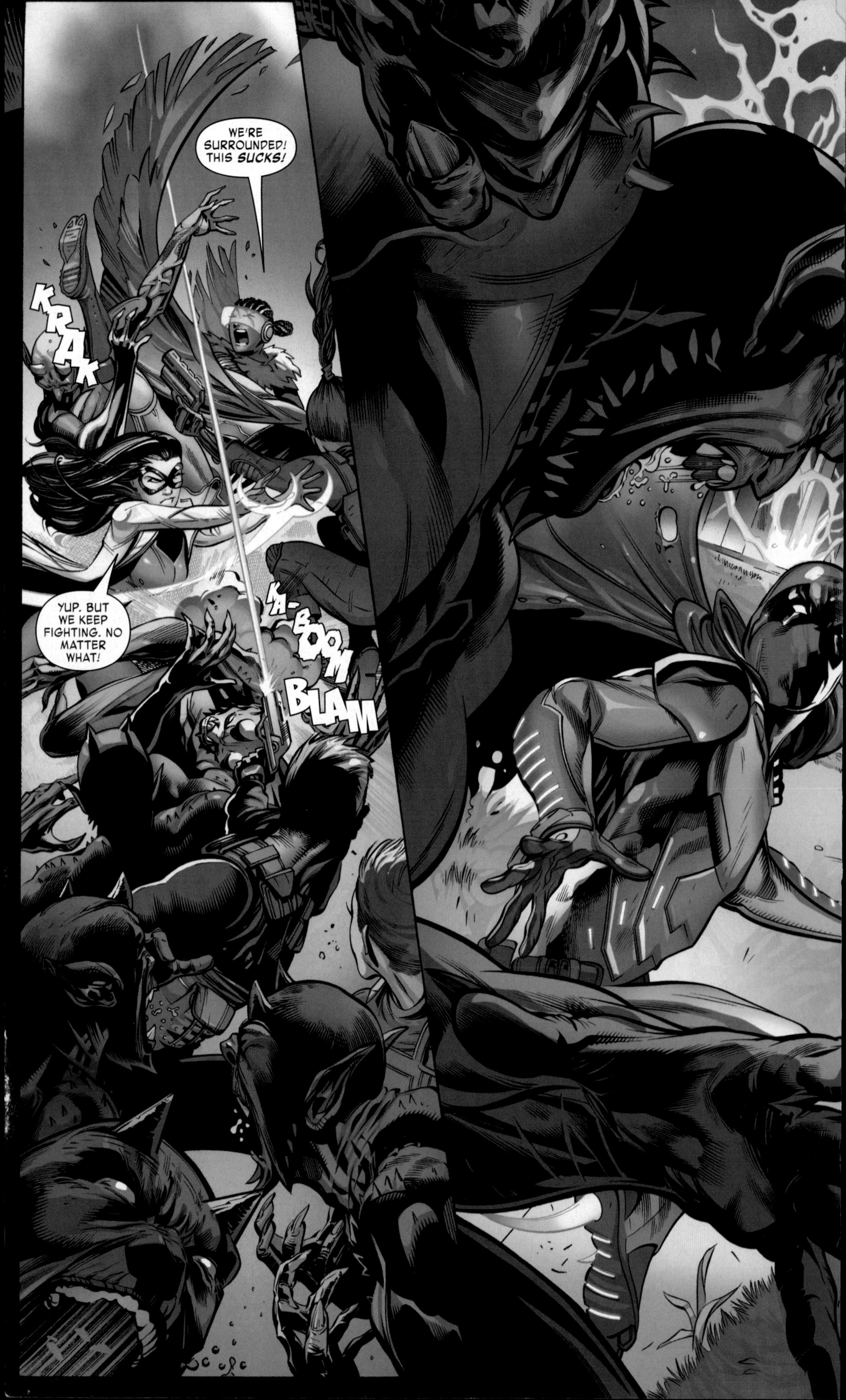
WE'RE SURROUNDED! THIS SUCKS!
KRAK
YUP. BUT WE KEEP FIGHTING. NO MATTER WHAT!
KA-BOOM
BLAM

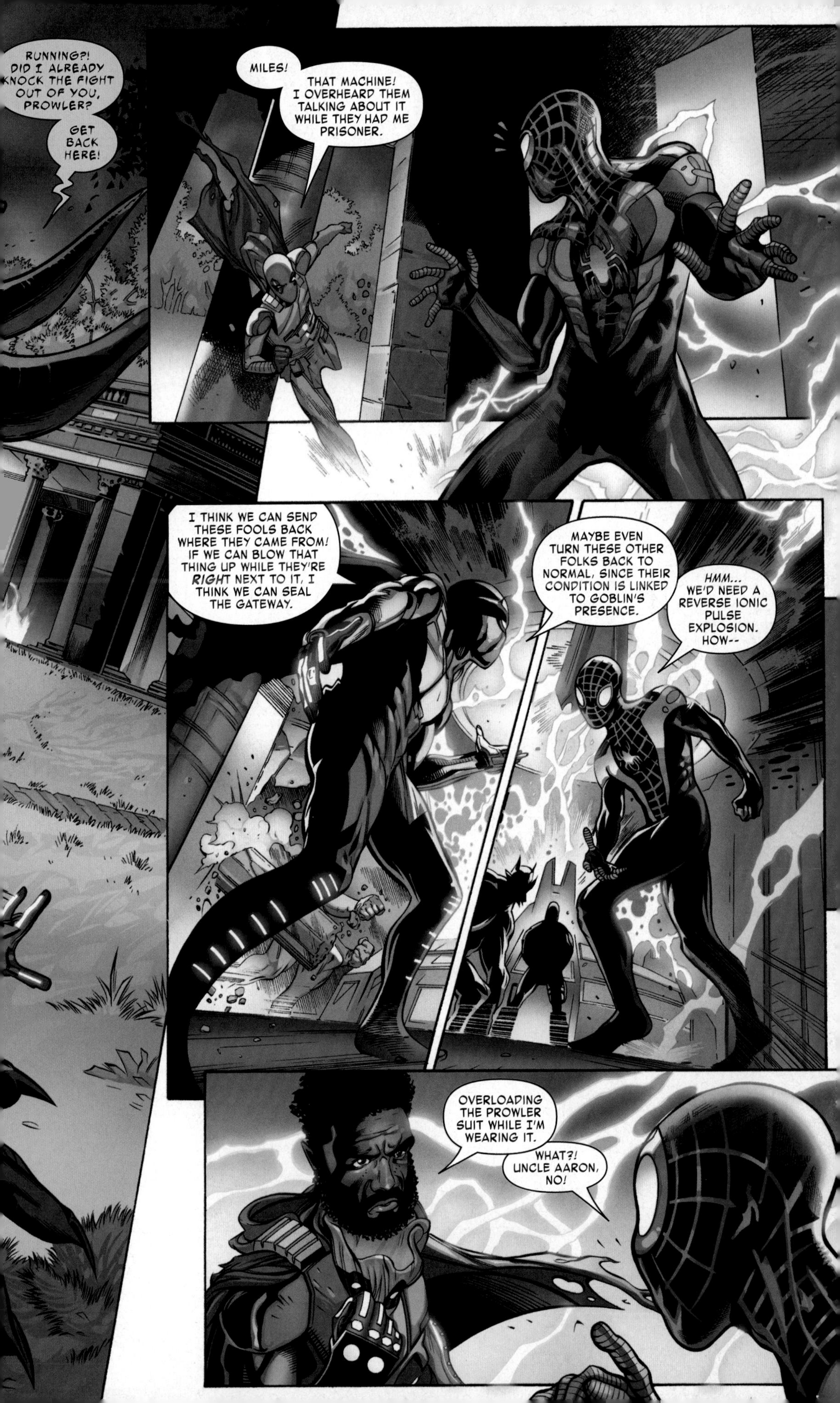
RUNNING?! DID I ALREADY KNOCK THE FIGHT OUT OF YOU, PROWLER?
GET BACK HERE!
MILES!
THAT MACHINE! I OVERHEARD THEM TALKING ABOUT IT WHILE THEY HAD ME PRISONER.
I THINK WE CAN SEND THESE FOOLS BACK WHERE THEY CAME FROM! IF WE CAN BLOW THAT THING UP WHILE THEY'RE RIGHT NEXT TO IT, I THINK WE CAN SEAL THE GATEWAY.
MAYBE EVEN TURN THESE OTHER FOLKS BACK TO NORMAL, SINCE THEIR CONDITION IS LINKED TO GOBLIN'S PRESENCE.
HMM... WE'D NEED A REVERSE IONIC PULSE EXPLOSION. HOW--
OVERLOADING THE PROWLER SUIT WHILE I'M WEARING IT.
WHAT?! UNCLE AARON, NO!

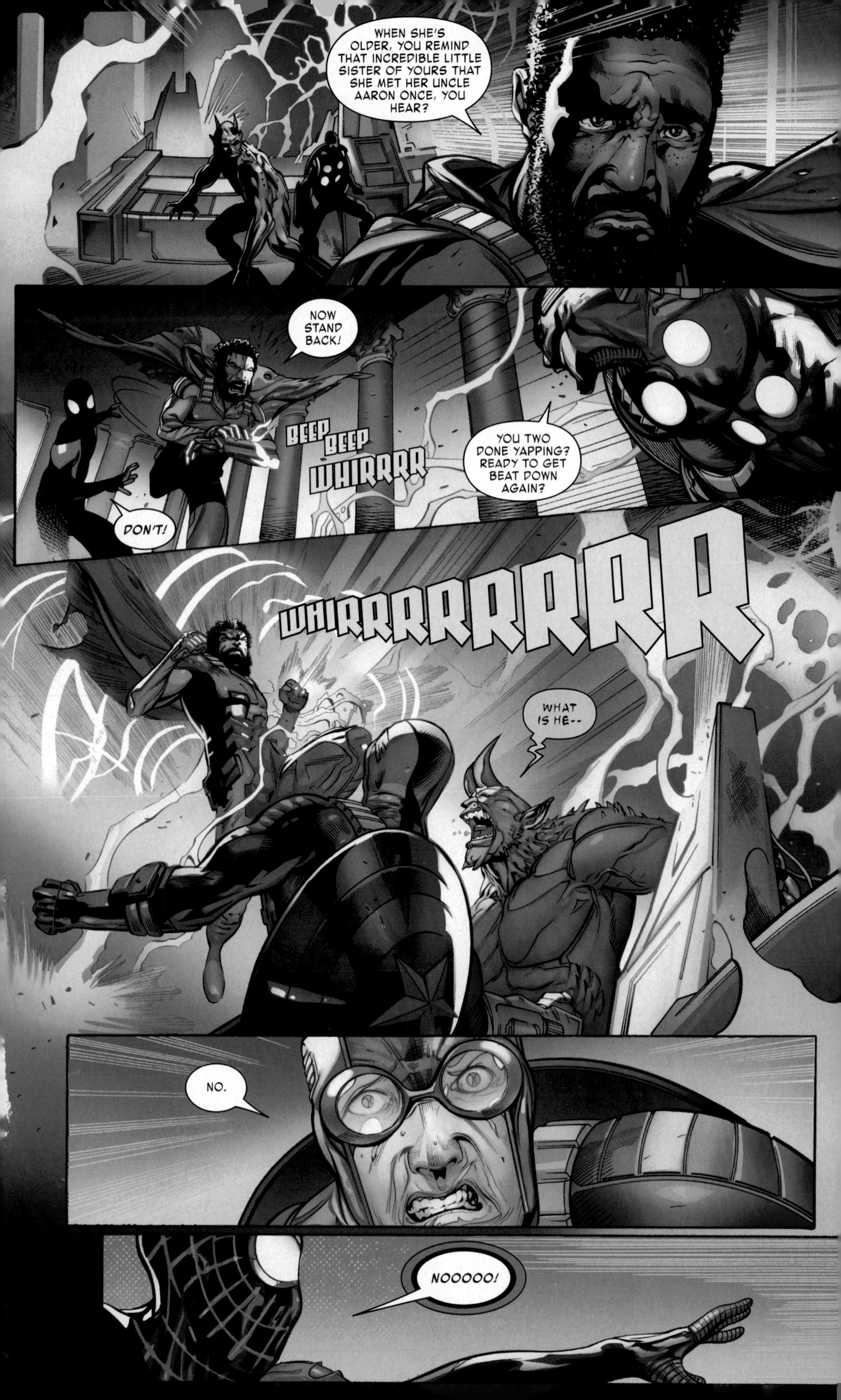

WHEN SHE'S OLDER, YOU REMIND THAT INCREDIBLE LITTLE SISTER OF YOURS THAT SHE MET HER UNCLE AARON ONCE, YOU HEAR?
NOW STAND BACK!
BEEP BEEP
WHIRRRR
YOU TWO DONE YAPPING? READY TO GET BEAT DOWN AGAIN?
DON'T!
WHIRRRRRRRR
WHAT IS HE--
NO.
NOOOOO!

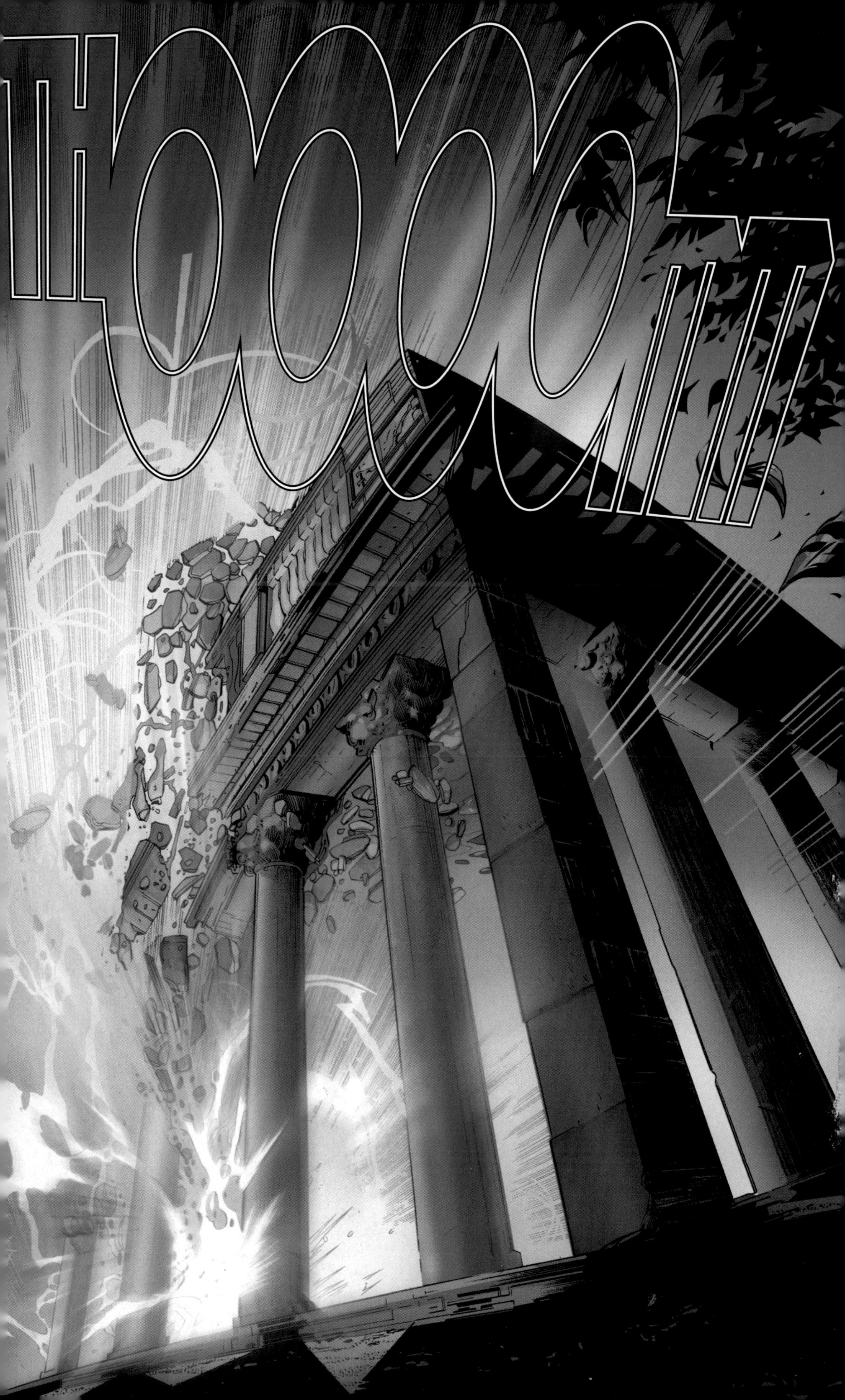
THOOOOMM

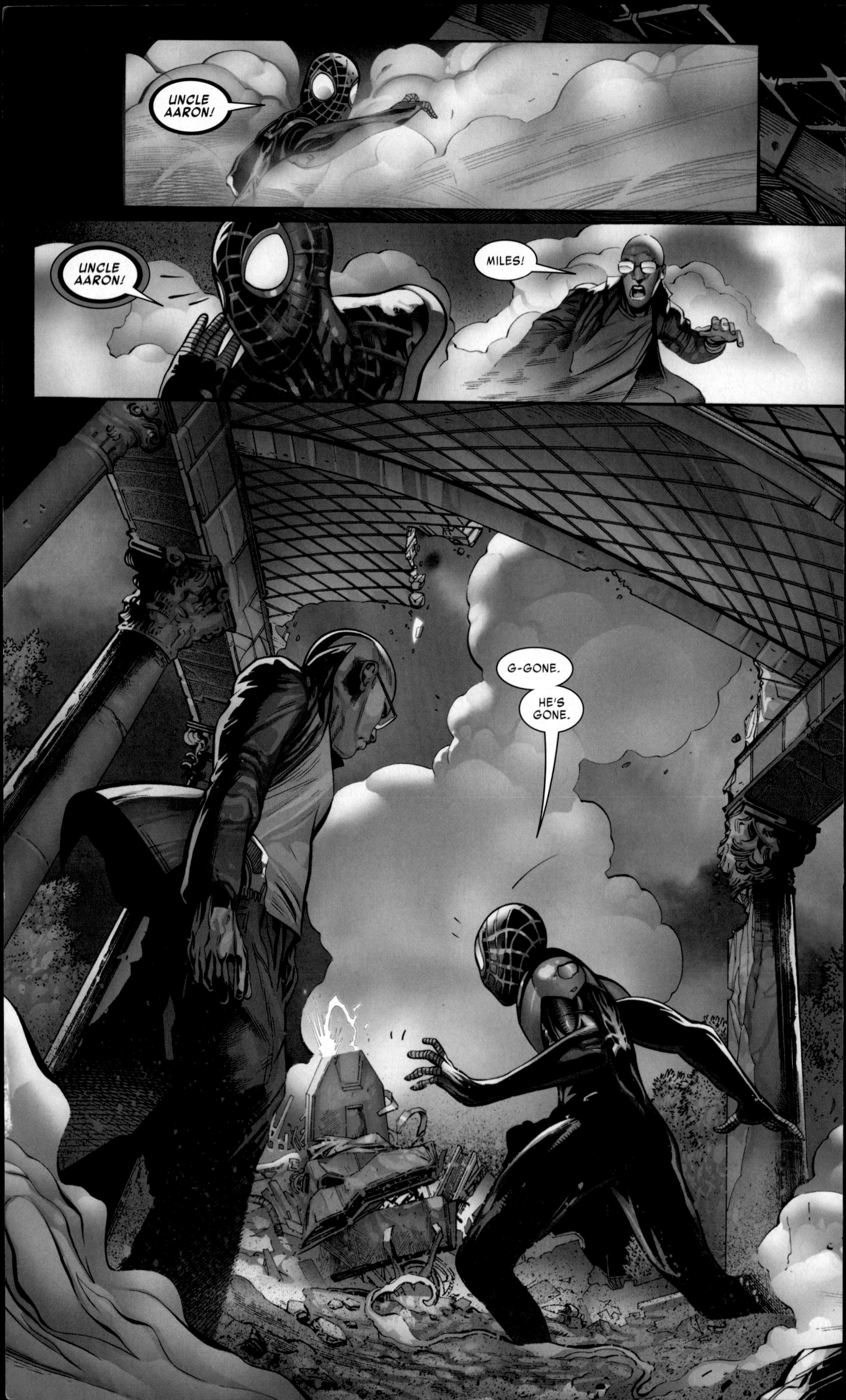
UNCLE AARON!
UNCLE AARON!
MILES!
G-GONE.
HE'S GONE.

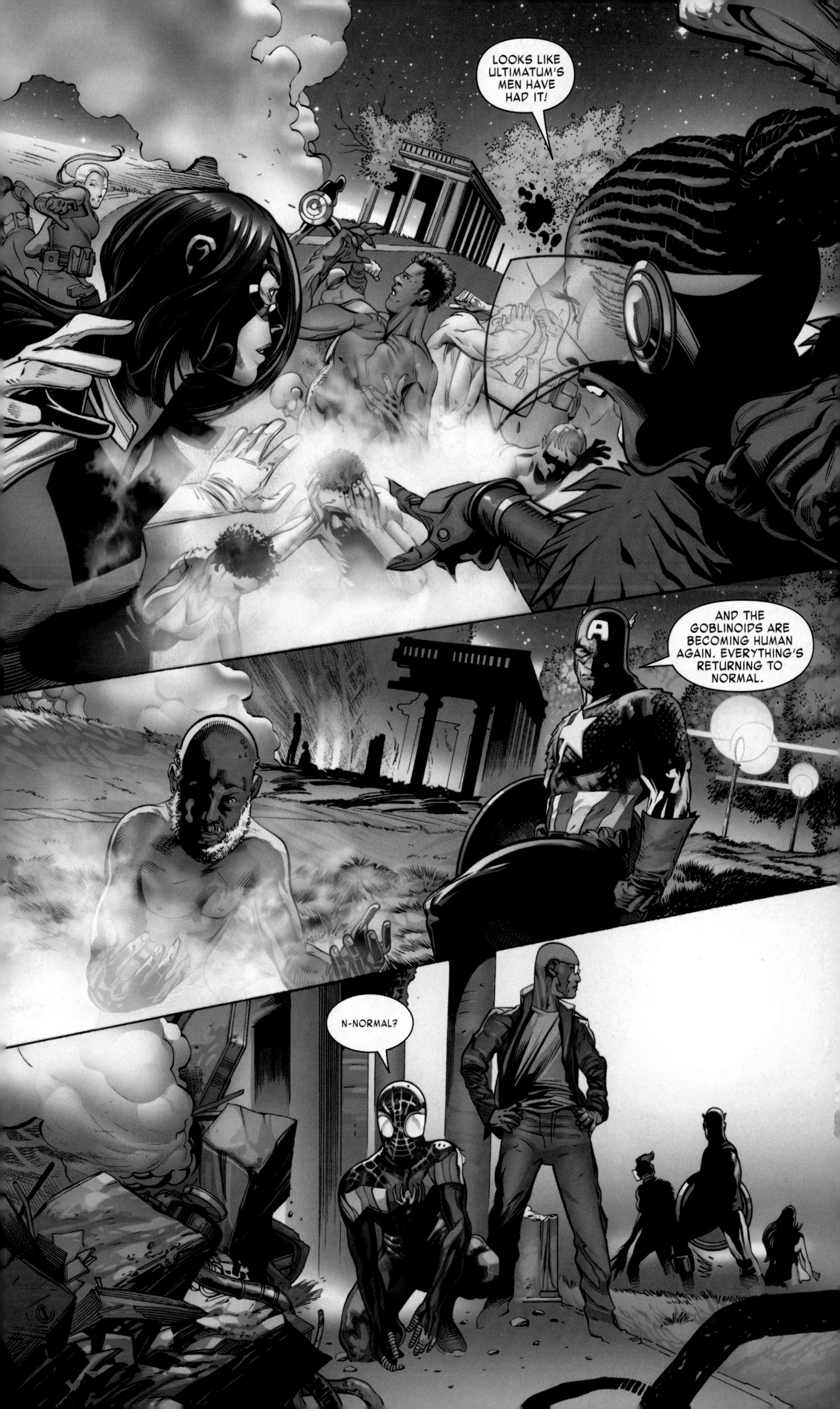
LOOKS LIKE ULTIMATUM'S MEN HAVE HAD IT!
AND THE GOBLINOIDS ARE BECOMING HUMAN AGAIN. EVERYTHING'S RETURNING TO NORMAL.
N-NORMAL?

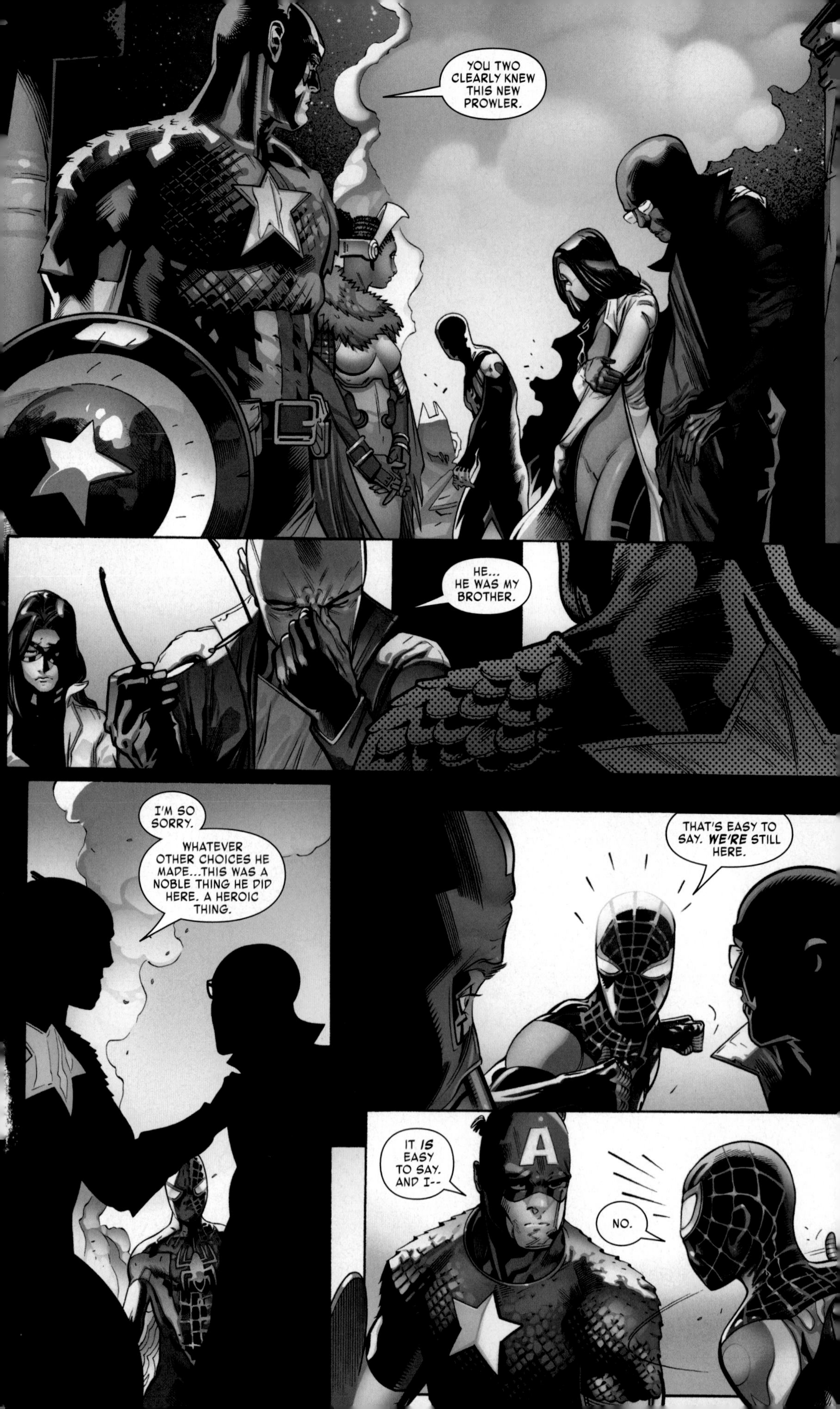
YOU TWO CLEARLY KNEW THIS NEW PROWLER.
HE... HE WAS MY BROTHER.
I'M SO SORRY.
WHATEVER OTHER CHOICES HE MADE...THIS WAS A NOBLE THING HE DID HERE. A HEROIC THING.
THAT'S EASY TO SAY. WE'RE STILL HERE.
IT IS EASY TO SAY. AND I--
NO.

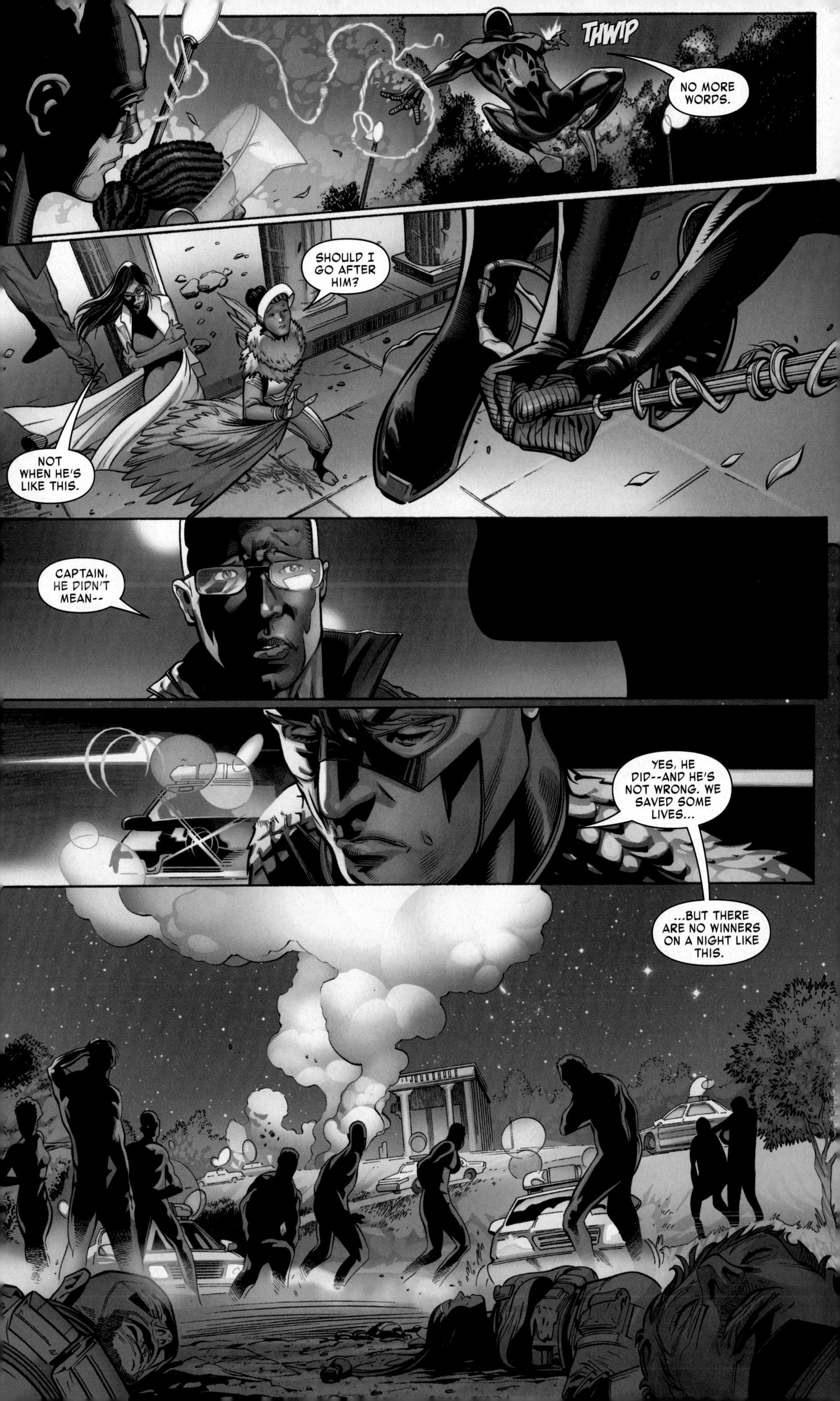
THWIP
NO MORE WORDS.
SHOULD I GO AFTER HIM?
NOT WHEN HE'S LIKE THIS.
CAPTAIN, HE DIDN'T MEAN--
YES, HE DID--AND HE'S NOT WRONG. WE SAVED SOME LIVES...
...BUT THERE ARE NO WINNERS ON A NIGHT LIKE THIS.

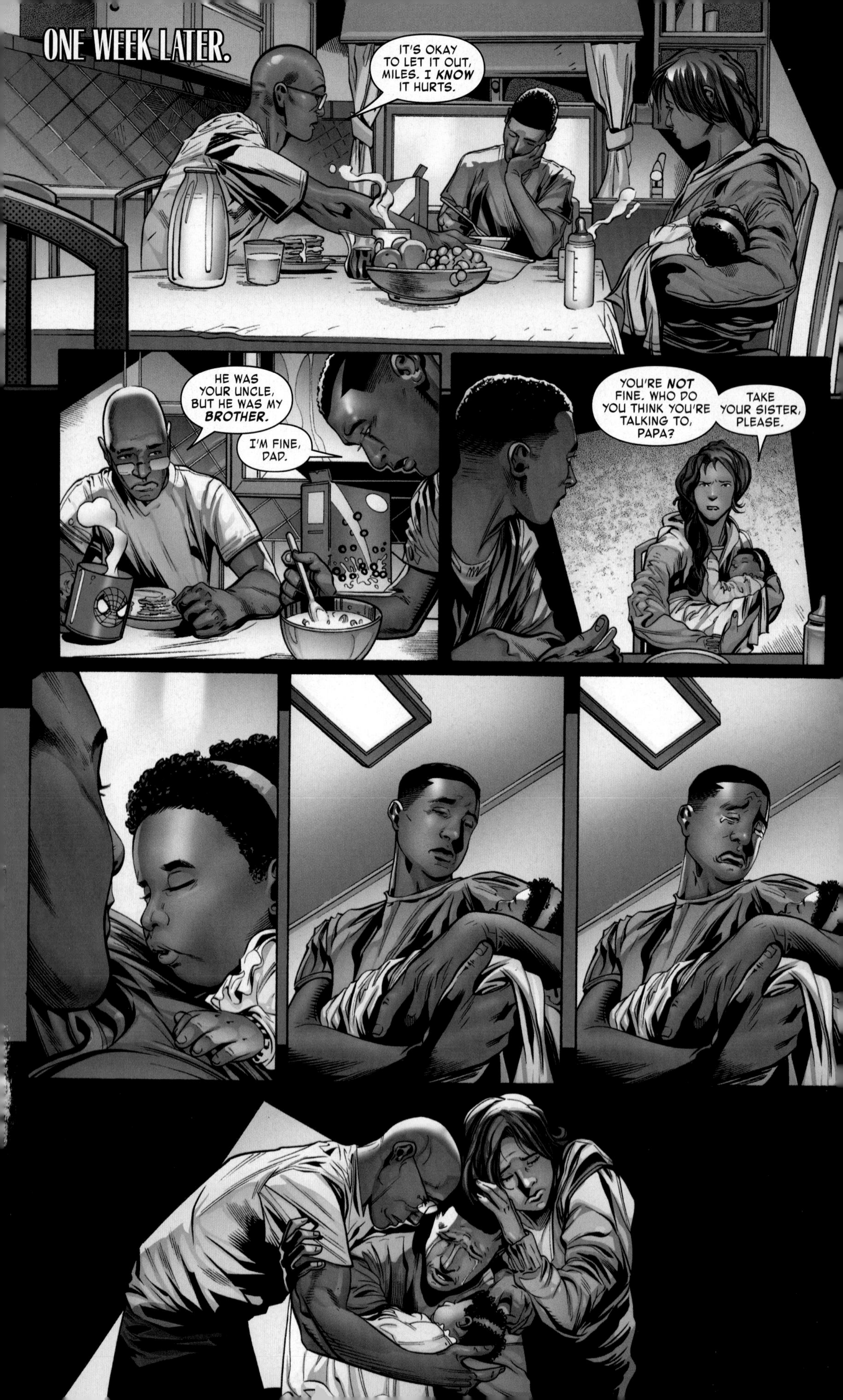
ONE WEEK LATER.
IT'S OKAY TO LET IT OUT, MILES. I KNOW IT HURTS.
HE WAS YOUR UNCLE, BUT HE WAS MY BROTHER.
I'M FINE, DAD.
YOU'RE NOT FINE. WHO DO YOU THINK YOU'RE TALKING TO, PAPA?
TAKE YOUR SISTER, PLEASE.

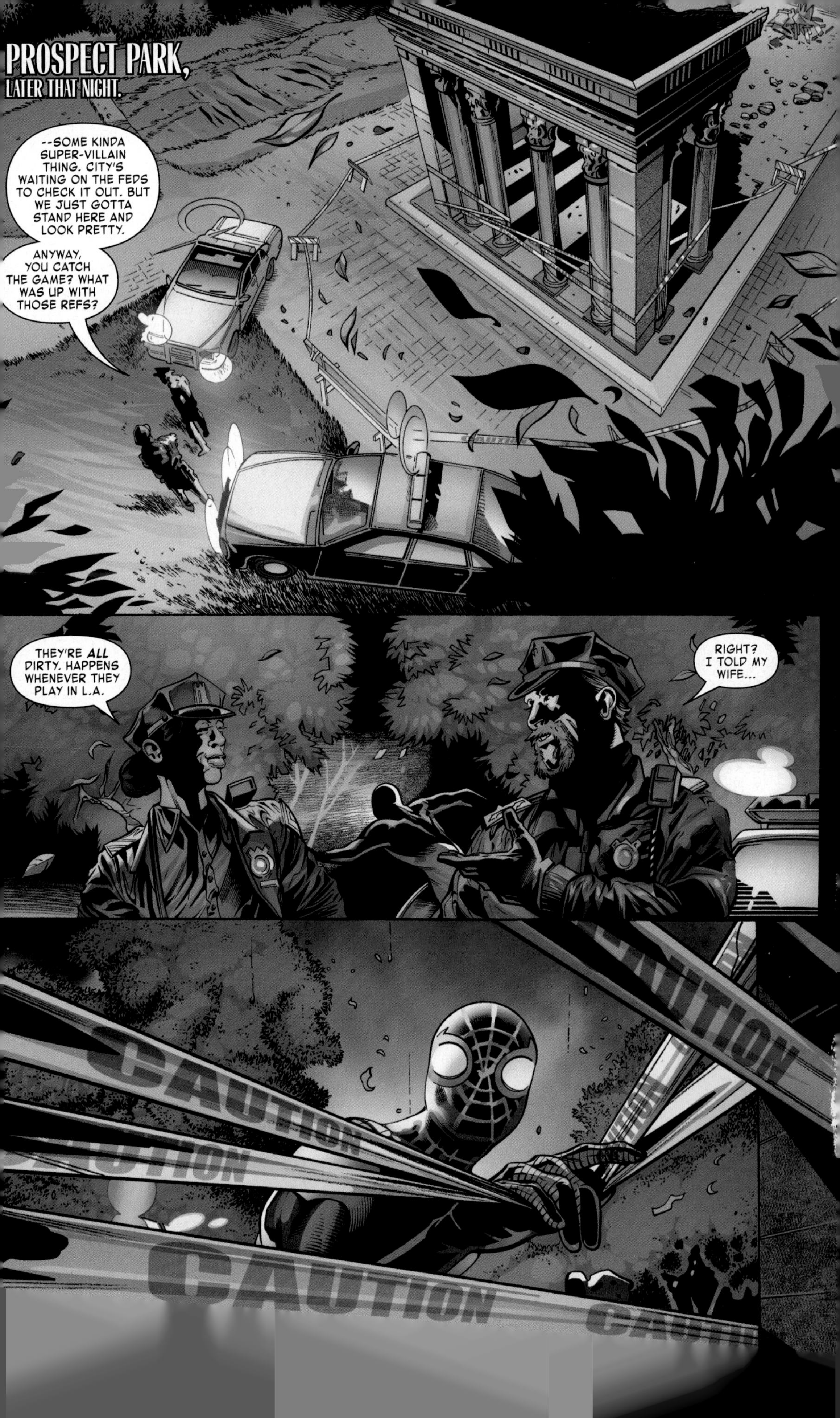
PROSPECT PARK, LATER THAT NIGHT.
--SOME KINDA SUPER-VILLAIN THING. CITY'S WAITING ON THE FEDS TO CHECK IT OUT. BUT WE JUST GOTTA STAND HERE AND LOOK PRETTY.
ANYWAY, YOU CATCH THE GAME? WHAT WAS UP WITH THOSE REFS?
CAUTION
THEY'RE ALL DIRTY. HAPPENS WHENEVER THEY PLAY IN L.A.
RIGHT? I TOLD MY WIFE...
CAUTION
CAUTION
CAUTION
CAUTION

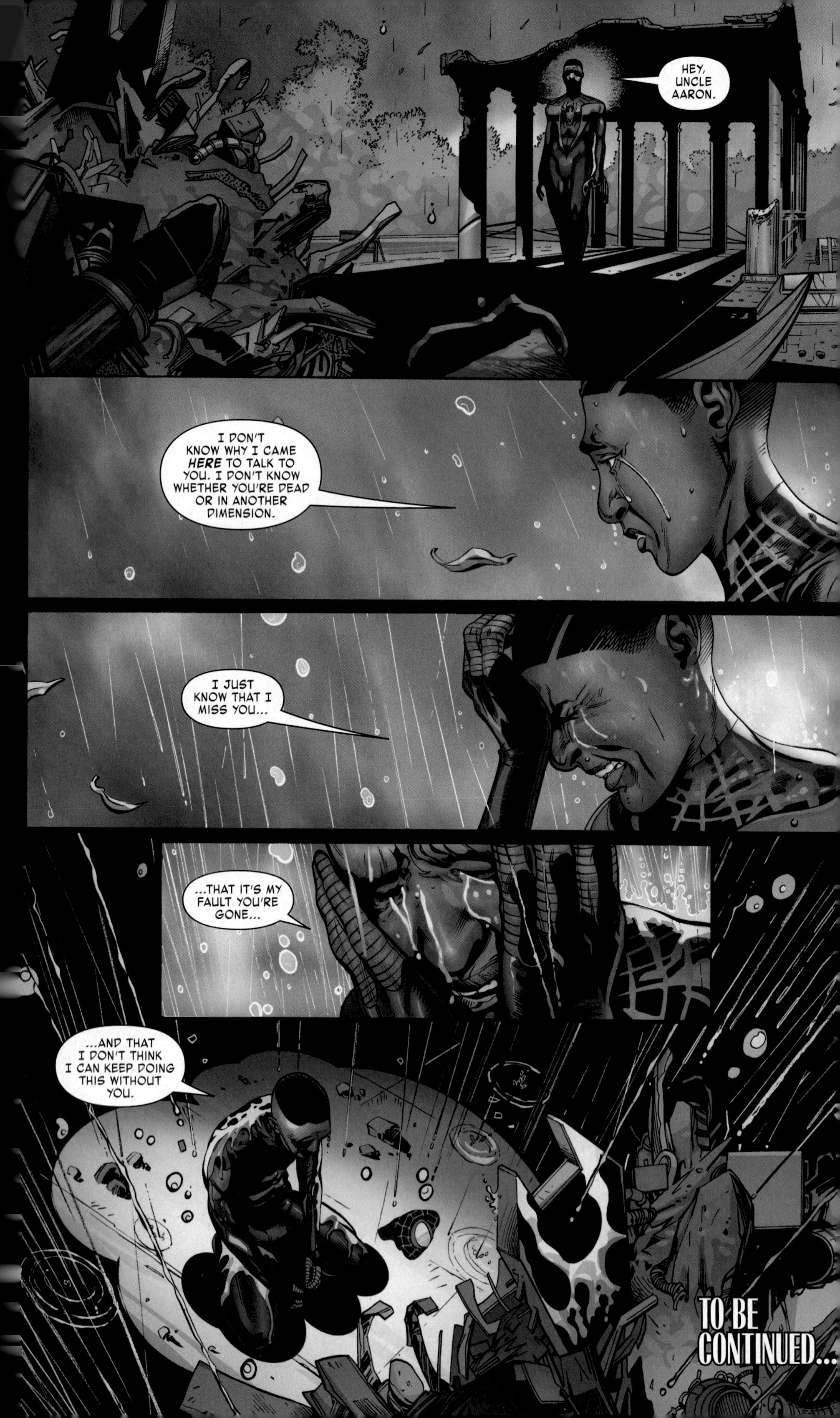
HEY, UNCLE AARON.
I DON'T KNOW WHY I CAME HERE TO TALK TO YOU. I DON'T KNOW WHETHER YOU'RE DEAD OR IN ANOTHER DIMENSION.
I JUST KNOW THAT I MISS YOU...
...THAT IT'S MY FAULT YOU'RE GONE...
...AND THAT I DON'T THINK I CAN KEEP DOING THIS WITHOUT YOU.
TO BE CONTINUED...

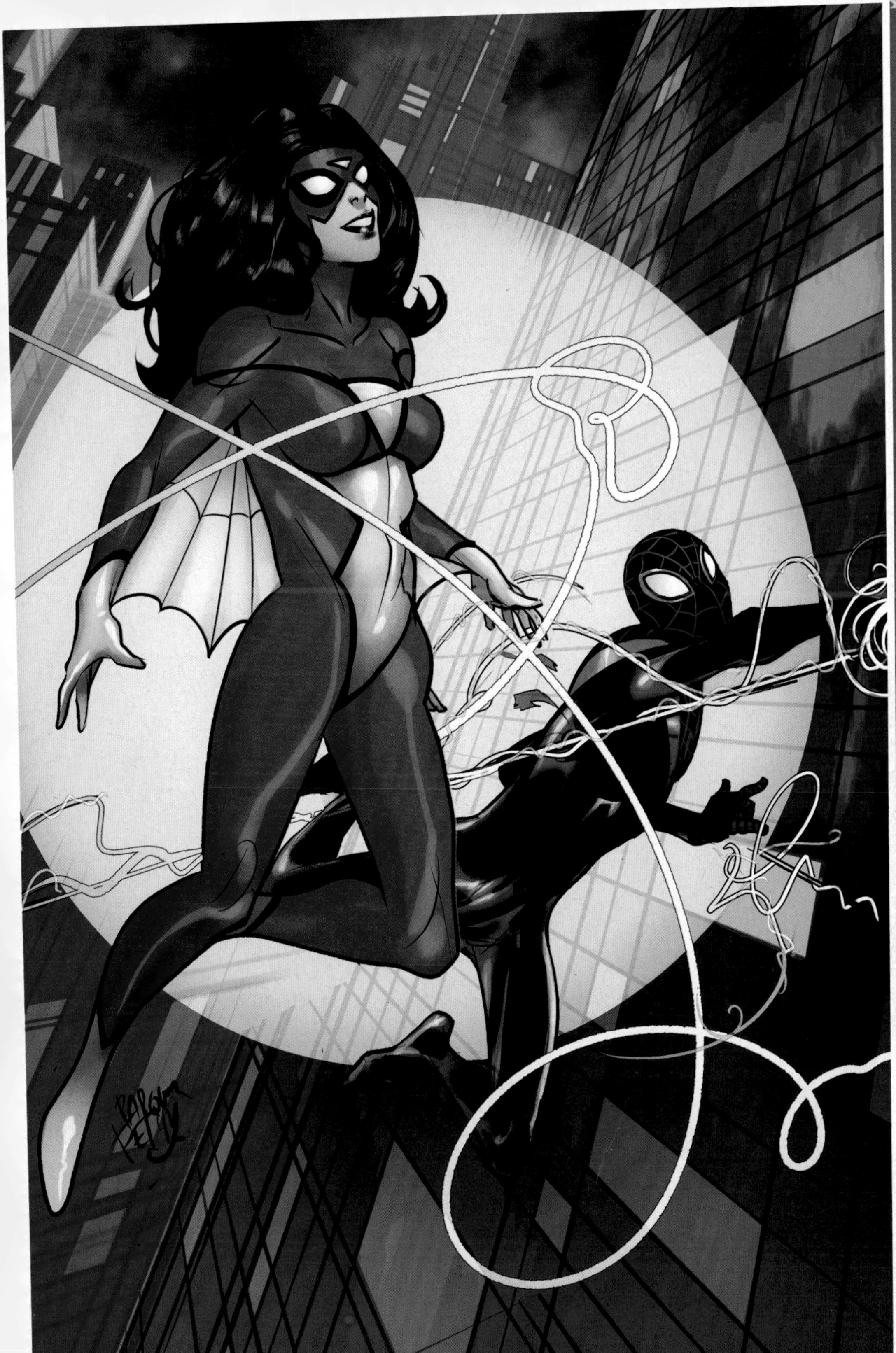

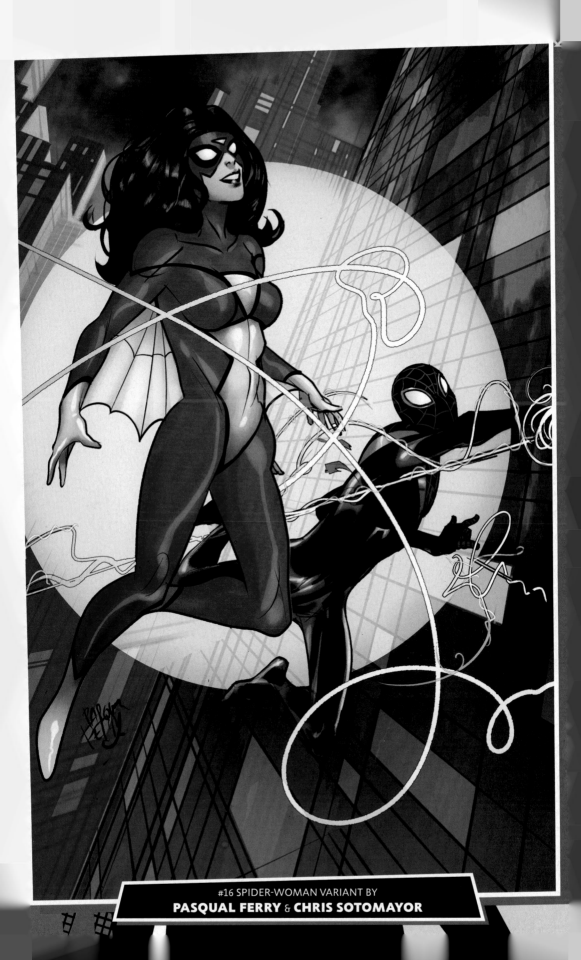

#16 SPIDER-WOMAN VARIANT BY
PASQUAL FERRY & CHRIS SOTOMAYOR

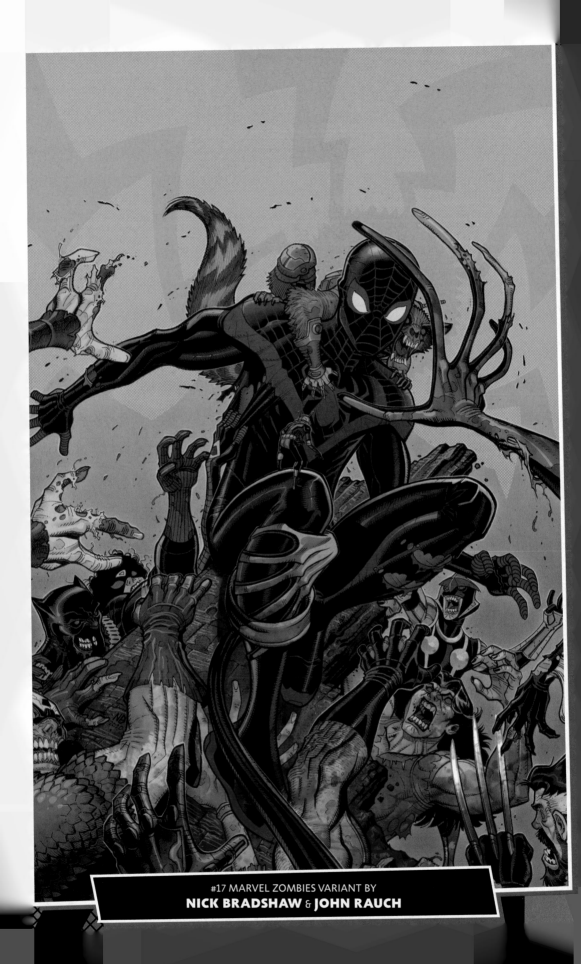

#17 MARVEL ZOMBIES VARIANT BY
NICK BRADSHAW & **JOHN RAUCH**

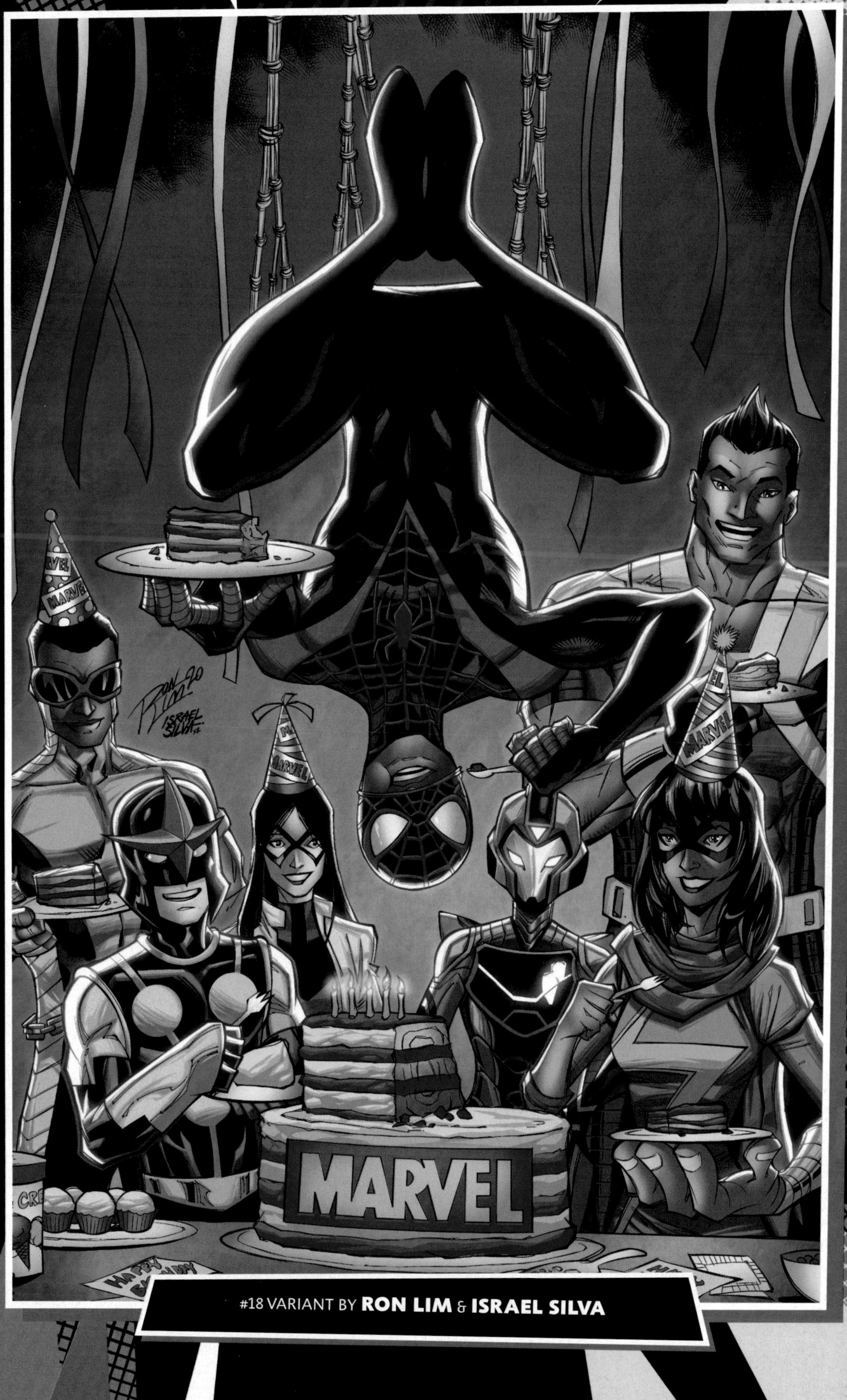
MARVEL
MARVEL
MARVEL
MARVEL

#18 VARIANT BY **RON LIM** & **ISRAEL SILVA**

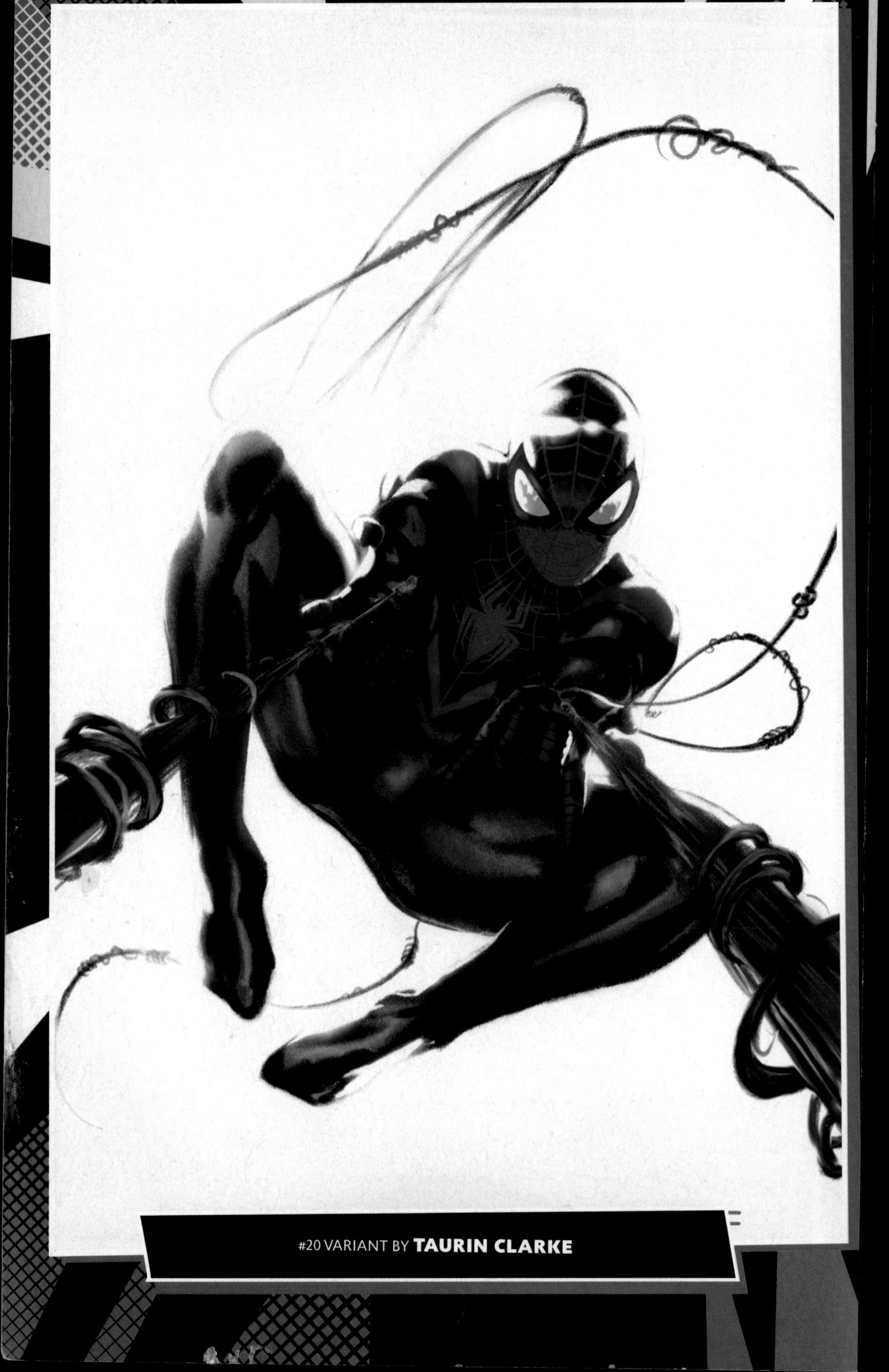

#20 VARIANT BY **TAURIN CLARKE**

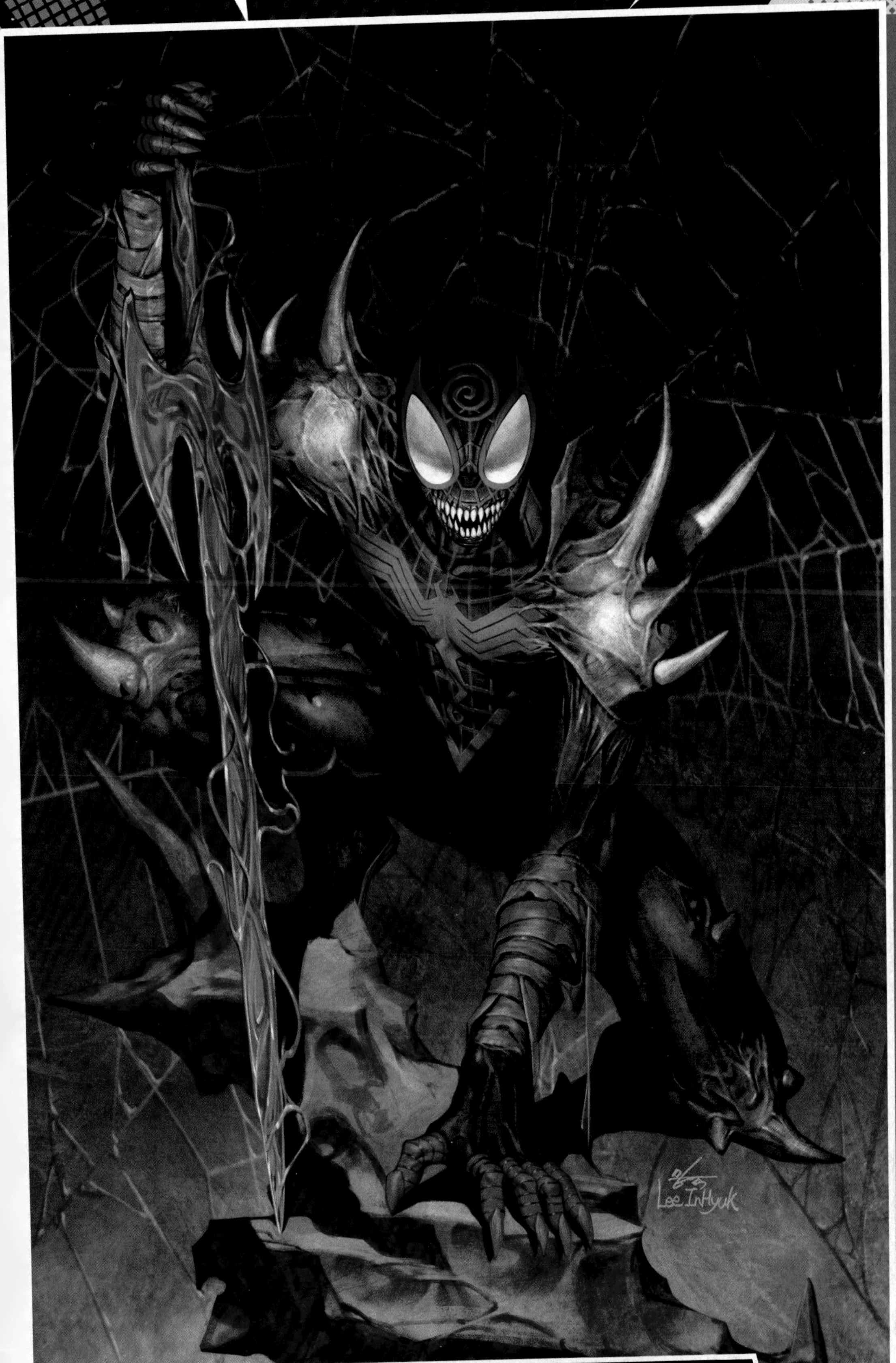
Lee InHyuk

#21 KNULLIFIED VARIANT BY **INHYUK LEE**

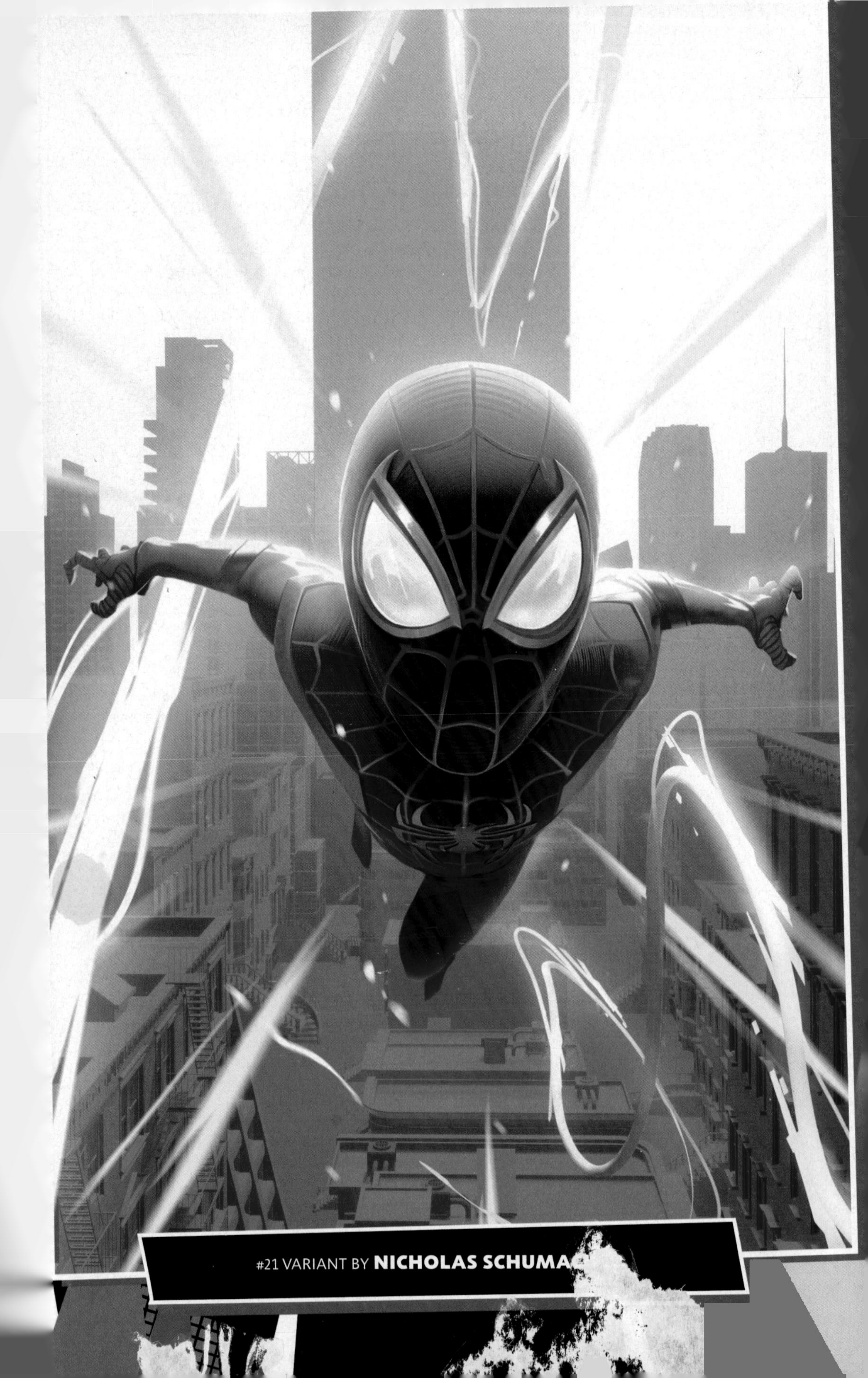

#21 VARIANT BY **NICHOLAS SCHUMA**